An Overview
of Writing Assessment

D0961730

An Overview of Writing Assessment

Theory, Research, and Practice

Willa Wolcott
University of Florida

with

Sue M. Legg
University of Florida

National Council of Teachers of English
1111 W. Kenyon Road, Urbana, Illinois 61801-1096

Staff Editor: Tom Tiller

Interior Design: Tom Kovacs for TGK Design

Cover Design: Barbara Yale-Read

NCTE Stock Number: 34904-3050

It is the policy of NCTE in its journals and other publications to provide a forum for the open discussion of ideas concerning the content and the teaching of English and the language arts. Publicity accorded to any particular point of view does not imply endorsement by the Executive Committee, the Board of Directors, or the membership at large, except in announcements of policy, where such endorsement is clearly specified.

Library of Congress Cataloging-in-Publication Data

Wolcott, Willa, 1942–
    An overview of writing assessment : theory, research, and practice
  / Willa Wolcott with Sue Legg.
        p.   cm.
    Includes bibliographical references (p.   ) and index.
    "NCTE stock number: 34904-3050"—T.p. verso.
    ISBN 0-8141-3490-4 (pbk.)
    1. English language—Composition and exercises—Ability testing—
United States.   2. English language—Composition and exercises—
Ability testing—United States—Methodology.   I. Legg, Sue M.
II. Title.
LB1576.W635   1998
808'.042'0287—dc21   98-17197
                                                                CIP

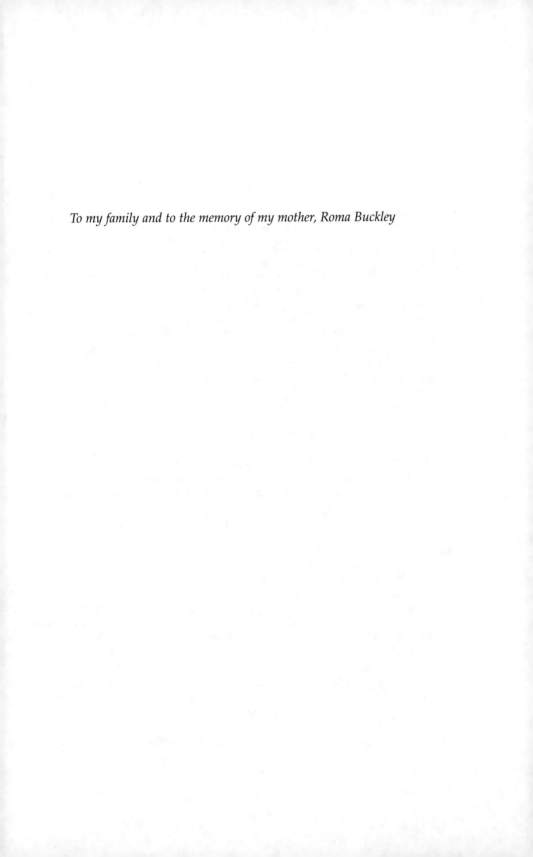

To my family and to the memory of my mother, Roma Buckley

Permissions

Appreciation is extended to the authors, journal editors, and publishers who gave permission to reprint excerpts or rating scales:

From "Beyond academic prose: Accommodating cultural differences in large-scale writing assessment" by R. Mountford in C. Cooper & L. Odell (Eds.), *Evaluating writing, 2nd edition.* National Council of Teachers of English. (In press). Reprinted with permission of the author.

From "Competency testing and the writing center" by R. Leahy. Reprinted by permission of the publisher from *WPA: Writing Program Administration,* 15.3 (Spring 1992). © 1992 by *WPA: Writing Program Administration.*

From "Defining and assessing competence in writing" by L. Odell in C. Cooper (Ed.), *The nature and measurement of competency in English.* © 1981 by the National Council of Teachers of English, Urbana, IL. Reprinted with permission of the author.

From *Assessing writers' knowledge and processes of composing* by L. Faigley, R. Cherry, D. Jolliffe, & A. Skinner, p. 105. © 1985 by Ablex Publishing Co., Norwood, NJ. Reprinted by permission of the publisher.

From *A framework for training teachers in portfolio assessment* by S. Legg, W. Wolcott, D. J. Henry, L. Bonnick, V. Christensen, R. Howland, S. Ketts, S. Martin, & A. Shaughnessy. © 1994 by the Florida Department of Education, Tallahassee, FL. Reprinted with permission of the Florida Department of Education. All rights reserved.

From "Holistic scoring: Past triumphs, future challenges" by E. White in M. Williamson & B. Huot (Eds.), *Validating holistic scoring for writing assessment.* © 1993 by Hampton Press, Cresskill, NJ. Reprinted by permission of the publisher.

From "Interdisciplinary portfolios" by B. Storm in *Portfolio News: Portfolio Assessment Clearinghouse,* 1(1). San Diego, CA: University of California Teacher Education Program. Reprinted by permission of the journal editor.

From *Individual student analysis version of CLAST analytic scale* by Writing Assessment Specialists. © 1992 by the Florida Department of Education, Tallahassee, FL. Reprinted with permission of the Florida Department of Education. All rights reserved.

From "The myth of assessment" by P. Belanoff in *Journal of Basic Writing.* © 1991 by the *Journal of Basic Writing,* Instructional Resource Center, Office of Academic Affairs, The City University of New York. Reprinted from the Spring issue, Volume 10, Number 1, by permission.

From "Portfolios" as defined by Northwest Evaluation Association in *Portfolio News: Portfolio Assessment Clearinghouse,* 2(3). San Diego, CA: University of

California Teacher Education Program. Reprinted by permission of the journal editor.

From "Primary trait scoring" by R. Lloyd-Jones. In C. Cooper & L. Odell (Eds.), *Evaluating writing: Describing, measuring, judging.* © 1977 by the National Council of Teachers of English, Urbana, IL. Reprinted with permission of the author.

From "Ranking, evaluating, and liking: Sorting out three forms of judgment" by P. Elbow in *College English, 55,* pp. 187–206. © 1993 by the National Council of Teachers of English. Reprinted with permission of the author.

From "Reliability issues in holistic assessment" by R. Cherry and P. Meyer in M. Williamson & B. Huot (Eds.), *Validating holistic scoring for writing assessment.* © 1993 by Hampton Press, Cresskill, NJ. Reprinted by permission of the publisher.

From P. Elbow as adapted from an essay in *Embracing contraries: Oppositions in teaching and learning.* © 1986 by Oxford University Press, New York. Adaptation reprinted with permission of the author.

From *Using the primary trait system for evaluating writing* by Ina V. S. Mullis. Published in June 1980 by National Assessment of Educational Progress, Educational Testing Service. Reprinted with permission of the author.

From *Teaching and assessing writing* by E. White. © 1985 and 1995 for the revised and expanded edition by Jossey-Bass, San Francisco. Reprinted by permission of the publisher.

From "Writing, student portfolios, and authentic assessment in science" by R. Freedman in *Portfolio News: Portfolio Assessment Clearinghouse, 4(2).* San Diego, CA: University of California Teacher Education Program. Reprinted by permission of the journal editor.

Excerpts from the literature review sections of the following reports prepared for the Florida Department of Education are used in Chapters 1–4 with permission of the Florida Department of Education, Tallahassee, Florida. All rights reserved.

Wolcott, W. (1988). *The effectiveness of essay topic formats.* Tallahassee, FL: Florida Department of Education.

Wolcott, W. (1992). *A feasibility study of large-scale writing portfolio assessment: Phase I, literature review and definition of issues.* Tallahassee, FL: Florida Department of Education.

Wolcott, W., with Hoffman, A. (1994). *Moving forward: A survey of alternative assessment in literature and current practice.* Tallahassee, FL: Florida Department of Education.

Wolcott, W., with Legg, S. (1990). *Issues in designing a direct eighth-grade writing assessment.* Tallahassee, FL: Florida Department of Education.

Contents

Figures and Tables

Figures

Tables

Acknowledgments

I am very grateful to Margaret Early, Professor Emerita of the University of Florida, for the care and thoughtful insight with which she reviewed an earlier draft of this manuscript.

I am also indebted to Jeaninne Webb, Professor Emerita and former director of the Office of Instructional Resources at the University of Florida, for inspiring and guiding my interest in all phases of writing assessment. I have been privileged as well to learn scoring principles from Rich Swartz of Educational Testing Service and to serve under Dan Kelly, Chief Reader for the State of Florida, who has modeled for us all what a good holistic scoring should be. I appreciate the guidance provided by two influential mentors in my life—Ruthellen Crews, who supervised my dissertation on holistic scoring, and Andrew Soule, who supervised my early years of English teaching.

I heartily thank Sue Legg, current director of the Office of Instructional Resources, for encouraging this project and for contributing the chapter on validity and reliability. I am also grateful to my colleague Diane Stevenson for suggesting the Tips for Teachers feature and for discussing assessment with me. I thank Anthe Hoffman for her help with portfolio assessment.

Special thanks go as well to Caroline Dennis for tracking down elusive bibliographic information; to Margaret Steptoe and Deborah Pickren for preparing several figures for this text; and to Carolyn Lyons for typing the final form of this manuscript. I also thank the students who graciously consented for their essays to be used, and I appreciate the help of instructors Dianne Cothran, Caroline Dennis, Jane Gibson, Lois Randolph, and Martin Simpson in applying the scoring instruments to student papers. I thank Tom Tiller of NCTE for working with me in editing this manuscript.

A tribute of admiration, affection, and respect goes to the many educators who collaborated with me on various projects so that we could learn more about assessment together—Beth Novinger and my other colleagues in holistic scoring throughout the state; the instructors in the Writing Center at the University of Florida; and several teachers in Alachua County, especially Gail Kanipe and Wendy Bice.

Finally, I thank my husband, Edward, and my sister, Sharon Buckley-Van Hoek, for reviewing earlier sections of this manuscript. I am deeply grateful to them and to all my family—Kedron, Charnley, Bill, Janet, and Brian—for their interest and encouragement which sustained me in this process.

———W. W.

1 Writing Assessment in the Changing Scene

The assessment of writing stands at the center of new educational directions being pursued as a result both of growing dissatisfaction with traditional testing practices and of changing views of the learning process. Because writing is intertwined with the learning process, the complexities of writing assessment serve as a microcosm of the assessment field in general.

The varied approaches currently used to assess writing reflect the changing beliefs of the past two decades about how writing should be taught and how assessment should be conducted. To some extent, the term *writing assessment* itself appears to juxtapose mutually exclusive elements—writing, with its susceptibility to debate as to what good writing is, and assessment, with its emphasis on what good measurement requires. Impromptu writing samples, while meeting many assessment requirements, are criticized for the narrow perspective of writing they provide, whereas portfolios, while providing the depth such samples lack, are criticized for their failure to meet the rigors of statistical measures. Thus, the current state of writing assessment often resembles rippled glass: the image that teases with promise still lacks the full clarity desired.

The problem is further compounded by the dualistic, almost opposing, terms in which discussions of writing assessment, as well as assessment in general, are often framed: internal or classroom assessment versus external, high-stakes assessment; "top-down" versus "bottom-up" assessments; formative versus summative evaluation; norm-referenced assessments that compare students against each other versus criterion-referenced assessments that evaluate students against standards; and indirect versus authentic or performance assessments.

The overall purpose of this monograph is to explore the state of writing assessment as it currently exists, its problems and potentials as revealed through research, and the ways in which it is often implemented. This text is directed primarily to fellow teachers, especially those at the secondary level, and to preservice teachers with the intent of providing information about a complex, changing subject that has an increasing influence on the classroom. Testing is, after all, a central way in which we measure the extent of a student's learning. It is also a means of reflecting in an ongoing manner upon how well we ourselves are doing in the classroom. By understanding the complexities of writing assessment, teachers might increasingly be able to influence the directions such assessments take in the future.

The "we" of this monograph can be at once narrowly and broadly defined. The "we" refers, first of all, to the two of us as authors, since we both have spent much of our lives in education and assessment. The "we" likewise refers to the groups of teachers with whom we have collaborated on portfolio assessment projects or in holistic scoring workshops, and the "we" finally refers, in the most inclusive sense, to all educators who, in classrooms at various levels, pursue the teaching of writing and thus witness directly the benefits and drawbacks of writing assessment. The "I" refers exclusively to myself, Willa Wolcott, as the author of eleven chapters; my colleague and supervisor, Sue Legg, wrote the chapter on reliability and validity. In writing the book, each of us brought perspectives derived both from practical experience and from research. I have taught secondary English and have spent many years teaching college-level developmental writers and supervising other writing teachers in the Reading and Writing Center at the University of Florida. Until just recently, students were placed in the developmental writing program here by means of holistically scored impromptu writing samples, and the program was evaluated annually through pre/post essays and portfolios. In addition to this firsthand experience with assessments, I have collaborated with secondary English teachers in several studies and projects to explore the benefits of portfolio assessment. My experiences with writing assessment include directing holistic scorings for state-mandated essay tests, conducting primary-trait scorings, giving workshops on assessment to teachers in two states, and researching, as part of grants, the literature on topic development, alternative assessment, and timed-writing samples. My colleague Sue Legg has done extensive work with assessment and measurement, including teaching college-level honors classes in measurement and serving as a consultant on assessment; in addition, she has collaborated with teachers on portfolios and other assessment projects.

The specific purpose of this chapter is to situate writing assessment within the framework of general assessment practices by providing an overview of the issues and controversies dominating assessment today. In this chapter, as well as in the remaining monograph, the term *assessment* is used interchangeably with the terms *testing* and *evaluation;* we have taken liberties in doing so, for the terms themselves do have specific uses and, in fact, are sometimes the subject of debate (see Grant Wiggins, 1993b).

Internal Classroom Tests versus External Tests

As teachers well know, internal classroom assessment differs from external assessment with respect to the context of the curriculum, the nature of the testing situation itself, and the reporting of results. In classroom tests, the test is often tied specifically to the knowledge and/or processes emphasized. Because of this integral link to curriculum, students are more apt to see the relevance of what they are being tested on, as, for example, when they are asked to write an essay discussing the symbolism in *A Separate Peace.* In external tests, however, any link to the curriculum of a specific course may be less apparent; in fact, the decontextualization of external tests is what some educators, such as Grant Wiggins, decry the most.

The testing situation also differs substantially in the care with which it is constructed and in the degree of formality with which it is administered. Classroom tests are often "homemade" and hence may include such weaknesses as poorly worded directions or questions or, on multiple-choice tests, obviously incorrect options. To compensate for such technical limitations, a teacher can provide additional explanations to any student who has questions about the testing task. Or a teacher can give additional time if the entire class clearly needs it. While teacher-made classroom tests may lack measurement rigor, the teacher can correct problems accordingly—by deleting a literature question that was misunderstood by most students, perhaps, or by curving the grades if test results indicate some identifiable flaws within the makeup of the test. Moreover, results of the classroom tests, unlike those of external assessments, can be interpreted within the larger framework of the teacher's broad perspective of a student—a perspective formed from observation of the student's class participation, homework, and oral presentations.

In external writing assessment, there is no such flexibility, nor is there necessarily an integral link to the curriculum of a specific class. Rather, if the purpose is accountability for classes, schools, or districts, the need for comparing the performances of students, classes, or districts requires that identical testing contexts be preserved. Thus, all facets of the test situation—directions, time allowed, and the questions themselves—must remain alike throughout, with the result that the individual student who encounters difficulty with the task usually receives little in the way of extra explanation. On the positive side, external assessments have usually been prepared with great care: topics and multiple-choice items are likely to have undergone extensive review and field-testing prior to their use, and attention has been paid to the wording and the ordering of the multiple-choice options.

Finally, the reporting of results is very different. Classroom test results usually go home with the student; in fact, parents can often view the test essay or paper itself. In external assessments, the score *results* are far more public, appearing on districtwide or statewide reports, but the actual tests or writing samples are usually not available for either the student or the parents.

Top-Down versus Bottom-Up Tests

The polarity that exists between classroom tests and external assessments is reinforced by the perception of who has responsibility for these assessments: external tests are seen as largely "top-down," imposed by school districts or state boards of education in order to hold schools and individual teachers accountable. Timed-writing assessments often fall into this category because they may be used to gauge the status of students' communicative ability within their schools. Teachers have little input into the tests themselves, and, even in large-scale writing assessments, teachers may not be involved in the scoring. The movement to portfolios, on the other hand, is credited by researchers Calfee and Perfumo (1993) as being "bottom-up," since it has originated largely with teachers. In fact, efforts to adapt portfolios to large-scale assessment have met with criticisms—albeit for very different reasons—from teachers and testing experts alike. Teachers feel that the standardization of portfolios required by large-scale assessments will diminish the ownership and individualization that characterize portfolios. Testing experts, on the other hand, are concerned about the technical difficulties entailed in scoring portfolios.

Formative versus Summative Evaluation

The dichotomy that appears in classroom and external assessments is echoed in the opposition between formative and summative evaluation. For example, Daniel Stufflebeam distinguishes between formative evaluation, which is ongoing and "proactive" in the sense that it allows for changes to be made, and summative evaluation, which is more fixed and "retroactive," bearing the connotation of finality in its sense of accountability (see Popham, 1988, p. 36). As explained by evaluation experts Davis, Scriven, and Thomas (1987), the purpose of formative evaluation is to *improve* instruction while it is still under way; summative evaluation, on the other hand, seeks to measure—generally for an outside audience—the effectiveness of instruction that has been completed (p. 3). According to the definitions of these evaluators, the prewriting and peer evaluation activities that students undertake during a writing class are largely formative, enabling students and teachers alike to see where progress has occurred and where problems remain to be addressed; summative evaluation, on the other hand, determines the effectiveness of classes and programs or indicates which students may need additional help (pp. 3–4).

As Popham (1988) notes and as the current educational reform movement suggests, attention is increasingly paid today to formative evaluation—to how instruction can be improved and to how assessment can influence the improvement. Thus, as states struggle with the issue of standards and with the intent to base diplomas on students' abilities to meet these standards (as opposed to merely fulfilling "seat time"), the issue of formative versus summative evaluation appears even more critical. Some of the testing programs currently under way, such as the new performance assessment program in Kentucky, have stipulated that schools with poor student performance be given the chance to improve before more drastic corrective action occurs.

Indirect Assessment versus Performance or Authentic Assessment

The most extreme polarity in assessment involves the nature of the tests themselves—that is, indirect assessment versus performance and authentic assessment. Thus, the norm-referenced, standardized tests that have dominated the educational scene for many decades are criticized for contributing to the decline of education in numerous respects: Lauren Resnick notes, for example, that such tests have fragmented and decontextualized knowledge (see O'Neil, 1993), while a 1994 report from the National Council of Teachers of English (NCTE) and International Reading Association (IRA) Joint Task Force on Assessment objects to present tests for their "centralization of data, their decomposition of tasks, and their standardization of pedagogy" (see Myers, 1994, p. 72). Multiple-choice tests are further criticized for their intrusion into classroom time, the limited empowerment they give teachers, their frequent lack of emphasis on higher-order skills, and, most particularly, their "'transmission view of learning' in which knowledge is delivered and memorized, not constructed and used" (Myers, p. 72).

Performance assessment, on the other hand, is direct. It attempts to evaluate a student's understanding by requiring the student to demonstrate, through actual performance, the solving of a problem or the undertaking of a project. As Calfee and Perfumo note, there are three key elements that distinguish performance assessment from indirect assessment:

1. Production rather than recognition—students must demonstrate competence rather than selecting an answer
2. Projects rather than items, i.e., a choice of depth over breadth—validity supersedes reliability as conventionally defined
3. Informed judgment rather than mechanical scoring—the teacher replaces the Scantron in the assessment process (1993, p. 532)

Performance assessment can be used in many subject areas, such as math or science or social studies, for example, with students being asked to undertake meaningful problem-solving tasks. The direct writing assessments to be discussed in Chapter 2 also exemplify performance assessment in that students are asked to demonstrate their competence in writing by actually composing. However, while performance assessment and authentic assessment are both considered as potential alternatives for indirect tests, the terms do not necessarily have the same meaning. The term *authentic assessment,* unlike *performance assessment,* implies that the context of the assessment approximates—to the extent possible—meaningful, real-life situations. In fact, educator Grant Wiggins (1993a) advocates the following criteria as essential to the development of authentic tests: meaningful, real-world kinds of problems; access to necessary resources; tasks wherein quality products result from the process; clear assessment criteria; and interactions between the examinees and the examiners (pp. 206–207). According to Wiggins, context is critical for authentic assessment, no matter how messy the context might be. In his view, impromptu writing assessments, both with time constraints that limit students' chances for revision and with restrictions against the use of resources, do *not* reflect authentic assessment even though students are being asked to compose.

The Role of Standards in Performance Assessment

In addition to the performance of problem-solving tasks, portfolios have become another alternate measure to multiple-choice or timed-writing tests for determining how well students understand and can apply concepts. A large part of the increased interest in portfolios as an alternative assessment approach stems from recent work on new educational standards for American schools. For example, a number of states and school districts countrywide have been involved in the New Standards Project to devise a coherent system of standards for English—and accompanying assessments for those standards—so that the educational system can, in the words of Simmons and Resnick, "help bring about better student outcomes—a different quality and higher level of student achievement" (see O'Neil, 1993, p. 17).

As part of the New Standards Project, various portfolio initiatives have been undertaken to develop literacy performance tasks that integrate reading and writing by asking students first to read a story and then to write a series of responses about it. Portfolios form the cornerstone for appraising the new standards largely because portfolios contain student work completed over a period of time. As envisioned by the project founders, the portfolios should contain work selected by the school, teacher, and student; specific projects and other examples of learning tasks; and what the founders call "performance-based matrix examinations" in several areas. The matrix exams require students to solve problems that integrate different subject areas, such as mathematics and writing, and that often include a collaborative, as well as an individual, component. Individual students take only subsets of the overall matrix examination, and these subsets become part of their portfolios. Various types of portfolios are being explored in the different state projects, so that the individuality of schools and the implications of portfolios both for classroom teaching and for scoring the portfolios will be fully understood. It is anticipated that professional training will take a "'trainer-of-trainers' approach," in which a few individuals are trained in scoring practices and then return to their home regions to train more teachers, who subsequently guide still others (Simmons and Resnick, 1993, p. 13).

General Work Standards

The work undertaken by the New Standards Project is but part of a larger debate about standards in many different subject areas. In the view of Simmons and Resnick, standards comprise three general types—content standards, which refer to the "desired outcomes in various subject areas" *for all students* [italics added]; performance standards, which signify, through both description and models, the level of performance needed for mastery; and school delivery standards, which denote the curricula, faculty, and other resources available to enable a school to implement the standards (O'Neil, 1993, p. 19). The development of national standards, led by the mathematics standards, is well under way in other subject areas; for example, the *Standards for the English Language Arts* document was released by NCTE and IRA in the spring of 1996.

The preparation of standards has required that many issues be resolved. First, there has been discussion about what subject matter the content standards should contain. The discussion has been particularly central in a subject area such as English, which encompasses reading, writing, and language use, and which must address the diversity of its students as reflected through their language and cultural backgrounds. Hence, educators grappling with the content standards in English have needed to come to terms with the various purposes and audiences for which communication is undertaken; with the challenges posed by differences between home and school languages; with increasing use of technology; and with the need for fostering student understanding not only of surface-level skills, but also of global, critical thinking skills whereby meaning is constructed through reading, writing, and speaking (*Standards Project for English Language Arts*, February 1994).

In addition, debate has arisen about whether special provisions should be made for some students—those with disadvantaged backgrounds or limited English proficiency, for example—in terms of the performance standards. A guiding principle of the New Standards Project, for example, has been that *all* students are entitled to a first-class education and that we must not hold lower expectations for disadvantaged children or for nonnative speakers of English; rather, in the view of the New Standards Project leaders, additional time and resources need to be provided to some students to enable them to succeed in meeting the same high expectations.

These issues of equity and excellence are central to the debate, for the question arises as to whether all students should be expected to attain similar standards of performance when they do not all have access to equitable resources in terms of schools, faculty, and even home environment—in other words, when the "delivery standards" vary so drastically from one school to another.

The very idea of having national standards has been troublesome to some educators. Eisner (1993) and Sizer and Rogers (1993) express their concerns that national standards might require schools to become standardized, thereby losing their individuality and diminishing the impact of parents and local communities on their schools. Like Sizer and Eisner, Grant Wiggins (1993b) is also troubled by national standards, emphasizing that standards instead must gauge individual performance in terms of a specific context and a specific purpose (p. 282).

Outcomes-Based Education (OBE)

The interest in alternative forms of assessment parallels the work being done on standards nationwide and the ongoing shifts in some states to outcomes-based education. Although the term has several definitions, the concept behind it is, as John O'Neil (1994) points out, "the simple principle that decisions about curriculum and instruction should be driven by the outcomes we'd like children to display at the end of their educational experiences" (p. 6). The impetus behind this movement is the idea that students are currently graduating without having experienced a demanding education—that many students have, in fact, put in "seat time" and accumulated the required units for graduation without being required to learn. Outcomes-Based Education stresses instead the importance of establishing common outcomes that *all* students will be required to demonstrate before graduating. William Spady (1994) carefully defines outcomes in the following manner: "Outcomes are high-quality, culminating demonstrations of significant learning in context. *Demonstration* is the key word; an outcome is not a score or a grade but the end product of a clearly defined process that students carry out" (p. 18).

Spady emphasizes the importance of having students participate at the end of their learning in a demonstration that is thorough and that is situated in a context with substantive content (p. 18). However, as O'Neil (1994) explains, the movement has generated controversy, largely because of the complexity in determining what the desired outcomes will be. Hence, it has been very difficult for those establishing the OBE plans to balance academic content that is challenging with the broader, interdisciplinary outcomes that define the human experience, such as the ability to communicate well or to solve problems (pp. 8–9). In view of these controversies, O'Neil speculates that the point of departure for new work on outcomes will become the academic subjects, rather than the interdisciplinary areas, and that school districts will move slowly in attaching high stakes to the outcomes, especially until performance assessments can be strengthened (p. 10).

Performance Assessment and the Role of Writing

The key to both the standards movement and the Outcomes-Based Education movement lies in the development of performance assessments to accompany the standards, assessments that will be appropriate for the "'inquiry view of learning'" (Myers, 1994). This view of learning, as the Pelavin Associates (1992) note, is a departure from the behaviorist school that has emphasized the acquisition of content and the recognition of "right" answers. The newer, constructivist theory emphasizes problem solving, critical-thinking skills, engagement, and cooperation. In this new view of education, according to the educator Costa (1993), the *process* of learning is of more importance than the *products* (p. 50). The challenge thus is to develop valid performance assessments that both capture these processes and, at the same time, allow generalizations to be drawn about students' understanding of a broader subject area; the challenge, moreover, is to develop assessments that can be scored reliably enough to enable "high stakes" decisions to be made about individuals.

For educators engaged in writing assessment, the broader challenge becomes that of balancing conflicting views, of creating workable harmony from the polarities, and of finding some way along the continuum to address the needs of all those who are stakeholders in writing assessments or, for that matter, in any assessments—parents, teachers, school boards, communities, states, and, most important, the students themselves.

2 Direct Writing Assessment

The sight of students hunched over their desks, with pens and pencils flying or stalling over blank booklet pages, has become common as school districts increasingly choose to assess students' writing by asking them to write. Although such direct writing assessments vary, students typically are asked to demonstrate their writing skill by producing "from scratch" a complete draft of an essay on an impromptu topic assigned under timed circumstances. Because the final evidence is *there* in the form of an essay, such on-demand writing tasks are viewed as representing real progress over the multiple-choice writing tests used previously to determine students' writing competence. Because, furthermore, everyone has been asked to perform a similar writing task, some basis exists for making comparisons among the writing skills of students at a defined grade level in any one school district. This task thus resembles that of asking chefs to produce, on demand, a specific type of entree or pastry to demonstrate their culinary skills. (To carry the analogy further, an actual lemon meringue pie is surely more indicative of a chef's ability than is a test asking about measurements, cooking time, or the virtues of various ingredients; at the same time, the very difficulty of judging the merits of the meringue pie versus beef bourguignon illustrates the need for some similarity of tasks if comparisons are to be drawn.)

Despite the advantages of direct writing assessments, limitations exist as well, ranging from the pressure that time constraints impose on students, to problems inherent in the nature of assigned topics and specific writing forms—problems that often short-circuit a teacher's effort to implement a writing workshop classroom. The purpose of this chapter is to clarify the issues behind direct writing assessments, to review their advantages and disadvantages, and to explore possible ways classroom teachers can help their students prepare for direct writing assessments.

The Context of Direct Writing Assessments

Most direct writing assessments, also called on-demand or impromptu writing, consist of asking students to write in response to a particular topic for a specified length of time. The topic is usually announced at the time of the testing, and students are often allowed neither to use resources, such as dictionaries, nor to confer with one another for explanations about the writing assignment.

The writing tasks may vary, depending on the topic, the age of the examinees, and the purpose of the exam itself. For example, third graders may be asked to write a story or to explain a situation or event, while high school students may be required to argue about a debatable issue or to respond to a passage or a quotation. At the end of the allotted time period, students submit their essays to be evaluated, sometimes by their classroom teachers, but often, in external assessments, by external scorers.

Such writing samples have been increasingly used in a variety of contexts, and in either partial or total replacement of the multiple-choice tests of grammar and usage that have fallen into disfavor. The samples have been adopted by some states seeking to determine the writing competence of secondary or college students. They have been used by individual, county, or statewide school systems to determine the effectiveness of their writing programs. They have been included as part of the General Educational Development (GED) test for high school equivalency diplomas. They have been used by some universities as a placement tool. Additionally, they have been incorporated into such professional examinations as the Law School Admissions Test (LSAT) or the Medical College Admissions Test (MCAT). In the former developmental writing program at our college, entering first-year students wrote sixty-minute essays on such topics as "A book, movie, or television program that made you think" as part of the placement procedures. The essays were scored by a group of experienced holistic scorers and the results combined with students' scores on an editing test. Six months later, at the end of the program, students wrote on similar topics, and their essays were combined with their placement papers and rescored by other holistic scorers as part of the program evaluation.

Advantages of Direct Writing Assessments

Because the on-demand essay requires students to perform a written task through which their writing skills will be judged, the impromptu writing sample has been a forerunner of the movement toward authentic assessment. Hence, a key perceived virtue of the writing sample is the appearance of credibility or what is known in testing terms as face validity.

In making students interpret the topic, write an organized response to it, and do at least a limited amount of revision or proofreading, a direct writing assessment reveals many facets of students' abilities: It indicates, for example, how well students can think through a particular topic, develop their ideas, express those ideas, and control their sentence structure and mechanics. Thus, unlike multiple-choice tests (and also unlike such structured writing exercises as sentence combining), the writing sample requires students to demonstrate their ability to deal in a limited time with virtually all the complexities that composing entails. To the extent that testing determines what is being taught, the increased use of direct writing assessments can be seen as encouraging more classroom effort to be expended on teaching writing.

Moreover, from the perspective of measurement experts, writing samples offer several clear advantages. First, with students being asked to do the same task under similar time constraints, writing samples provide relatively controlled testing conditions whereby comparisons can be made between students. That is, because the number of possible variables that can influence a writing performance are kept as identical as possible—namely, the topic, testing context, availability of resources, and scoring methods—the writing performance of any one student can be evaluated in terms of the performances of all other students. Second, because the writing is done under the instructor's eye, the writing remains clearly the student's own; hence, questions of authorship or of collaboration do not arise. These questions do, of course, arise occasionally with other forms of writing assessment, such as the portfolio; therefore, the certainty of authorship that direct writing samples provide is significant, especially in those situations in which individual competence is being assessed. Still another advantage is the cost, for even though scoring costs remain high regardless of the scoring method used, timed single essays can be scored more efficiently than can longer works, such as portfolios.

Finally, even though writing samples cause the focus to be placed strictly on the *product* the student creates rather than on the *process* involved in its creation, defenders of direct writing samples argue that such focus is not entirely negative and that, in fact, products are what ultimately matter in most communications or transactional writing (Gorrell, 1988; Lederman, 1986).

Objections to Writing Samples

Despite the advantages and the prevalence of using writing samples to assess students' writing, many educators object for both philosophical

and practical reasons. Specifically, objections involve the following issues: restriction of the writing process, the purpose behind the sample,
the choice of topics, the mode of discourse sampled, the effect of time
constraints, and reliability.

Restriction of the Writing Process

Because of time restrictions, such writing samples are often criticized
for preventing students from using the writing process fully as it has
been defined and illustrated by teachers in the classroom. Educators
argue that such assessment of a product stands in opposition to the
process theory of writing, a theory that depicts writing as a series of recursive stages entailing deliberate goals and choices on the part of the
individual (Flower & Hayes, 1981). Moreover, direct writing assessments contradict the social constructionist theory of writing which, according to Kenneth Bruffee (1986), emphasizes the social nature of
writing that links us all to our communities. In light of the important
instructional changes that have occurred as a result of these theories in
the past two decades—instructional practices that encourage the recursive stages of prewriting, drafting, and revising, or that emphasize by
means of peer groups the collaborative nature of the writing community—educators view with misgivings the importance that timed writing samples place on the written product. They point out that
examinees are given little time either to generate ideas about their writing or to do more than a superficial proofreading; that students who are
allowed no access to resources often produce shallow or mechanical
writing; and that students are even denied the chance to collaborate
with others in talking through ideas about their topics.

Precisely because of concern that direct writing assessments collide
with key instructional precepts, some testing programs have attempted
to adapt their assessment procedures to reflect the writing process
more accurately. Applebee, Langer, and Mullis (1989) note that "one
[approach] is to design tasks that lead students through a panoply of
process-related activities; another is to provide smaller, more focused
tasks that may assess one or another process-related skill" (p. 34). Certainly, some testing programs have attempted to reduce the differences
between the writing process and product assessment either by announcing topics ahead of time or by extending the task over a three-day
period. Other programs also employ a set of detailed prewriting questions to help their students think about the topic.

Whereas prewriting strategies can be adapted to direct assessments,
the possibilities for revision within a timed assessment period, especially for revision of such higher-order elements as organization and

development, remain more limited. Some testing programs provide dictionaries and similar resources for revision purposes. However, other testing programs continue to prohibit such resources from being used, arguing that not all schools can provide their students with similar materials and that too much testing time may be consumed by students who become stalled over looking up a single word.

Thus, only to a very limited extent can the writing process as it is practiced in many classrooms be applied to the direct assessments of writing samples.

The Purpose Behind the Sample

Another serious philosophical objection to the writing sample lies with the purpose for which it is sometimes used. Educators such as Edward White (1985) and Lee Odell (1981), for example, express concern over using writing samples to measure the minimal competence of individual writers. For Odell, the issue is how such competence is defined. Stressing that minimal competence should not be equated with merely observing the conventions of writing, Odell argues rather that competence must be defined broadly to mean "the ability to discover what one wishes to say and to convey one's message through language, syntax, and content that are appropriate for one's audience and purpose" (p. 103). For White, the issue is how to link testing more closely with teaching. Hence, he argues that instead of having writing competence at the college level determined by writing samples alone, rigorous upper-division writing courses with "public standards" should be implemented. For White and Odell, then, as well as for many other educators, single writing samples remain an insufficient way of measuring students' larger writing competence.

Topics for the Samples

Not only do objections arise about the purposes, such as determining writing competence, for which samples are sometimes used, but also criticisms are levied against the tasks themselves. In particular, the topics used in direct assessments, often called topic prompts, have become a source of debate. For example, Garth Boomer (1985) argues against the arbitrariness of the typical topic prompt, noting that assigning a topic "cuts across the basic condition for good writing: having something to say and wanting to say it" (p. 63). Referring to research that shows the importance of owning a topic, he cautions that problems may arise in the writing of students who are not involved with a topic. The result, according to Boomer, is that the type of tests used in large-scale assessments in which topics are given to students may not accurately indicate writers' abilities. Regardless of those occasional testing programs that incorporate extra time for revision or proofreading purposes, the basic "stimulus-response" model of such impromptu assessment is, in his eyes, basically flawed.

Some test writers have attempted to correct this potential lack of topic ownership by providing examinees with a choice of topics, hoping thereby to make at least one prompt both accessible and engaging for the students. However, as will be seen in Chapter 3 on topic development, this practice also has its limitations in that the choices offered may not make equal requirements of the students. Odell (1981), for example, points out that similar-sounding topics can make very different demands of students, and he cautions that unless topics require similar writing skills, students' work cannot be compared. Research by Ruth and Murphy (1988), as well as by Hoetker and Brossell (1986), has further underscored the complexity of the way that topic prompts are presented in writing assessment. Thus, the issue of topic prompts, to be explored more fully in Chapter 3, is a major cause, for both philosophical and practical reasons, of some educators' dissatisfaction with direct writing assessments.

The Writing Mode

Another serious objection to the writing sample is the limitation it necessarily places on the mode of discourse to be tested—whether narrative, persuasive, expository, or descriptive. The mode can not only affect the testing outcome but also clearly influence the nature of the writing instruction that occurs. For example, a study by Engelhard, Gordon, and Gabrielson (1992) of eighth-grade students participating in large-scale writing assessments found that mode of discourse was a significant factor in predicting writing quality: narrative writing tasks received the highest scores, with descriptive tasks next and expository tasks last. Similar results have been reported in studies by Pamela Kegley (1986) and Cantor and Hoover (1986). The seventh graders in Kegley's study performed better on narrative papers than they did on persuasive papers, and students in Cantor and Hoover's study often chose to write narratives even when they were given topics that required other modes of discourse; thus, Cantor and Hoover note that "students in the upper elementary and middle school grades seem to receive most of their writing instruction and most of their writing practice in the narrative mode" (p. 9).

Still other research, notably a study by Raley (1986) and a pilot study in Utah (see Duke and Strong, 1988) in which middle schoolers had difficulty with the persuasive mode, confirms that the narrative mode may be developmentally easier, or at least more common, for younger students.

Clearly, then, the mode of discourse required by the writing sample has consequences for the examinees and must be carefully considered beforehand. As Kegley (1986) stresses, "The modes of discourse cannot be considered interchangeable" (p. 153).

Not only may the mode of discourse used in the writing sample affect the student writers, but also it may influence the scorers of the samples. Rosemary Hake (1986) cautions, for example, that scorers may become more subjective in their evaluations when they are asked to score narratives based on personal experience. Furthermore, as Hake notes and as an early study by Crowhurst and Piché (1979) revealed, narrative writing, as opposed to descriptive and argumentative writing, demands least from students in terms of syntactic complexity. Because the organizational pattern for narratives is typically chronological, there are fewer elements for scorers to consider in making their evaluations.

As particular modes of discourse can create potential problems both for the students and for the evaluators—and as the mode tested will surely have an effect on instructional programs—it seems clear that designers of testing programs must thoughtfully consider what mode or modes will best suit the purpose of the exam.

To minimize problems, some large-scale testing programs assess a variety of writing types. Alternately, some programs require their students to write on two discourse forms. Still others schedule one type of writing to be tested each year for students in different grades, sometimes announcing the type beforehand, and sometimes not. For college-level writing proficiency assessments, the expository mode (or the persuasive mode) is tested most often. Not only is this form typical of the academic writing required in most college courses, but expository writing also requires students to use other discourse forms to develop their ideas and to draw upon their general knowledge. Such professional examinations as the MCAT for medical school often require expository writing of their applicants, while the LSAT, not surprisingly, asks law-school applicants to demonstrate their proficiency in argumentative writing.

Time Constraints

Another major objection to using writing samples for assessment arises from the artificiality of the testing situation and the imposition of time constraints. As Carlson and Bridgeman (1986) thoughtfully point out, time restrictions may cause some students anxiety by limiting the amount of prewriting and revising anyone can do. The researchers caution that "it may be possible that some students do well under such 'first draft' conditions, whereas others, who might be equally good writers, do not" (pp. 142–143). Certainly, our own classroom experiences underscore the pressure some students feel about timed writing: one young woman, in particular, moaned, groaned, fumed, and twitched as she wrote the two, timed essays required by our curriculum; although normally a poised and outgoing student, she literally fell apart when confronted by pressure of that kind. Many testing programs give students a full hour in which to write, but some major writing assessments, such as those formerly given by the National Assessment of Educational Progress (NAEP), allow less than twenty minutes.

Empirical studies on the effect of time on students' writing performance have been limited. A 1989 study of South Carolina's assessment was initiated because of concern that the sixteen minutes allowed for the original NAEP study had been too limited. For one part of the study, the experimental group of students was given fifty minutes to write on one topic and sixteen minutes on another; the control group of students was allowed sixteen minutes for each of the two topics. Results showed that while students with more time to write on the topic did perform better than their peers in the control group, the difference was not as clear as might have been expected. Interestingly, the better writers, rather than the weaker writers, seemed to benefit more from the additional time (see Applebee et al., 1989, pp. 32–34). Although the results were not definitive, the National Assessment of Educational Progress now allows longer periods for their writing assessments.

Admittedly, as our own assessment experiences have shown, providing additional time does not guarantee that students' writing will be better. Students who retake the essay portion of a college examination in our state are given double time, or two hours, for their writing. Although this extra time benefits some students, for others it just results in longer—but equally poor—essays. Similarly, we sometimes saw stronger essays written for the twenty-minute SAT-II placement samples formerly used at our university than we do for the sixty-minute state examination essays, even though the latter essays are often considerably longer.

But while increased time does not ensure better writing, it is important to realize, as Lee Odell (1981) cautions, that a typical writing prompt requires students to do many tasks: "contemplate a topic *to which they have likely given little previous thought*; identify their audience and purpose; decide upon the rhetorical strategies they will need in order to achieve their purpose with their intended audience; write a first draft; reconsider and, where necessary, revise that draft; edit their draft to make sure it corresponds to the conventions of standard written English" (pp. 108–109). Given the scope of the tasks that timed-writing assessments require of students, it seems critical to provide them with sufficient time.

Multiple Samples

Even when the mode of discourse is carefully chosen or when time constraints are adjusted to provide more flexibility, one writing sample from a given student remains inadequate from the perspectives both of the student writers and of the scorers. First, as Odell (1981) warns, students may not be writing their best on any given day (p. 118); moreover, precisely because of the variables just discussed, such as the mode of discourse or the topic, students' writing ability may not be fully reflected in a single writing sample.

More important, with one sample, the issue of score reliability arises—that is, the question of whether a given piece of writing would receive the same scores on a different occasion; this issue has, in fact, been called by researchers Breland, Camp, Jones, Morris, and Rock (1987) "the Achilles heel of essay assessment" (p. 23). (We saw evidence of this problem when a few of our students' early essays received different scores during our December program evaluation from the scores the same essays received when they were scored six months earlier for placement purposes.) The researchers suggest that score reliability can be improved either by giving several essays or by combining an essay with other types of exams, such as multiple-choice tests (p. 57). Hence, some major content-area assessments require students to answer several questions, and professional exams that have recently incorporated essays in their testing procedures may require two writing samples in similar modes from the examinees. Those testing programs in our state that require only one sample note that examinees who fail the writing portion can retake the exam, usually without charge.

Scoring Issues

As the score-reliability issue suggests, the scoring of writing samples, whether for direct writing assessments or for portfolios, is a major issue in itself, and consequently, three chapters will be devoted to the problems and potentials of methods currently used. Within the context of this chapter, suffice it to say that giving students a choice of topics can also create potential problems in the scoring of the essays. It raises the issue of whether readers should be trained separately for each topic or whether a generic scoring rubric—which stands as an abstract representation of each scoring point—can be used for multiple topics. Ideally, readers should be trained separately for each topic, just as separate scoring guides should, in the view of Edward White (1985), be developed according to the topics given and the level of students' writing (p. 125). But practicalities often preclude doing either; hence, testing programs may compromise by conducting one training session in which essays composed on both topics are simultaneously presented. Or they may use one common, generic scoring guide through successive scoring sessions, implicitly using the guide as a criterion-based measure that indicates whether students' writing reflects certain criteria.

Such compromises do not mean that something shoddy is occurring in these large-scale assessments, because most scorers, like most teachers, can balance the two topics quite readily; moreover, as will be seen in Chapter 5, formal scoring sessions contain several provisions for training and for monitoring. But despite the safeguards, the very idea that practical exigencies require testing programs to depart from the ideal in their scoring approaches only serves to underscore the complexity of evaluating writing. It reinforces the concern with which the holistic scoring of direct writing samples is viewed (Charney, 1984; Greenberg, 1992; Huot, 1990), a concern that arises both from the current emphasis on the importance of the reader's individual response to a text and from research on the various factors influencing those responses.

The Role of Classroom Teachers in Direct Assessments

Notwithstanding the limitations associated with direct writing assessment, writing samples do have positive features. Writing samples give, if not the whole picture, at least a glimpse into students' writing; as such, they show us where students' composing strengths and weaknesses lie, albeit under constrained circumstances. To return to the analogy noted at the start of this chapter, tasting a lemon meringue pie will not, in itself, reveal how good a chef is at preparing a six-course meal. But if the pie is light and delicious, it conveys the likelihood, at least, that the rest of the dinner will be a success. Moreover, just as the effort and the ingredients that we expend on cooking are judged ultimately by how a final dessert or meal tastes, so, too, do writing products, and not the processes alone, matter. Indeed, in this electronic age of e-mail, products represent the writer—products written, moreover, in haste, without much collaboration, and without much chance to "go back in" to erase or correct. In this sense, creating opportunities for students to practice timed writings periodically throughout a year seems an appropriate element for classroom instruction.

Teachers can, for example, provide opportunities for students, no matter what their school level, to write in various modes of discourse or periodically to write on topics that are assigned. Occasional practice of this nature does not negate the instructional value of the writing-workshop classroom, with its emphasis on topic ownership, on writing as discovery, or on the importance of revision. But it does mean that some efforts can be made to adapt process approaches even to timed-assessment contexts. That is, even if students do not truly "own" the topics that a direct writing assessment assigns to them, they can be shown how to use their prewriting strategies—their clusters, trees, or questions—to find that indeed they do still have something to say. Likewise, they can be shown how to read topics critically to determine what is being asked and how to make effective use of their time. (To anyone familiar with the student who "finishes" an essay ten minutes after the timed writing starts and then waits, with leg swinging impatiently, for the assessment to end, the notion of helping students use their time efficiently is, in and of itself, challenging.) Finally, students can be taught how best to apply to their own timed essays the evaluative skills they have learned in the peer-review groups and revising steps of their writing workshops. Even though the time constraints likely will limit students to surface proofreading alone, their practice in editing the final drafts of their outside papers may help to alleviate their anxiety by giving them practical ways to approach the task.

In addition, teachers can respond to the increasing use of direct writing assessments for external accountability purposes by becoming actively involved whenever possible in the development of topics, in the creation of scoring guides, and in the scoring of essays themselves. As teachers increase their understanding of the complexities entailed in writing assessment, such professional involvement ensures greater likelihood that teachers' voices will be heard and acted upon.

Certainly, a direct writing assessment is an imperfect measure with notable limitations, often reflecting what Alan Purves (1992) calls "PDQ" or "perceived drafting quality" (p. 118). Nevertheless, the writing opportunities a teacher provides in a classroom can only serve to benefit students in meeting that task—by giving students the confidence to believe that, even within the restricted context of the impromptu writing sample, they have the skills necessary to succeed. Furthermore, by participating in a knowledgeable way in external writing assessment programs—through scoring essays, through developing topics, modes, or guides, and through strengthening the links to the writing process—teachers can help to align direct writing assessments more closely with classroom instruction.

Summary

Direct writing assessments, also called impromptu essays, are being used increasingly for a variety of examination purposes. Because direct assessments require students to compose essays under controlled conditions, they permit comparisons to be made across or within classes, schools, and districts. Timed essays allow at least a glimpse into a given student's ability to write under particular circumstances, and they can be scored quickly and efficiently. However, they have several limitations, one of the most serious being the artificial conditions under which most impromptu essays are given. That is, students generally must compose on an assigned topic, and often they are not allowed access to resources of any kind during the testing period. In addition, there is little opportunity for students to revise or to apply other writing process approaches. As impromptu essays are often used for external accountability, teachers can help students practice for such timed assessments, and teachers can become involved in various aspects of direct writing assessments from designing topics to developing scoring guides.

TIPS FOR TEACHERS

What Teachers Can Do to Prepare Students for Direct Writing Assessments

1. Students need to be given a number of varied opportunities to practice writing in timed situations within the classroom. These tasks can include the full spectrum of writing modes—narratives, descriptive scenes, persuasive letters or editorials, expository essays, and reports—for various purposes and audiences. These timed writings can then serve as an instructional focal point for numerous writing and revising activities.

2. In most direct writing assessments students are given one or two topics from which to choose; this practice differs from that of the writing workshop in which students choose what they wish to write about. Sometimes, however, students in a workshop can be

given the topic beforehand, so that they can think about it and plan; at other times, they need to be given the topic on the spot. Whatever the procedure, students need to be shown how to read carefully and understand an assigned topic before they begin to write. They need to learn how to say to themselves, "What is this topic asking me to do?" or "What approach should I take with this topic?"

3. The importance of planning one's use of time needs to be stressed to students, especially because many students' first instinct seems to be to pick up their pens and write. Students should experiment with some simplified prewriting strategies on a few topics—playing with "trees," abbreviated outlines, clusters, or whatever works for them to generate ideas on the spot. Sometimes the prewriting can be done one day and the actual timed writing the next; this practice should be balanced with tasks that require students to do both under time constraints. Students need to realize that prewriting—far from wasting the time they need for the essay—instead enhances the effectiveness of their final work.

4. Once the kernels of ideas are jotted down, students can use arrows or numbers to quickly organize their prospective material, and they can consider what their controlling idea or main point is. Students need to know how to tackle an introduction quickly, but they also need to know that they cannot labor too long over getting the paper started. For too many students, writers' block paralyzes them at the opening paragraph and prevents them from getting under way.

5. The importance of *developing with specifics* needs likewise to be stressed. One useful exercise—after an initial timed writing is done—is to put on strips of paper a series of general statements drawn from the students' original timed writings and then have pairs of students select a strip to work on together and to develop with specific details. The class as a whole can subsequently examine these revisions to see how the specifics have improved the writing. (For example, when asked what advice they would give first-year students, our students—older by one term—wrote such general statements in their essays as "Find your way around the school" or "Learn to balance your studies and your recreation." Later, when students, working in pairs, developed one of the generalities, paragraphs with many more details appeared.)

6. Finally, students need to be given tips on proofreading and revising. They need to know, for example, that they cannot spend time "copying over" their material—that, rather, corrections can be

made on the original draft provided they are done neatly and legibly. Students need to know how to add or cross out material carefully so that potential scorers can still read their essays clearly. They also need to be shown how to proofread their papers from the last paragraph first so that they actually focus on and identify the errors they most often make. Opportunities for true revision rarely exist in timed writings, but students can work, either individually or in groups, with their practice essays afterward and can revise them extensively in much the same way that they can with papers written out of class or in a workshop setting.

3 Topic Design

The chronic complaint of students in class—"I don't know what to write about"—underscores the need for carefully designed topic prompts in direct writing assessments in order to elicit students' best possible writing under constrained circumstances.

Interest in the role that topic prompts play is not new; such early composition researchers as Braddock, Lloyd-Jones, and Schoer cautioned in 1963 that attention must be paid to the topic when any writing was to be evaluated. But interest in topics as an influential variable in writing evaluation has increased during the last dozen years or so as both researchers and teachers have explored the complexity of this issue.

The way that many writing assessments prescribe a specific topic troubles those instructors who, in the tradition of Donald Graves and of Nancie Atwell, believe that students' best writing occurs when students truly have something to say—when their writing has a purpose and an audience. Such ownership is lacking, many feel, when students are assigned a topic or are given a choice among two or three on which they are asked to demonstrate their writing competence. The result is often mechanical, with students' real voices missing.

But topics given in the testing context of a large-scale writing assessment must meet different conditions from those imposed by classroom assignments. In an external testing context, there exists an interplay among the student, the test developer, and the scorer, all of whom have their own requirements and perspectives. From the point of view of examinees, for example, topics must, first and foremost, be accessible. That is, especially in a timed assessment, students must be able to understand the topic and respond to it quickly in writing; as a result, the topic must be stated clearly, so that students—who are usually unable in a testing context to ask for additional explanation—can interpret the topic and the task. Moreover, given the varied backgrounds of students, suggested topics must be broad based, so that all students have an equal chance of addressing the topic. While the topics ideally should be so engaging that students become involved with their writing task, the topics should not elicit such an emotional response that students lose control of their writing.

From the point of view of the test developer, topics must meet other stipulations as well. Topics must fulfill the goals of the program by encouraging students to do the type of writing that is sought. Furthermore, if topics are to be given for comparative purposes across assessments—such as pre-post growth, program evaluation, individual student competence, or overall class performance—they must be parallel in structure and comparable in difficulty. (Asking students to write a narrative in September and an informative report in December is, for example, quite different from asking students to write a narrative in September and another narrative in December. The first instance shows whether students are able to handle different modes of writing, whereas the second instance might indicate whether any change has occurred in students' abilities to handle the narrative mode.) As new topics in the same format are often needed for successive writing assessments, the *type* of topics (e.g., a letter in response to a problem, the analysis of a quotation) must be replicable. Moreover, topics must be neither so bland nor so difficult that good writers cannot be distinguished from weak writers.

From the scorers' point of view, the topics must meet other requirements as well. Because scorers of large assessments are reading hundreds of essays, the topics must generate some varied responses in order for scorers to discern levels of writing performance. (Topics that elicit virtually the same response from every writer—e.g., ways to deal with stress—can have a numbing effect on the reader and make it difficult to distinguish strong responses from weak ones.) At the same time, the topic should not elicit an overemotional response on the reader's part any more than it should on the writer's part, or the reliability of the score conceivably could be affected.

As can be seen, then, all participants involved with topic prompts have different—and sometimes incompatible—requirements for topic design. The purpose of this chapter is to explore the complexities of topic design as they relate to the three parties just identified—test takers, test developers, and test scorers.

Accessibility of the Topic

The key criterion in most direct writing assessments is accessibility of the topic, or how readily the student writers can grasp the task, think of something to say on a given topic, and proceed to write. According to the researcher Carl Bereiter (1980), "thinking of what to write" can be a major obstacle for students who might otherwise be able to write fluently on a topic about which they have ideas. Judith Langer (1984) also points out that better writing might be produced if students have knowledge of a topic. She observes, "Intuition and experience suggest that when students write to a topic about which they have a great deal of well integrated knowledge, their writing is more likely to be well organized and fluent; conversely, when students know little about a topic, their writing is more likely to fail" (p. 136). Accessibility is influenced primarily by two factors: the subject matter and the wording of the topic prompt itself.

Subject Matter

Determining the subject matter of the prompt is especially critical in large-scale writing assessments. Unlike the classroom context, for example, wherein topics develop naturally from class discussions or from material read, topics in these large assessments must be broad based, appealing to writers from different backgrounds and experiences.

Because of the need for accessibility, many assessments use personal topics, or at least specify that personal experience may be used as part of the development of the essay. Advocates of personal experience topics point to many advantages, among which are the possibility that students will "own" the topic and hence, in the view of such scholars as Donald Graves and Janet Emig, become more engaged with their writing. In addition, with personal experience topics, the support students give in their essays is apt to be genuine. Karen Greenberg (1981) stresses the likelihood that personal experience topics will generate "fresh and lively" writing and will, more importantly, allow students to express their own views rather than relying upon some vague authority (pp. 30–31). Moreover, as Catherine Keech (1982) has found in her work with topics, students' writing tends to be more fluent and to reflect their own voices (p. 140). Still another advantage is the freshness or uniqueness of responses, which may help to sustain readers' interest—a factor, which, as just discussed, is important in large-scale assessments wherein scorers must evaluate hundreds of essays.

But if personal topics appear to offer clear advantages for large-scale assessments, research suggests that there are drawbacks as well. In the first edition of his major work on writing assessment, Edward White (1985) notes that "personal experience topics may be more accessible to most students, but they are not 'easier' for all students" (p. 67). Certainly, some studies confirm this observation. In one study, Karen Greenberg (1981) hypothesized that first-year college students would do better on topics requiring personal experience than they would on more abstract forms of similar topics. Not only did she find that students' writing was *not* statistically better on the personal experience formats, but also, to her surprise, students even avoided using the first person pronoun in their writing (p. 93). In another study at the University of Texas, Witte and Faigley (1983) found that writers who were very concerned about their writing did less well on personal experience essays than they did on their argumentative papers (p. 83).

Still other educators express concern about the potential impact that personal experience topics can have either on students from different cultures or on students with disadvantaged backgrounds. Ruth and Murphy (1988) note, for example, that teachers of ESL students have commented on the difficulties some of their students experience in writing about topics dealing with themselves. Some state testing programs avoid personal topics precisely so that students from low socioeconomic backgrounds will not be put at a disadvantage. Nor are all personal experience topics necessarily even accessible. Topic prompts that deal with questions about heredity, background, or "home" are apt to pose problems for a number of students. (Certainly, in my own experience with the developmental writing program, such a caution seems significant. When, for example, I asked the students in an in-class writing assignment to respond to the line from Robert Frost's poem "Home is the place where, when you go there/ They have to take you in," the other instructors and I were not prepared for the unhappy intensity of the personal experiences a few writers revealed.)

Strong emotions can adversely affect the quality of writing students produce precisely because, as colleague and published poet Diane Stevenson points out, the students are reliving the experience itself rather than trying to craft the writing and transform it. If a student is writing about an unhappy experience, that student might not have the necessary distance or desire to be concerned with the way he or she has written about the experience; instead, the writing process becomes a catharsis for the writer, and the written product on which the student will then be evaluated is merely secondary. Sandra Stotsky (1995), arguing that too much emphasis has been placed on personal writing in the overall school curriculum with the result of neglecting other genres, suggests that even the context of writing assessment does not justify emphasizing personal writing exclusively. She states, "If the goal of an assessment is writing ability, not academic achievement, students can be asked to write on something other than their experiences, beliefs, or attitudes if they are provided with sufficient written information, such as case study information, or pictorial information" (p. 770).

Just as writing in response to personal topics may be difficult for some writers, so too can reading such personal papers pose difficulties for the scorers. For example, when local scorers and I were asked to score a series of middle school papers from another state, we were all stricken by the paper from a young girl who wrote painfully of her grandmother's recent death; because this youngster's mother was also dead and her father was in jail, we were left with the question of who was caring for her now. The score on the paper seemed a minor issue. A similar difficulty occurred several years ago when we scored a paper written by a young Cambodian refugee whose family had been massacred. Having to assign that paper a low score because of its severe language problems seemed almost a travesty in view of the suffering he had already endured. Despite their advantages, then, personal topics risk making uncomfortable not only some students who are asked to write about their own experiences, but also some readers who are asked to read—and ultimately evaluate—the very personal responses that occasionally result.

Still another potential drawback of personal topics derives from the rhetorical mode they almost exclusively encourage. As Stotsky (1995) notes, "experience-based writing may stimulate an excessive use of narrative structure because of teachers' and students' tendency, especially in the early grades, to turn experience-based writing into storytelling" (p. 765). Stotsky worries that students may have little practice in trying other ways to organize their information. The *purpose* of the assessment thus becomes critical in determining the topic of the assessment. Carlson and Bridgeman (1986) caution, for example, that "if the writing is expected to provide a sample of how well students will perform in the classroom, the stimulus should be representative of that type of writing" (p. 141), and they note that in their survey of various *college* departments' attitudes toward writing, "personal and creative writing" was not valued as highly in other disciplines as it was in English courses.

Of course, personal experiences work well as one of several means of support for a generalization. In fact, Edward White (1985) endorses those topics which require the writer to "relate the self to knowledge, find personal meaning in external objects, and communicate internal truth to an outside reader" (pp. 118–119). Often, major testing programs encourage students to use personal experience, in addition to readings, to support their discussion of a particular topic. Such "expository narratives" seemingly can be scored more readily. In research done by Rosemary Hake (1986), for example, the scoring done for "expository narrations" was more objective than it was for narratives alone, leading her to conclude, "If we do want to measure a writer's skill and we continue to encourage writers to use personal experiences when they write, we should certainly create topics and test directions that elicit expository narrations rather than pure narrations" (p. 161).

Thus, although personal experience topics offer great accessibility to most students, such topics may be troublesome to those writers who feel uncomfortable in revealing themselves; moreover, topics in this format lend themselves to a narrative mode of writing that may not—unless it is linked to an expository thesis—be appropriate for the particular purpose of the assessment.

General Knowledge Topics

But if personal experience topics can be problematic, general knowledge topics for writing assessments present difficulties as well. Because of the critical role played by background knowledge, it is difficult to find common topics which all students, regardless of background, can tap into and which will not penalize students with cultural differences from the norm assumed by the topic. Even those topics about which it is often assumed everyone will have something to say—television, for example—can present a stumbling block for students from home environments where television is unimportant. Still other general knowledge topics, such as those dealing with current controversial issues, can arouse students' emotions to such an extent that the quality of their writing may be obscured. Papers on such topics can also trigger readers' biases.

Further, general knowledge topics give rise to problems with the accuracy of students' knowledge. Papers in which factual knowledge is erroneous are troublesome to score, particularly if the purpose of the exam is to illustrate students' ability to write, rather than their recollection of specific events. Readers who must deal with wars that are situated in the wrong decade, with inventions attributed to the wrong century, or with factual statements that are blatantly wrong must struggle to ignore or minimize such knowledge gaps. Even when the writing itself comprises an integral part of a subject-area exam, the issue of accuracy or of legitimacy in a response must be addressed: despite the various interpretations encouraged by reader response, an analysis of a poem that wanders in an entirely irrelevant direction can cause concern to readers who must deal with content as part of the quality of writing in an English subject-area exam.

Finally, even though a general knowledge topic might be accessible, students may not become fully engaged in their approach to the essay and may respond in mechanical, similar-sounding ways. Such predictable essays can be difficult for readers to score, especially when there are hundreds of identical responses. Other papers that may be tedious to score are those written in response to "negative" topics, such as a problem that needs correcting in the environment or in the country; depending on the maturity of the writer, responses may be shallow, glib, or simplistic. Certainly, the evaluator's interest in a topic should not be as major a concern as the student's interest. Nevertheless, just as interest plays a role in how well students might respond to a topic, it may also affect for a few readers the accuracy with which they are able to evaluate the writing quality that results.

The Issue of Topic Wording

The subject matter of a topic is not the sole problematic issue in topic development. Both the wording of the topic and the amount of context provided can be critical factors in how well students are able to respond.

Confusion may, according to Catherine Keech, arise from a single word. In our own writing tests, we have seen students misinterpret *values* for *valuable* or *fiction* for *nonfiction*, thereby creating distortions in the resulting responses. Because a single word can be so crucial, it is imperative that attention be paid to the level of vocabulary reflected in the topic prompt (see Carlson & Bridgeman, 1986).

At the same time, several studies have suggested that wording variations may not play as critical a role as is sometimes believed. In one study, for example, Brossell and Ash (1984) manipulated the wording of two versions of twenty-one topics in a Florida state-mandated examination for college students; some topic directives included a personal address stated as a command or question, whereas other topics were presented with neutral directives. When the essays were scored afterward, significant differences were not attributable to the topic variables. Brossell and Ash concluded, "We came away feeling that as long as topics do not require special knowledge and are suited to the characteristics of the test takers, neither small syntactical variations nor subject matter has much of an effect on essay examinations" (p. 424). In a similar vein, Karen Greenberg (1981) found that including the personal "you" in the topic to student writers did not make a substantial difference.

But despite these research findings, it does seem advisable to pay attention to the ordering and vocabulary level of topics. Furthermore, the wording of the instructions can be especially significant. Catherine Keech (1982) points out, for example, that some instructions, such as "'Support your opinion with specific examples'" and "'Write a well organized essay,'" are helpful in that they remind students of the criteria for a good essay. Other helpful reminders may include instructions to focus on one part of a problem. But she cautions against instructions that are either too elaborate or too general, as in the directive to "Describe what you see in the picture," a command which does not give students enough information about their task (p. 175). She also cautions against specifying the number of words or paragraphs that the essay should contain; in Keech's view, such specifications cause students to waste time counting words, or they emphasize the paragraph as a distinct unit, rather than as an integral part of the overall essay.

The Context and Audience in Topic Prompts

Related to the issue of wording is the amount of context provided in topic prompts and the audience for whom the essay is written. The issue of reader-as-audience is fundamental both to writing instruction and to writing assessment, for a primary challenge facing every writing teacher is helping students realize that, because they are writing to be read, they have the obligation to be clear and coherent for their readers. But despite the growing use of peer groups in the classroom—and the growing importance of reader response—students continue to struggle with the notion of audience and with the entailed obligations to their readers. In fact, both the British scholar James Britton and the American researcher Arthur Applebee have found that most students continue to see their writing audience as their teacher in an examining role. In writing assessments, the notion of audience becomes even more complex in that students recognize, no matter who might be specified as the audience for a specific topic prompt, that the true audience consists ultimately of the "judges" or "raters" who will be evaluating their essays.

The effect that the specification of audience might have on students' writing assessments has been explored by several researchers. In a 1980 study by Woodworth and Keech, for example, three ninth-grade classes and three junior/senior classes were given—at random—different versions of a similar test topic in which the degree of audience specification varied. All had to write about a first experience, but students in one group had no audience specified at all; the second group had as the audience "someone who is about to experience this activity for the first time"; and the third group was told to write for "a particular person (brother, sister, friend, etc.) who has not had such an experience" (p. 63).

When the essays were each scored holistically by two readers, no differences were found in the mean scores given to students writing to the three audiences. In the researchers' view, students might have viewed the audience as the essay evaluators, especially as over half the students wrote an informal essay in response, rather than a letter such as might be expected for the familiar audience. Many of the students could not specify a particular person to whom they were writing. Thus, the authors conclude that "audience specification of this sort does not necessarily result in simple and direct improvement of student writing" (p. 34).

In another study—one involving college students—Hoetker and Brossell (1986) also found that specifying the audience in great detail did not have a positive effect on the students' writing. Papers written in response to the most detailed audience specification not only were the shortest but also received the lowest holistic scores. Thus, even though the specification of a particular audience is sometimes advocated by writing specialists as a means for making the test more realistic, it does not always produce the best results.

In fact, James Hoetker (1982) calls attention to Gordon Brossell's observation that writing processes, while helpful to students who are learning how to compose, may not assist students confronted with the constraints of an assessment context. Hoetker himself concludes his review of studies on examination topics by noting that "teaching writing is not assessing writing skills is not doing research on writing" and that, because the different purposes of each undertaking require different methods, "the use of elaborate fictional topics, which are effective in setting assignments in a writing class, may, in a testing situation, serve to confuse and hinder student writers" (p. 389).

The extent of context or structure that should be given to students is another issue that must be addressed in any writing assessments. The formats used in large-scale assessments vary enormously, from sentence fragments to elaborate scenarios and even pictures or audiotapes. Whereas some use simple phrases, such as "a memory from childhood," as a point of departure for students to begin their writing (Keech, 1982, p. 136), others supply students with a task, audience, and purpose with which to fulfill their task. (One testing program even supplies the opening sentence and suggests possible directions for the essay to follow after that.) Both the simple and the elaborate topic prompts contain disadvantages as well as advantages. In their work on topic development, Ruth and Murphy (1988) note that if students have to determine their own audience and purpose for writing, a broad range of interpretations may occur, thereby adding to the scoring challenge. At the same time, they caution that every specification that is added to the topic creates another constraint for the writer and may limit what the writing task measures. Other assessment experts, such as Carlson and Bridgeman (1986), likewise stress the need for a balance in topics—a balance that both allows for a sufficiently broad range of student responses, so that all students do not produce virtually the same-sounding essay, and yet provides for a commonality of structure so that there is some basis for comparing the essays.

Research studies into the effect of context and structure on student responses to topics have not produced clear-cut results. In a recent study of advanced seventh-, ninth-, and eleventh-grade students and first-year college students, Eileen Oliver (1995) found that the degree of specification in the writing-assessment prompts for topic, purpose, and audience did affect the quality of writing to varying degrees depending on students' age and grade level. In Oliver's view, "effective and rigorous composition instruction" with well-designed assignments enables students to produce better writing (p. 444). Christine Hult (1987), after studying Michigan's elaborate college placement essay prompt, concluded cautiously that the complex structure might have worked in students' favor, although she acknowledged the presence of several variables (p. 25). Kinzer and Murphy (1982) examined two of eight topics that had been randomly given to students in three different schools to see why these two topics produced the greatest difference in score results; they found that higher scores seemed related to the extent to which students could recognize the prompt's explicit and implicit demands.

But not everyone reads a prompt the same way. Just as reader-response theorists have shown that interpretations of any given written passage can vary widely, so may the demands of a given prompt be interpreted differently, depending on the role of the person reading it. For example, a pilot study by Kinzer, Carroll, and Murphy (1982) showed that the test writers and scorers interpreted the requirements of the task quite differently from the way the students understood their task. The researchers stressed the need for providing clear prompts not open to misinterpretation. As will be seen in Figure 5 (Chapter 6) of this text, one of our students interpreted the placement essay topic prompt far more generally than the topic writers intended.

Summary

As this chapter illustrates, then, the development of topic prompts for writing assessment presents a special challenge if the topics are, in fact, to meet the requirements of all the parties involved—the test writers, the test readers, and, most important, the test takers themselves. While research results regarding the importance of audience, context, and wording are not always clear-cut, they do indicate the need for paying attention to all the elements of prompt development as they relate in particular to the purpose of a given assessment. These research results underscore the importance not only of careful design of the topic type but also of an equally careful review of any prospective topics that are written subsequently using that design. These results also illustrate the need for a comprehensive, carefully done field testing that includes minority students and nonnative speakers of English, as well as other students with a range of backgrounds. The essays written on the field-tested topics must then be carefully scored, with the scorers paying close attention to some of the issues raised by topic development experts. Scorers must look at the range of essays that results, at possible misinterpretations students have made of the topic, at potential vocabulary difficulties, and at the quality of the essays that result. Finally, as Edward White (1985) and Eileen Oliver (1995) suggest, research into topic development underscores the need to pay closer attention to the assignments we devise for our writing classes.

TIPS FOR TEACHERS

Topic Design

Whenever possible, teachers need to become involved in the development and review of topics for writing assessments, because teachers bring to the task a familiarity with their students' interests and their students' vocabulary level that few outsiders can share. Writing themselves on the topics they generate will help teachers know how difficult a particular task might be.

1. Teachers can have their students practice reading sample topics and interpreting the tasks that are required. Together, the class can discuss the implications of the various instructions and testing vocabulary terms that are used. Through these test-taking strategies, students become aware of the need for staying on topic and dealing with the task at hand.

2. Students can also practice writing various essays in response to the types of topics anticipated in an assessment. If detailed contexts are to be used, then students need to know how to frame their writing within similar contexts; if, on the other hand, stu-

dents might be encountering quotations, phrases, or pictures, then students need practice in composing essays that respond to those requirements.

3. Finally, students can practice their prewriting strategies on a variety of essays that respond to potentially different topic formats, so that students feel, regardless of the topic type, that they do indeed have "something to say."

4 Portfolio Assessment

A common sight in classrooms today, especially at the end of a semester, is the array of brightly covered folders containing essays, colorful illustrations, and perhaps a videotape or two. These portfolios, whether in composition or other subject areas, represent a different type of performance assessment from the direct writing samples. They sometimes serve in place of, or in addition to, other forms of assessment as a way to measure students' progress. But portfolios differ from the ubiquitous folders long used in English classes to store nonselective collections of student work. Rather, the concept of portfolios, as derived from the fine arts, implies that students' best or most representative pieces are displayed, that students have a choice in selecting what goes into the portfolio, and that their selections are based on knowledgeable reflections about their own work done over a period of time. While each portfolio undertaking is unique, and while, as Murphy and Smith (1990) emphasize, there is no one right way to do portfolios, these key attributes of student selection, student reflection, and revision of work completed over a span of time commonly underpin portfolio projects. The purpose of this chapter is to explore these concepts as they apply, first, to portfolios used for instructional assessment *within* classes, and second, to portfolios used for external assessment purposes *across* classes, schools, or districts. The chapter also reviews controversies that can arise with portfolios used for external assessment and highlights various methods used in scoring portfolios.

Because definitions of portfolios vary, we have found especially useful the Northwest Evaluation Association's (NWEA's) description of a portfolio as a

> *purposeful* collection of student work that exhibits to the student (and/or others) the student's *efforts, progress,* or *achievement* in (a) given areas(s). This collection must include: student participation in selection of portfolio content: the criteria for selection; the criteria for judging merit; and evidence of student self-reflection. (Northwest Evaluation Association, 1991, p. 4; cf. Meyer, Schuman, & Angello, 1990)

The process of initiating a portfolio program—whether within or across classes—can be viewed as analogous to the writing process itself: the external vehicle which the portfolio process constitutes serves as a metaphor for the internal writing process it embodies, both in the attention that must be paid to purpose, audience, and capacity for revision, and in the understanding that must be fostered of criteria, ownership, and self-reflection.

Portfolios in the Classroom

Portfolios have been used primarily for instruction and internal assessment—that is, within classrooms. Although portfolios are used most often in writing, they are also used in other subject areas such as math, science, and social studies; in some schools, cross-disciplinary portfolios that include selections from several fields have grown in popularity. Some portfolios include tests and reading logs; others contain only work directly produced by the students. In some school systems, portfolios may travel with a given student throughout the years of the student's career, providing the student at graduation with an ongoing record of his or her growth and progress; in other cases, portfolios are used for a single term or a year.

Purpose and Procedures

Just as the idea of purpose is central to writing, it is also critical to portfolios. Indeed, purpose is one of the key distinctions between portfolios and the commonly used writing folders that contain everything a student does or random pieces of student work. As the NWEA definition suggests and as some educators have stressed (e.g., French, 1991), the purpose behind the portfolios must be carefully considered before teachers undertake portfolios with their classes. Teachers must explore whether the portfolios are intended to show students' progress over time, to depict only their best work or their most representative work, or to reveal students' ability to handle various types of writing assignments. In addition, they must give thought beforehand to the specific role or function that portfolios will have in the classroom: For example, will the portfolios be used for grading purposes, comprising either a major or a supplementary part of the student's grade? Alternately, will portfolios have more of an illustrative function by providing evidence of a student's work and hence forming the basis for a conference with parents? These are the issues that teachers need to weigh *before* undertaking a portfolio project, even though, as Murphy and Smith (1990) stress, allowances for change must always be incorporated. Despite the importance of flexibility—of the capacity for

Time Entailed

Finally, allowance must be made for the time required to work with portfolios. The extra time is needed not so much for the reading and writing activities themselves; as Tierney, Carter, and Desai (1991) have aptly noted, such activities should, in a writing workshop atmosphere, be in progress anyway. Rather, time is needed for the preparatory part of the portfolio process when the portfolio concept is introduced. Time is needed as well for the ongoing practice stages of the portfolio process when students use guides to "peer edit" each other's work, when they are given opportunities to develop their own reflective skills through dress rehearsals, when they conference with their teachers, or when teachers review the ongoing drafts. Time is needed, finally, for all the evaluative parts of the portfolio process—both for students to reflect upon their own progress and choose their portfolio selections and for teachers to review the showcase portfolios and assign the grades or scores.

Collaborative Work

Collaboration in a variety of forms is a frequent characteristic of class-room portfolio programs. Often, the articulation of the purposes and goals of the portfolio program can incorporate suggestions from the students themselves. Even very young students can become engaged in deciding what they want their portfolios to contain and reveal about themselves. In fact, the collaborative nature of such goal setting is con-sidered a great asset of portfolios because students thereby become in-volved in their own educational process. (D. J. Henry, who has used portfolios with both her high school students and her community col-lege students, lets her students determine the percentage of credit that will be given to the final "presentation" or "display" portfolio versus the "working" portfolio, which contains their exercises and practice drafts. She has remarked how heated the discussions can become as those students who have worked hard and attended regularly may want more credit given to the working portfolios than do their coun-terparts who may have worked only in a desultory manner [see Abbot et al., 1994].)

Within a classroom, the teacher and students may collaborate in making a number of decisions: They may explore, for example, what the requirements for portfolio content will be—such as whether a range of entries might be expected and, if so, the types that should be in-cluded. They may also discuss the various forms of media that might be employed as options. Because one hallmark of portfolios is the creative individualization they encourage, students often choose to embellish their portfolios with colorful illustrations, videotapes, audiotapes, and graphs in addition to the more traditional papers, letters, and reports. But even allowing for creativity, teachers may still want to provide students with guidelines to follow, especially in terms of the instructional purpose. Otherwise, a teacher may receive portfolios that either range from very skimpy to overflowing or contain only one type of writing or one medium. The classroom discussions that address these issues can, therefore, help to broaden students' understanding not only about what is required but also about what is possible.

Collaboration may also be involved in the preparation and revision of selections for the portfolios. In the writing workshop atmosphere that often prevails with portfolio programs, students may receive input from their classmates during peer editing sessions, or they may confer with their teacher about possible changes. As papers usually need several revisions before they are ready for portfolios, students can benefit from the encouragement and varying perspectives that such collaborative environments provide.

Finally, the collaboration within a classroom may extend to discussions about the standards by which the portfolios will be evaluated. The very definition of portfolios as articulated by the NWEA stresses the importance of students' knowing this information. Students' familiarity with the assessment criteria not only demystifies the evaluation process for them but also gives them the foundation on which to build their own self-reflection skills and become better able to assess their own work. In this manner, when students must make decisions about their "best" work—as portfolios often ask them to do—they have some objective basis for making their choices and need not rely solely on what their "favorite" work might be.

Revision

Revision is another central concept of portfolios. Unlike direct writing assessments, portfolios encourage students to see their writings as works in progress that can undergo multiple revisions throughout a term. Thus, portfolios often contain, in addition to the polished draft of one or more entries, stacks of rough drafts that convey the process the student underwent in reaching the final stage. In this respect, portfolios provide a much fuller picture of a student than a timed-writing assessment ever can.

This emphasis on revision in portfolios has both advantages and disadvantages. On the one hand, students are often pleased that an unsuccessful piece can be revised—that, in effect, they have the chance to "try again." In some cases, this knowledge gives the students freedom to experiment and to risk failing on a first try. Because they work on the same piece in various stages, they often develop more of a sense of ownership of their work. For example, Judith Leder (1991) recounts the pride that business majors at one college felt upon completing a major portfolio assignment and the importance they placed on being allowed to learn from their mistakes and revise their work (pp. 130–132). Similar observations came from our own developmental writers: One first-year student wrote upon completing the portfolio, "Portfolio taught vital revision tools. Now I revise papers two or three times before I turn them in. Portfolio system very helpful." Other reflective comments we received included this observation: "I have done six papers so far, and I have lost count of revision." Another student remarked, "As I have revised my papers, they seem to get better because I have a chance to see my mistakes and correct them."

On the other hand, some students may be discomfited by the need to revise a given piece several times. Their view of revision is limited to correcting occasional words or other surface features, and they may become discouraged at repeatedly having to revise for higher-order concerns. As one of our own instructors observed, revision is viewed differently by better writers who examine "their writing more self-consciously" during revisions than it is by weaker writers who, instead of truly revising, spend "15 minutes in front of a computer screen, adding three commas and two sentences." Accustomed to tossing something off, these latter students dislike having to return repeatedly to the same tired work. They want their work to be graded so they can dismiss it and move on, rather than struggle with recursive revisions. Still other students argue that they revise as they write, and they remain resistant to making changes afterward.

For teachers, too, the emphasis on revision may be two-sided. On the beneficial side is surely the improvement made visible when a student's drafts are laid side by side. As Mills-Courts and Amiran (1991) note, evidence of the teachers' successes are plainly visible: "Nowhere else can teachers see with such clarity the effects of their efforts in the classroom. It's all there, from awkward first draft to the clear demonstration of the growth of analytical, evaluative, and decision-making skills evidenced by students' selections and reasoning in the introduction, the process of revision, and in the final drafts" (p. 107). Winograd and Jones (1993) stress a similar idea by noting that the value of portfolios for teachers lies precisely in the students' growth that teachers can see through the multiple measures contained in the portfolios (p. 11). Rewarding, too, for the teachers is the sense of ownership that some students appear to acquire through their engagement over time with the same work. Furthermore, the "coaching hat" that teachers can wear during this time is beneficial; relieved of the need for grading every paper as though each one were a final product, teachers can, instead, convey how they have responded *as readers* to the students' texts and make suggestions for improvement.

On the negative side is the time involved in coaching the students through these multiple drafts (while new assignments, more likely than not, may be underway at the very same time). Still another negative is the fact that the teacher's coaching hat ultimately must be removed in order to evaluate students' final portfolios—a shift that constitutes a real change in roles. Furthermore, some students may rely too heavily on receiving teachers' feedback before making any improvements and then limit their changes only to those noted by the instructor; or students may not bother enough with their first drafts, relying on their opportunities to revise. Still other students, especially weak writers, do not always improve with multiple revisions and may need instead to start afresh with an entirely new assignment. One of our instructors wrote that what was hardest about her participation in portfolios was "keeping up the 'energy' level—for both student and teacher." She added, "Toward the end of the term, we were getting a bit tired of the same work and 'rework'!"

Thus, the emphasis on revision inherent in portfolios carries with it a challenge for teachers and students alike: the challenge is to structure the opportunities for revision in such a way that students can appreciate the benefits, rather than the drawbacks. Sometimes, providing students with interim grades on their portfolios can help them see where they stand in the overall process, especially if they are troubled by the lack of specific grades on individual entries. If the portfolios span a semester and teachers must give grades at the end of the quarter, then these interim grades can serve that function as well.

Reflection

Closely related to the concept of revision in portfolios is that of reflection. Ideally, portfolios encourage students to reflect upon their own work and develop their self-assessment skills. Regardless of whether the portfolio is done for a math or writing class, or whether it is the work of a senior or a third grader, a common thread in most portfolios is the inclusion of a reflective piece—often written as a letter to the readers of the portfolio. These reflective pieces may form the most engaging part of a portfolio, where the honesty and individuality of the student are readily apparent as he or she struggles to identify strengths and weaknesses or to provide rationales for why particular entries have been chosen. Such metacognition—or the student's self-awareness not only of progress made but also of areas yet to be learned—indicates higher-order thinking and is critical in order for students to develop.

Educators MacIsaac and Jackson (1992) identify three major stages of reflection typically contained in portfolios, from the student's first basic recounting of what has been done, through the second stage in which the student explains and illustrates what has been learned, to the final stage in which the student considers new goals and indicates what subsequent direction to pursue. Cautioning that "portfolios are more than activity records, [in that they] provide documentation of accomplishments representing growth in a learner's skill or understanding over time," MacIsaac and Jackson stress the valuable link that portfolios forge for students "between finished works and particular personal futures" (pp. 12–13).

These stages have been apparent in excerpts from reflective letters written by several developmental writers in our former program: One reflective letter began, "'I hate writing.' I made this statement in the beginning of the semester, however; being forced to do it in your class has changed my view point on my writing dramatically. . . ." Another student began his reflective letter with the straightforward statement, "My writing experiences this past semester have been a little like a roller coaster ride, up and down." The agony of a third student writer's struggle is apparent both in the form and content of the message itself: "The honest truth of my improvement in Writing hasn't exceed very far. For many reasons, I don't seem to know how to get my point across very well. . . .The revision has definitely influence myself to risk and try something new. But I still seem to be facing the same problems. . . ."

As portfolio advocates Kathryn Howard (1990) and Camp and Levine (1991) have noted, such reflection does not come easily to students, and they need to have several opportunities—in addition to time—to practice evaluating their own work. Helping to build students' confidence about their own perceptions of their work is, therefore, an essential part of the portfolio process. This need may be particularly acute for younger students, who, as Howard has noted, may be unduly influenced by the teacher's grade in determining their own strengths and weaknesses (p. 6). Even older students need practice. As one of our developmental first-year writers observed in the opening paragraph to the reflective letter, "To play the role of critic of your own work sometimes it is not that easy. Usually, when it comes to criticizing yourself, you either do it too easy or too hard (depends on the honesty of that person)." Endorsing nonetheless the idea of reflection, he commented, "It makes us to use our spirit of responsibility and shows the sense of criticizing."

In many classrooms, teachers periodically ask their students to look back over their portfolios and to answer a series of guided questions as a means of developing the students' self-evaluation skills. As Figure 1 and the writing sample below illustrate, the guides provide students with the preliminary structure they need for learning how to critique their own work; the questions force students to weigh the reasons that make a particular work "best," as opposed to being "favorite" or "representative." The reflective component of portfolios, then, is a key element in moving students toward an internalized self-assessment that is the ultimate goal of evaluation. Figure 1 and the writing sample below show a preliminary reflective exercise and a reflective letter written by a student in my first-year developmental writing course.

Reflective Letter Written in Class

Dear Dr. Wolcott,

Entering college I knew how to write decent, average papers. When writing the papers, I always came across the same problems like; writing my ideas down on paper, awkward sentence structure, and writing weak introductory and conclusion paragraphs. With the help of the writing class I improved greatly.

College Freshman Writing
Preliminary Reflective Guide for a Portfolio

The purpose of this exercise is to give you the opportunity to look back over the papers you have written so far this semester and to reflect on their strengths and weaknesses. Try to answer each question carefully. This exercise will not be graded, but it will give you practice in assessing your own writing before you compose your final reflective letter for the portfolio.

1. Of all the papers that you have written so far this term, which one do you consider to be your best? Why?
2. What is the greatest strength of that paper?
3. Do you think it still needs some improvement? In what areas?
4. What paper gave you the most difficulty in writing this term? Why do you think that was so?
5. How do you plan to improve that paper?
6. In what areas do you feel you are making progress as a writer?
7. In what areas do you think you need to improve as a writer?
8. Have you felt as though you could take some "risks" in your writing this term since you usually have the chance to revise? Why or why not?

Figure 1. Preliminary reflective guide from the Writing Center, University of Florida.

Other voices acknowledge the possible use of portfolios for both external and internal purposes. Jon Davies (1991) cautions against "the tendency by some educators to reduce complex debate on portfolios to an 'us versus them' phenomenon" (p. 8) and suggests that more research is needed to explore the variety of uses for portfolios, including that of statewide assessment. In a similar vein, Winograd and Jones (1993) admit that portfolios represent a significant improvement over former testing practices but, nevertheless, stress their belief that "portfolio assessment is *most* powerful and *most* appropriate when it is used by individual students, teachers, and parents" (p. 11).

External Assessment Purposes and Consequences

Regardless of the debate over internal and external uses of portfolios, as of 1995 portfolios used for external assessment purposes continued to remain in the minority. For example, Calfee and Perfumo found in a 1994 study that of 150 instructors sampled nationwide, about 60 percent were using portfolios within the classrooms; another 20 percent were using portfolios throughout the school; and 10 percent were using portfolios for district or state purposes (pp. 1–4). In a nationwide study we recently completed, we found that portfolios were used predominantly within classrooms for instructional and internal assessment purposes (Wolcott with Hoffman, 1994). In those programs that do use portfolios for external assessment purposes, serious consequences may or may not be involved for individual students or for the program, school, or district. Some colleges use portfolios from entering first-year students to determine where the students will be placed in targeted courses; hence, a student with a strong portfolio may be exempt from traditional first-year composition, whereas a student with a weak portfolio may be enrolled in a college preparatory course. Other colleges use portfolios as part of their exit criteria to determine whether students can progress to subsequent courses; some schools even use portfolios as alternatives to required competency exams. In all these cases, the portfolio has external consequences for the individual students above and beyond the internal practice of a classroom grade for a course.

At the secondary level, portfolios are increasingly being used as *part* of the requirements for students' graduation. These graduation portfolios are, in some cases, presented to a panel as part of the seniors' culminating rites. With the exception of those programs in which portfolios are used to meet partial graduation requirements, portfolios at the secondary level tend to have a less severe impact on individual students than those at the college level. (One school district that attempted in 1994 to use portfolios alone—in place of the more traditional graduating units—as the sole basis for determining students' readiness for graduation encountered severe resistance and was forced to change its procedures and return to more traditional criteria after the election of a new school board that emphasized the need for traditional, credit-based requirements [see Davis and Felknor, 1994].)

In other school systems, portfolios serve as a means of gauging the success of a program, an individual school, or an entire school district. Vermont, for example, led the way in the early '90s with its math and writing portfolios that served to indicate how well that state's students were performing in those areas. As teachers were heavily involved and not all schools chose to participate in the program, the portfolio assessment, albeit external, was not considered high-stakes. The subsequent introduction of portfolios in Kentucky, however, was clearly high-stakes (see Guskey, 1994). Incorporated as part of an overall school reform program that has included multiple dimensions, the writing and math portfolios have been used to indicate the extent to which schools—and individual teachers within those schools—have contributed to overall improvement from their baseline collection point. Schools that do not show sufficient improvement over time are scheduled to receive sanctions, whereas those schools and teachers that do show substantive improvement will be rewarded.

Differences between Internal and External Portfolio Assessment

As can be seen, then, external portfolio assessment comes in many different shapes and forms with varying consequences to the parties concerned. Because external portfolio assessment differs in several important categories from the portfolio assessment used within classrooms for internal instructional purposes—categories such as goals, contents, selection, process drafts, and scoring procedures—the remainder of this chapter will explore the differences and their implications.

Goals

The goals for external assessment often differ from those for internal classroom assessment, in which students and teachers together may decide common purposes. For external assessment, the goals may reflect the concerns of a larger entity. Accordingly, whereas an internal portfolio may emphasize representative works or demonstrate a student's progress over time, portfolios prepared for external assessment may be required to demonstrate a student's ability to compose in a variety of discourse modes. Thus, while the individual goals of students and teachers may be included, the purpose of the external assessment, which is likely to be program or school evaluation, becomes the overriding factor in determining the goals of the individual student portfolios.

Contents

For an external assessment program, the types of content and the number of entries often need to be standardized. Some educators, such as Paulson and Paulson (1991), decry this need for standardization, which, in their view, negates the individualization that is the hallmark of portfolios. At the same time, there must be some basis for comparability if portfolios are to be evaluated in relation to one another, as is the situation with most external portfolio assessment programs.

Similarly, external portfolio assessment programs may list their specifications in terms of broad types that reflect the goals of the particular program. For example, if the purpose of the portfolio is to show a student's ability to write in different modes, the requirements for the portfolio may ask students to include an argumentative piece; an expository piece; an in-class, on-demand piece; a personal narrative; a creative piece; and a reflective letter. If the purpose of the portfolio is to show growth over time, the specifications may ask students to include an early work, a late work, and a "best" work, as well as the reflective letter. Or again, if the purpose is to show a student's ability to write in a variety of contexts, the specifications may ask students to include pieces written for other courses. Structuring the portfolio requirements to identify broad *types* of entries to be included, then, is a common means by which external assessment programs allow both for individuality and for comparability across students or classes.

Student Selection

The extent of student choice may also differ in an external assessment program. While students usually do—and, in fact, should—participate in the selection of at least some of the entries for their portfolios, in an external assessment program they may not necessarily be able to choose all their entries. Teachers whose instruction is reflected through the students' portfolios may seek to have some say in the selections. And the instructor's point of view may be valuable: not only may students have initial difficulty in learning to distinguish between their "favorite" and their "best" work, but also the teacher may have a deeper understanding than the students have of the criteria against which the portfolios are being evaluated. Thus, to a greater extent in an external portfolio assessment program than in an internal portfolio program, choices about the entries are likely to involve some collaborative decision making on the part of both the teacher and the student.

Context for the Assignment

Because readers for external portfolios are not as familiar with the students' assignments as are the readers for most internal portfolios, the context of assignments must be explained clearly in each student's cover letter or table of contents. Whereas in internal portfolio assessments it may suffice to have a student merely note "observation assignment" next to the title in the table of contents of the portfolio, in external assessments it is helpful to have a more in-depth explanation of what the assignment entailed, how the observation was chosen and conducted, and what the other parameters of the assignment were. Similarly, if an impromptu writing has been included, readers of external portfolios should be given a history of its origin. They need to know whether a choice of topics was provided, whether resources were available, and whether revisions were allowed. Even when the drafts are included, readers need to have a feel for why particular entries have been included in a given portfolio in order to have a more complete sense of the writer's intentions.

Cover sheets that provide explanations of the origins behind the assignments are often necessary in external portfolio assessments to enhance the portfolios for both the writers and readers. Otherwise, assessment may be hindered by the concerns expressed by Despain and Hilgers (1992) that "teacher-readers find assessment problematic when they do not know the contexts of individual essays' production" (p. 27). Certainly when our teachers assembled to score portfolios for a program evaluation, they had more difficulty scoring portfolios from those classes whose curriculum differed from their own. Unless students provided some context for their entries, the teachers had less grounding for their evaluation.

Authenticating Student Work

In external portfolio assessments, authenticating authorship of the portfolios may become important if high stakes, such as a competency requirement, are involved for the individual student. However, as a number of educators have noted, authenticating authorship is not easy, especially when collaborative learning environments are created as in peer editing, conferencing, and group prewriting. To improve their performance in a portfolio, some students may obtain extensive help. Irene Clark (1993), for example, writes of students who crowded her college writing center with multiple visits to different tutors just before their portfolios were due in an overzealous attempt to obtain a better grade. As Pat Belanoff (1991) has noted, in such instances the questions thus arise as to when the help given is too much or when the work ceases to be the student's own (Belanoff & Elbow, p. 31).

These questions have no easy answer. That the extent of collaboration can have great impact on portfolios is suggested by Claudia Gentile (1992), who, in discussing the first portfolio study completed by the National Assessment of Educational Progress, calls attention to the problem of comparing across students and across classes if some students have participated in more collaborative activities than have others. To clarify student authorship and to minimize potential problems of authentication, some high-stakes portfolio programs require students to include notes from their classroom instructor certifying that a particular entry is theirs; other programs require students to include more in-class writing, in addition to the reflective letters, as a means of demonstrating each student's own writing (Holt & Baker, 1991). Still another means for authenticating authorship is to require students to include all the drafts of at least one entry; the drafts reveal the work in progress as the student interacts with peers or conferences with the instructor.

Scoring the Portfolios

When portfolios are prepared for external assessment purposes, a sampling of portfolios is often selected at random to be scored by readers other than the classroom teacher. Several decisions need to be made about the scoring—whether, for example, a single score will be assigned for the overall portfolio on the basis of a holistic approach or an analytic approach, or whether individual entries will be evaluated instead to ascertain if a sufficient number of entries meet the passing criteria.

Several educators argue against using holistic scoring for something as complex as the portfolio. Hamp-Lyons and Condon (1993), for example, suggest that merely having the additional evidence that a portfolio provides, or more *types* of evidence, does not result in a "broader basis for judgments, making decisions easier" (pp. 180–181); rather, they argue that the complexity of portfolio scoring requires readers to balance parts against each other, making the ultimate decision harder. They caution, furthermore, that significant "cognitive changes" are involved when readers shift from reading fifty-minute impromptu essays to the much more complex task of balancing all the entries in a portfolio. Their view is underscored by other educators (Sommers, Black, Daiker, & Stygall, 1993), who stress how important it is for scorers to read a portfolio completely in order to avoid being influenced by the "roller coaster" effect of uneven entries or the "glow" effect of a single strong entry.

In our own portfolio scorings we have tried several different approaches, and the advantages and disadvantages of each have been readily apparent. For example, as part of one pilot study in which secondary English teachers from eleventh- and twelfth-grade classes used portfolios with their students, the portfolios were scored both holistically and analytically. The portfolios of the different classes were similar in that they contained common pre- and post-impromptu writings, reflective letters, and common types of assignments such as an academic essay or a personal, informal writing; moreover, the portfolios had been prepared over the same time span and with all teachers meeting frequently to discuss any issues associated with implementing the portfolios. Despite these similarities, the portfolios were quite different, representative as they were of an Advanced Placement twelfth-grade class and of several regular eleventh- and twelfth-grade classes that included basic writers. The teachers, together with other experienced holistic scorers, first evaluated the portfolios analytically. They used an analytic guide in which they rated each entry individually on a wide variety of criteria—from sentence variety to depth of content—and achieved a summed score for the final portfolio. This approach provided extensive feedback to the students; it was, however, time-consuming, and the agreement among raters on the individual elements of the individual entries was not always strong.

Subsequently, the readers scored the same portfolios holistically (with each reader rating different portfolios from those he or she had scored analytically). Given that our readers were experienced holistic scorers and that a four-point scale was used, the agreement between the two readers of each portfolio was, not surprisingly, higher than when the analytic scale was used. Feedback was much more limited, although in these circumstances scorers did rate a few key elements of the portfolios overall so that the students participating in the study would have some sense of why their portfolios had received a particular score. Even though such feedback typically is not given when single essays are scored holistically, some portfolio assessment programs, such as Kentucky's, do give overall ratings of specific elements within the portfolio. Our readers did not experience much difficulty scoring the portfolios holistically, but one or two readers commented that it was

important to know that "the technical quality of the assessment is good enough to yield a truthful picture of student abilities" (p. 448), especially if high stakes are involved. Indeed, in a similar vein, Calfee and Perfumo point out that "on the surface, collecting student work seems simple enough, but the reality of interpreting a folder full of writing samples into a valid assessment is not simple at all" (1994, p. 4).

The training necessary to evaluate single writing samples is even more essential when readers are dealing with the complexities of port-folios. As will be seen in Chapter 5, such training must occur more than once. Even when scorers are experienced at using a particular scoring method, they need to be reoriented *at the time of the actual scoring* with the scoring scale and with training samples that are periodically intro-duced throughout a reading. The scorers need, moreover, to be moni-tored throughout a reading in order not only to prevent the inadvertent, upward "drift" of scores that can come from fatigue or from individual biases but also to provide a source of guidance for the troublesome de-cisions that scorers must make. As previously emphasized, the training ideally should come from "one voice" so that the same message is being given to all participants. The initial reliability problems associated with some external portfolio assessment programs may have arisen in part because of insufficient or weak training practices.

But the teacher training that is essential for portfolio scorings is also vital for the *implementation* of portfolios in a classroom. Citing several researchers, Winograd and Jones (1993) stress that in order for teachers to know how to use portfolios effectively, they must have a solid un-derstanding not only of the processes involved in effective learning and teaching, but also of "the construction, management, and interpretation of portfolios" (p. 13). The authors point out that "the issue of staff de-velopment is crucial when teachers are *required* to use portfolios as part of a high-stakes accountability assessment program" (p. 13, emphasis in original).

Reporting

Still another frequent difference between external and internal portfo-lio assessments is the issue of reporting. The results of external portfo-lio assessments are often reported in terms of single scores, whether analytically or holistically derived. In fact, the use of "numerical values on portfolios for class-to-class and school-to-school comparison" (p. 4) was precisely one of the objections to external assessment expressed by commission member Dixie Dellinger of the Commission on Composi-tion of the National Council of Teachers of English (NCTE) (as cited in a reprint of the NCTE Council-Grams, 1991). (It is important to note that, in actuality, the portfolios for Vermont's program are evaluated on a verbal scale of "frequently to seldom.") Results of internal portfolio assessments, on the other hand, may be given in terms of letter grades, or, as Calfee and Perfumo note, the quality of performance may be expressed in descriptions or narrations; the narrative form, as advocated by Linda Rief (1990), has received particular attention. The difference in the reporting form is closely related to the difference in the purpose and the audience of the two portfolio assessments: Internal portfolio assessments are integrally connected to the curriculum of a class, and letter grades or narratives are appropriate in conveying the teacher's evaluation of the student's work. External portfolio assessments, on the other hand, are often divorced from the classroom context, and the scorers may have no personal knowledge of the students. Hence, narratives are less effective and more time-consuming for external portfolio assessments. In fact, numbers or their verbal equivalents are often used for comparative purposes, as in, for example, a tally of how many students received scores of "frequently" on a particular characteristic.

Thus, despite the commonalities between external and internal portfolio assessment, differences exist as well, largely in terms of the roles that the individual student and teacher play in the process and in terms of the importance that scoring and technical issues assume.

Summary

At all educational levels and in various disciplines, portfolio assessment has become increasingly popular. The definition of portfolios varies, as do their type, purpose, and contents. However, some commonalities exist. Because portfolio assessment allows for a full, in-depth display of students' work, it is viewed as more meaningful and even more valid than many other kinds of assessments. Because, too, it at once affects and reflects the curriculum, it is more integrally tied to instruction than many other assessment forms. Furthermore, portfolio assessment empowers both students and instructors by giving them a voice about the goals of the program and the overall requirements for the portfolios and for the individual entries. The reflection and revision processes that portfolios encourage promote the development of higher-order thinking skills over time as students learn to evaluate their own entries and to make necessary revisions; in this manner, students begin to take responsibility for their own learning. From the collaborative processes that serve as scaffolding for the works in progress, students move toward becoming independent and critically aware learners with portfolios that reflect their individuality.

Because of the inherent value of the portfolio process, portfolios have been advocated increasingly for external assessment purposes, including some that are high-stakes for schools. Thus, portfolios may be used as a means of program evaluation, as a partial graduation requirement, as a replacement for competency exams, or as a placement measure. Portfolios used for these purposes still represent a varied body of work done over a period of time, and they still usually require students to include some evidence of reflection or self-assessment. However, when portfolios are used in external contexts, more standardization becomes necessary, and students may have less choice and, ultimately, even less voice in the entire process than likely would be the case with internal portfolio assessment. Issues such as authenticating authorship and providing full contexts for readers may become important. Essential, too, are the scoring decisions that must be made when portfolios are used for external assessment purposes. These decisions include the evaluation approach to be used (such as holistic versus analytic or primary trait); the breadth of the scoring scale; criteria; appropriate training procedures; and reporting methods. Because portfolio scoring is complex—even for experienced scorers—the rate of agreement among readers may not be as high as that obtained among raters of single essays. In fact, precisely because this technical issue of interrater reliability is so troublesome, some testing experts view external portfolio assessment with concern. Such assessment is also a source of concern for those educators who fear that many virtues of the internal portfolio assessment process—the ownership and individualization and empowerment both for teachers and for students—will be subsumed by externally imposed and standardized requirements.

In our own experiences, portfolio assessment is a valuable instructional tool within the classroom. As we have found in our program evaluation and in our pilot study with a local high school, portfolios can also be used effectively for external assessment purposes—provided that training is given to teachers implementing portfolios, that the technical limitations concerning reliability and validity are recognized, and that the purposes for the portfolios, consequently, do not carry high stakes either for students or for the school.

TIPS FOR TEACHERS

Preparing Students for External Portfolio Assessment

External portfolio assessment differs from internal, classroom portfolio assessment. However, if teachers distinguish between working portfolios and the presentation or final display portfolio, then some of the potential problems of external portfolio assessment can be minimized.

1. Although the purpose behind an external assessment often determines the final portfolio goals, teachers can still discuss with students the portfolio process and consider subgoals for the working portfolio. At the very least, students need to have a good idea both of what the portfolios will entail and of how the procedures will be implemented.

2. While the need for standardization of external portfolios may require a specific number or type of entries, teachers can ensure that a sufficient number and variety of assignments are given to allow students practice and choice.

3. If a class or program is being evaluated through the external portfolios, teachers should provide guidance or input into student selection. However, student choice should still be an important element in at least some of the entries.

4. The cover letter or table of contents should be detailed enough to provide external readers with a clear picture of what each portfolio entry is trying to accomplish.

5. As students need practice at reflecting upon their work, teachers can provide opportunities throughout the term—along with reflective guides—to enable students to evaluate their progress.

6. Drafts should be an ongoing part of the working portfolio; thus, if rough drafts are required for any (or all) of the final display portfolio, they will be available. (The drafts can also indicate how effectively students are doing revisions.)

7. Because common criteria are likely to be used for scoring portfolios in external assessments, teachers can discuss with students what the criteria mean and how they are generally applied. Classes can practice applying the criteria to a common set of papers.

8. Although individual entries are unlikely to receive grades, interim portfolio grades or progress reports may be helpful in showing students where they stand before the final portfolio grade is given. Teachers may choose to provide their own students with narrative reports as supplements to the uniform scoring reports that may be required for an external assessment.

5 Training

Integrally related to the issue of what form a writing assessment should take is the issue of how best to evaluate student work in that assessment. In large-scale assessments, the most common evaluation approaches are holistic scoring, primary trait scoring, and analytic scoring, each of which will be discussed in subsequent chapters. Regardless of which scoring approach is chosen, however, special attention must be paid in large-scale assessments both to training the scorers and to monitoring them throughout the scoring process. Given the hundreds of papers that most English teachers have graded, the need for such an emphasis on training may appear surprising. Yet, in much the same way that individual jogging differs from running on a cross-country team or that recreational sailing differs from participation in the America's Cup race, so, too, group scoring differs from classroom grading. Whether the context is jogging, sailing, or scoring papers, the dilemma is the same: even while the principles entailed in the individual and the group event may be similar, the greater stakes entailed in the group context often require that expectations, procedures, and criteria become more formalized. In the case of writing assessment, any scoring approach places such demands on the readers that thorough training, in addition to monitoring, is necessary if the scorings are to be reliable and fair to all students. Thus, the training entails familiarizing the readers with the nature of the particular scoring process itself, helping them to internalize the established criteria of the scoring program, and exploring how the criteria can be applied to students' most recent writing efforts.

As many teachers are expected to participate in school-level, district-level, or state-level assessments, the purpose of this chapter is to review the various training procedures, the theories underlying these processes, and their implications. Although this chapter focuses on training approaches for scorings, it is important to point out that training is essential as well to familiarize teachers beforehand with the writing assessments themselves. No matter what form the assessment ultimately takes—whether it is a direct writing assessment or a portfolio assessment, for example—staff development needs to be provided to teachers. As noted in Chapter 4 by Winograd and Jones (1993, p. 13), staff development is critical when high stakes are attached to the assessment. Thus, teachers need to be informed about the underlying theoretical precepts behind the assessment, and they need to be trained in appropriate instructional practices that will ultimately enable their students to perform successfully in the writing assessments.

The Need for Training

Attitudes Toward Training

Some researchers view the need for training as an indication of the artificiality of scoring methods. Davida Charney (1984), for example, in a seminal article critical of holistic scoring, argues that attempts to "calibrate" readers—that is, to train them to score papers in accordance with specified criteria—implicitly show the difficulties that readers experience in adhering to such imposed criteria, and thereby illustrate how such scorings depart from the normal reading process. Peter Elbow (1991), too, arguing for the importance of "getting good pictures of what we are trying to test" rather than "good agreement among interpreters of those pictures," says that reliability has to yield "if assessment is to bear any believable relationship to the actual world of readers and responders" (p. xiii). Pat Belanoff (1991) labels the process by which readers are trained to agree on texts as "a form of brainwashing for sure" and notes that "we need to beware of valuing some scheme simply because it produces interreader reliability" (p. 59).

But not everyone agrees that concern for reliability among readers—that is, making efforts to obtain agreement among scorers—is destructive. Edward White (1985), for example, stresses that in holistic scoring "the training of readers, or 'calibration' as it is sometimes called, is not indoctrination into standards determined by those who know best (as it is too often imagined to be) but rather the formation of an assenting community that feels a sense of ownership of the standards and the process" (p. 164). For White, the development of a consensus among readers is a vital and collegial part of the training process; it entails the creation of an "interpretive community" that understands and adopts the scoring criteria.

The Importance of Training

The need for such training is illustrated not only by those studies in which training produced positive results, but also by those in which the absence of training contributed to a lack of meaningful results. For example, the early work of Diederich, French, and Carlton (1961) revealed the problems that can occur when readers of essays are given neither assistance nor criteria in scoring. In this study, the researchers asked over fifty readers from six fields to grade three hundred essays written at home by new first-year students at different colleges. The raters were first instructed to sort fifty papers into three piles signifying their level of quality—average, above average, and below average. Next, they were to sort each pile into three more stacks, for a total of nine. They then placed the remaining papers in one of the appropriate piles and wrote comments about what they liked or disliked in the essays. The extent of disagreement was shown when every essay received at least five of the nine possible scores on the scale, and one third of the essays received the entire range of scores. Similar findings occurred in a later study by Elaine Hrach (1983) in which fifty-nine secondary English teachers sorted twenty papers written by secondary students into scoring categories of their own choice. As in the study by Diederich, French, and Carlton, the readers in Hrach's study were influenced by qualities either present or absent in the essays and *the readers differed in what they considered to be important*. While Hrach endorsed the realism of her study, she suggested, nevertheless, that a lack of training in writing evaluation might explain the wide variability of her results.

The use of training in other studies further confirms its importance. In a study designed to explore the validity of holistic scoring, Brian Huot (1988) compared the talking protocols of four expert readers and four novice readers as they scored eighty-five essays each. The novice readers had neither training nor a scoring rubric to follow, whereas the expert readers trained with anchor papers and with a modified scoring rubric. From the comments of the two groups of readers, Huot concluded that the training procedures and the use of a rubric actually freed the readers to become more fully engaged with the essays by providing them with a set of "expectations, justification or explanation" (p. 223) to rely upon, in contrast to the novice readers who had to concentrate on the evaluative task at hand.

The need for training is thus confirmed both by those studies that depict what happens when it is not available and by those studies that illustrate what happens when it is provided. The major reason that such training is imperative lies in the individuality of reader interpretations. As recent work on reader response has shown, readers bring individual frames of reference to their interpretations of work. These frameworks include, first, the individual biases that everyone has: For example, whereas one reader might dislike the use of rhetorical questions in an essay, other readers might find them particularly effective. Whereas someone might respond positively to a religious paper, other readers might be bothered by it. Still others might be overly influenced by a good conclusion, and thus have to work at not letting an effective closing sentence dominate their impression of the essay as a whole. Training helps readers become knowledgeable about how their own biases can influence their judgments and, more important, how they can counteract these biases in their scoring procedures.

In addition to the variability of normal human biases, scoring is also affected by differing interpretations as to what exactly constitutes good writing. Pat Belanoff (1991) identifies the problem:

> In truth we don't always agree on which characteristics of a good piece of writing are most significant in making us judge the piece positively.
>
> I've often sat with groups of teachers and worked out what we could agree on as the traits of a good piece of writing—they'll come out something like clarity, effective organization, contextual awareness, coherence, correctness of language, and so on; probably the same set of traits any group of good teachers would come up with. In the abstract, they sound fine. The problem comes when we get around to applying them to actual papers. What I think is clear, someone else doesn't. What I see as well-organized, another doesn't. Or I value the work because it's well-organized and another reader agrees, but thinks the good organization is overshadowed by superficiality of content. (p. 58)

Belanoff's concerns seem exemplified by those studies that show the influence of particular qualities on readers' judgments. For example, several studies have found the quality of content, along with the organization of those ideas, to be a major factor in readers' evaluations of essays (see Breland et al., 1987; Diederich, 1974; and Freedman, 1979). In contrast, other studies have found that such factors as mechanics, spelling, syntactic maturity, and vocabulary, as well as the length of a piece, affect some judgments of writing quality. To illustrate, researchers Rafoth and Rubin (1984), upon finding that mechanics affected eighty composition instructors' ratings more than content did, speculated that graders may not distinguish clearly between the domains of content and mechanics in making their writing judgments. Still other scorers, in studies by both Stach (1987) and Harris (1977), gave more weight to such elements as mechanics and neatness than they believed they would. As a result, Harris observed with her own study that there "came the conviction that form is so integral a part of content that in some ethereal way form is content and content is form" (pp. 180–181).

In addition to readers' disagreements about what constitutes good writing and about how those elements of good writing actually get applied, there remains, as still another source of complexity in writing evaluation, the attitude that readers hold toward the writers of the essays. Research by Sarah Freedman (1984) and by Barritt, Stock, and Clark (1986) suggests that readers of essays have mental approximations of the identities of the writers; hence, the readers become bothered when the writers do not fulfill their expectations of what the appropriate tone or role is that these student writers should adopt. In Freedman's study, for example, four experienced holistic scorers were given packets of essays that contained, in addition to student writers' essays, an essay by a professional writer on the same topic. Unaware that professional writers' work had been included, the scorers gave only slightly higher scores to the professionals' work. When Freedman sought to discover what qualities characterized the professional essays, she found a tone of familiarity, scholarly references, and an initial rejection of the assignment at hand. Because these qualities are not likely to appear in most students' writing, Freedman speculated that scorers might have negatively interpreted these characteristics as "overstepping" on the part of some students. Given the complexity of writing, then, as well as the complexity of the reader-writer interaction, training can play an essential role in enabling readers to score essays with some uniform, and thereby fairer, perspective.

Training of scorers becomes even more critical when scorings are conducted in multiple, decentralized contexts. Training is especially imperative in order for scorers to maintain the scoring standards when either individual scorers or small groups of scorers must evaluate essays or portfolios against some external standard. This need was dramatized in one of my studies conducted a few years ago in which a group of twelve highly experienced scorers were given the task of holistically scoring *at home* a group of essays similar to ones they had scored together as a group many times. Though the scorers were basically successful in assigning the scores, several readers expressed, through their logs and taped protocols, hesitation about the scores they sometimes assigned, and the results also showed a tendency for some readers to drift higher as they scored independently (see Wolcott, 1989).

But even though such decentralized scorings are less than ideal, "remote scoring" is, as Breland and Jones (1988) suggest, apt to become ever more likely as technological advances continue to be made in communication and as the costs of a centralized scoring increase (p. 5). In their study of remote scorings, Breland and Jones compared the scores assigned by experienced readers who received the essays along with instructions and sample papers in their offices with the scores given by monitored readers in what the researchers called a conference setting. Breland and Jones found that even though the reliability was not as strong for the remote scorers as for those readers who came together to score under the guidance of table leaders, it did offer a possibly viable alternative in those cases when "cost or convenience [might] be relatively more important than reliability" (p. 1). Certainly, a modified application of this decentralized scoring movement can be seen in the statewide portfolio assessment practices of Vermont and Kentucky, where teachers are grouped together into smaller, regional "clusters" or "networks" not only for informational purposes but also for the purpose of scoring their students' portfolios.

Thus the complexities entailed in assessing writing require that training be provided to scorers if fair responses are to be achieved. The need for training as a way to militate against variable reader responses is further underscored if, as is likely to be the case in the future, more assessments are scored in decentralized locations, such as schools or school districts.

Training Procedures in Formal Scorings

As the results of these previously discussed studies suggest, such training is not a one-time occurrence. Rather, training must be provided with each new scoring occasion to all scorers—including the experienced ones—and it should, moreover, include provisions for ongoing monitoring. In actual practice, training may be skimpy. A single training session may be given, with the expectation that teachers will know how to do the scorings later. Alternately, a brief training session may be provided at the end of a workday when teachers are likely to be tired and unreceptive to the training.

Such practices contrast with those followed by the large-scale, formal scorings where extensive training is done at the start of every scoring session. In fact, in most scoring contexts that have serious consequences for students, scorers undergo repeated training. In the recent past, for example, we conducted two separate placement scorings for developmental writing classes and two separate SAT-II placement scorings for first-year composition courses. In all four scorings (which were held only two weeks apart), the readers underwent training both prior to and during each of the scoring sessions, despite the fact we share many years of scoring experience among us. As noted at the beginning of the chapter, this training entails familiarizing the participants with the process, the criteria, and the current topics and essays—an important issue as the scoring scale and topics often differ substantially.

Nature of the Training

Training may vary with the size and formality of the scoring, with the type of scoring approach used (such as primary trait or holistic scoring), and with the purpose and type of assessment; there are, however, commonalities. Generally, for example, experienced scorers, as well as novices, undergo training for each scoring occasion—even though novices often participate in an additional introductory session. In a typical training session for holistic scoring, the training entails several stages: (1) linking scorers to previous sessions through the use of old papers; (2) familiarizing scorers with selected papers that exemplify the score points on the new topics; and (3) practicing the application of score points to new samples at periodic intervals throughout a session.

The scorers begin the training session by scoring model writing samples or portfolios from the preceding session; this practice of beginning with old samples allows scorers to "anchor" themselves to the standards used in the past. Next, after discussing the characteristics of the topic in the forthcoming task, the scorers rate new samples selected as anchor papers for their current session.

The story behind the anchor papers illuminates how consensus can be reached in a holistic scoring session. These anchor papers, sometimes called range finders or benchmarks, are chosen a week or two prior to the actual scoring by a sample selection committee that usually includes the chief readers and one or two table leaders. The papers are chosen by consensus, after the sample selectors have independently scored each essay (or perhaps each portfolio). Once anchor papers are chosen to represent each of the varying score points, the essays are presented to a group of table leaders at a meeting that precedes the scoring itself. The anchor papers *may or may not* be accepted by the table leaders as good exemplars of a particular score. If the anchor papers are not validated, then other papers that have fared better during the table leaders' meeting are chosen as replacements. As can be seen, then, the anchor papers are not autocratically imposed, as is sometimes believed; rather, the anchor papers that are chosen represent, from the perspective of both table leaders and chief readers, strong exemplars of a particular score range on a specific topic. Significantly, the range finders or anchor papers do *not* represent the best or the worst of a particular score point—the best *6*, for example, or the worst possible *1*. If such were the case, no other paper would be deemed good enough to receive a *6*, nor, conversely, would another paper be considered poor enough to receive a *1*. Rather, the anchors represent the typical, midrange score of each point, thereby leaving room for other papers to receive similar scores.

During the scoring itself, the presentation of the selected anchor samples is then followed with additional samples for readers to use in practicing their scoring. In each case, the scores that readers have assigned to the practice samples are tallied publicly, so that readers have a chance to see where they are scoring in relation to their colleagues. Time is then allotted for brief discussions of problem papers and problem scores. This public tallying and brief discussion period constitute an important feedback mechanism for scorers so that they can see if their response to a given work varies too much from those of their colleagues; they can see, for example, if their concern for correctness has caused them to undervalue the content of a given piece, or if their fondness for a good conclusion causes them to overlook serious problems in other parts of the essay.

Time is also allotted at the start of each training session to remind readers of the conditions under which the writing assessments were produced and to suggest appropriate scoring procedures. Hence, readers are urged to discuss with their table leaders any papers that appear problematic to them, and they are urged to turn over any papers that are illegible. If written descriptions of the criteria are available, as is usually the case with modified holistic scorings, then readers are urged to evaluate the papers they score both against these criteria and against the range finders that exemplify how the criteria have been translated into practice. The training continues throughout a scoring session, and practice samples are presented after breaks and after lunchtime, so that readers are constantly being reminded of the scale to which they must adhere. Thus, the training process is careful and deliberate in order both to help readers adopt the scoring standards and to strengthen the confidence the readers themselves feel.

Research Basis for Training Practices

To ensure a successful training session, scoring leaders usually follow certain precepts derived from research. For example, a study by Godshalk, Swineford, and Coffman (1966) in which holistic scorers evaluated each of five essays written by about 650 eleventh and twelfth graders illustrated the value of holding training sessions at the beginning of every scoring session in order to prevent readers from initially giving scores that are too high. Still another precept is the value of training with "one voice," a value that runs counter to the common "trainer-of-trainers" practice wherein one trained reader trains others who, in turn, branch out to train succeeding readers. As some states have discovered, this kind of training can become altered as the message is transmitted. (In fact, earlier research by Sarah Freedman [1981] suggested the effect that a trainer could have on the scoring. Two different trainers trained two pairs of raters, providing them with sample essays for each topic. The four readers—all of whom were highly qualified— graded the papers consistently with each other and were not affected by such other variables as the time of day or their particular rating session. However, when Freedman replayed tapes of the training sessions, she found that there were differences in the discussions the two trainers conducted. Whereas one trainer might indicate that adjacent scores of 2 and 1 were acceptable on a particular sample, the other trainer might find the 1 not acceptable at all. Such training differences could conceivably have an impact on the scores assigned.) To improve the consistency with which all readers are trained, some programs have sought to provide "one voice" by making more training videotapes. Thus, research findings suggest that training in the scoring of writing assessments—no matter what the scoring method used—must be timely, early, consistent, and, above all, carefully done.

While other models may exist, in many scoring programs the development of a consensus is a central part of the training approach. That is, rather than decreeing that certain samples must receive certain scores, the chief reader works at building a consensus of appropriate scores among all the participants. Using this philosophy, chief readers will not insist that the scores they gave certain essays during the sample selection process must be the "true" scores. Rather, if table leaders subsequently assign a different score during the table leaders' meeting and are able to defend this score during discussion, then the paper is likely to be presented to readers as emblematic of both scores—as representative of a 4/5 paper, for example, rather than the 4 that the chief readers might have envisioned or the 5 that the majority of table leaders might have given it. Such consensus building underscores the value placed on the expertise of the teachers participating in the scoring.

Monitoring Procedures in Formal Scorings

A corollary of training, although one rarely discussed, is monitoring. During formal scorings, several monitoring practices are invoked to sustain the impact of the initial training throughout a day and to guide readers in maintaining their adherence to the standards. Table leaders fulfill much of the monitoring role by independently scoring those essays they have randomly selected from their readers' folders as a verification of the readers' scores. If the table leaders' scores differ from those of their readers, then the leaders discuss the papers with the readers, suggesting that the readers look the essays over again. While this practice may imply some harsh "quality control," in effect, it actually provides readers with a consultant or a guide to whom they can turn with problematic papers. It gives the readers, moreover, immediate feedback as to how their reading is progressing. What is important to emphasize is that the table leaders never make the readers change their scores.

Another common way to monitor formal scorings is the check reading. In this phase, table leaders submit to the head table selected essays that they and their readers have independently scored. The chief readers at the head table, in turn, independently score these same essays to ascertain whether everyone is scoring consistently. This approach provides one way to corroborate that all parties—readers, table leaders, and chief readers—are scoring to a common standard. If there is disagreement among the three parties, then the paper can be reviewed.

A third monitoring procedure, which may be less common, is the use of "seeded" papers in some scorings. In this practice, which is designed to show how well the individual scorers are maintaining the standards throughout a scoring, essays that are prescored by the committee may be included at various intervals in readers' packets of essays to ascertain how well the individual reader's score matches the predetermined score.

The monitoring procedures thus serve to buttress the training by providing an ongoing means of ensuring that readers are scoring papers alike. Although some researchers point to these various procedures as indicative of the problems entailed in "forcing" scorers to adhere to arbitrary standards, these practices are important. Scoring accuracy can be affected by such external factors as fatigue, the heat in the room, or the time of day, and the table leaders' guidance can be useful in preventing a general drift upward in the scores. In my study on the effectiveness of monitoring, I found that experienced scorers who rated essays at home with only a scoring guide as their resource tended to give higher scores to papers than when those same scorers participated in a monitored group scoring. In their logs and on questionnaires, not only did the twelve participants in the study indicate that they consulted their guides frequently during the unmonitored scoring, but also a few scorers expressed regret that they had no anchor papers and no table leader to consult. Thus, despite being highly experienced scorers, these readers clearly felt the need for standards to anchor their scoring. When these same readers then scored matched papers in a monitored setting with three table leaders and two chief readers, the readers tended to consult with table leaders about problematic papers, and their overall average scores were lower than in the unmonitored setting. Nearly two-thirds of the readers responded afterward that it was "almost always" easier to score papers in a structured, monitored setting than it was to score at home.

Because, additionally, 60 percent also said they felt free to disagree with their table leaders, the readers clearly viewed table leaders as guides or consultants rather than as authority figures. In this vein, Edward White's emphasis (1985) on the importance of a congenial, supportive atmosphere in a scoring session suggests the value of the following observations that two participants in my study made about monitoring. One table leader wrote:

> As a table leader, I have observed the monitoring process as a tempering of our individual prejudices and preconceived notions about how the papers should be graded. We must set aside our whims, caprices, and dogmatism in the interest of fairness and competency. Readers, table leaders, and chief readers balance papers against group standards adjusting skillfully as we proceed. (Wolcott, 1989, p. 162)

A similar view is offered from the perspective of a reader:

> As a reader, I find the structure useful, supportive, reassuring, and congenial. I feel in touch with the standards. I have resource people available to me when I have questions. I think the formal setting helps me deal with essays fairly. The monitoring process makes the effort a collegial attempt to establish and share certain standards and values among professional colleagues, and the students benefit ultimately from that. (p. 163)

As can be seen, then, training—and its corollary, monitoring—are important in any scoring of a writing assessment. Training that is done in a timely, thorough manner helps readers to overcome individual human biases and to work together to achieve a common understanding of what good writing entails, while the monitoring provides an additional, ongoing source of support for readers. Through individual interactions with table leaders and through group tallying of samples and range finders, the participants in a scoring negotiate their individual responses to student texts in accordance with a framework of standards they not only recognize but also, in many cases, adopt as their own.

Summary

Thorough and continuous training is essential to the success of any scoring approach used for a large-scale writing assessment. It is, likewise, essential to the success of the writing assessment itself. If the goal of writing assessments is to improve students' writing skills, training must be provided with depth and continuity both to the teachers who prepare students for the assessments and to the scorers who do the assessing.

6 Holistic Scoring

Teachers often employ an analytic approach in grading students' essays in the classroom; however, in direct writing assessments, and sometimes in portfolio assessments as well, holistic scoring is the more commonly used evaluation method. Because holistic scoring is so widely used for statewide external assessments, program evaluations, and placement tests, the purpose of this chapter is to review the premises and procedures involved and the meaning behind the scores. There will also be a discussion of holistic scoring's application to the classroom in fostering students' understanding of writing criteria and their self-assessment skills.

The Meaning of Holistic Scoring

As Miles Myers (1980) explains, holistic scoring is based on the premise that the whole is worth more than the sum of its parts; this scoring approach hence seeks to focus on an entire piece rather than on its individual components. Thus, an essay is not evaluated in terms of its specific features, e.g., its development, creativity, sentence structure, or mechanics; neither are ratings derived by mentally adding together scores for the individual features. Instead, a paper is scored in terms of the overall impression—the synergistic effect—that is created by the elements working together within the piece. (In this respect, one can see echoes of the whole language movement or of the holistic health movement that stresses the interdependence of elements and the need for viewing the patient in totality.) Although holistic scoring emphasizes the "general impression" that the reader receives, the term should not convey that holistic scoring is a quick and easy way to handle writing assignments. Rather, the overall impression is derived from the reader's thorough understanding of the criteria and training in applying those criteria to papers.

The holistic scoring approach basically rewards students for what they do well (College Board, 1993). This emphasis on the positive does not, however, mean that problems are overlooked or minimized. Rather, insofar as problems either mar the impression the reader receives or interfere with the writer's communication, they may call attention to themselves and become factored into the final impression. If, for example, scorers encounter a few mechanical errors in an impromptu essay, they tend to disregard the mistakes, recognizing that these essays represent first drafts written under pressure. In such a case, the mechanical problems do not affect the final outcome of the paper. If, on the other hand, a paper is so riddled with mechanical errors that the readers have to work extra hard to discern the meaning, then the mechanical errors are likely to lower any score assigned. Similarly, an occasional sentence fragment or faulty pronoun reference will not prevent readers from assigning the highest score possible if, at the end of reading an essay, they are impressed with its fluency, development, and thoughtful content. If, conversely, the same sentence fragments or pronoun reference problems occur in an essay that is poorly organized, undeveloped, and shallow, then the grammar problems will aggravate the readers' reaction and further lower the score. Conversely, an essay that is mechanically strong may still receive a lower-half score if it is rhetorically weak, with little content or with limited development.

Thus, holistic scoring is a matter of the reader's mentally absorbing and balancing all the elements—rhetorical as well as mechanical and grammatical—that contribute to the overall impression a paper makes. Because balancing these elements together is never easy to do, training is essential in order to enhance the agreement among readers. As noted in the chapter on training, even when all the scorers are writing teachers, enough differences can exist in their perspectives to warrant training. Although the instructors in our developmental writing program followed a similar curriculum and employed similar texts, when we came together for a group holistic scoring of students' portfolios, training was necessary to moderate our individual perspectives. Indeed, in formal holistic scoring sessions, readers undergo continuous training so that their scores are determined on the basis of criteria that are either conveyed implicitly through the model papers used for training or depicted explicitly in operational definitions that describe each score level.

Principles of Holistic Scoring

In the pure form of holistic scoring, essays are rank-ordered against one another, not against an ideal. That is, the best papers within a discrete set of essays are given the highest score, while the weakest papers are given the lowest score; papers in between are given the middle range of scores. The concept of rank-ordering is important, for it means, as Edward White (1985) points out, that a given score is not an absolute. The score of 3 that a paper receives will be meaningless unless it is understood in the context of the entire scale against which the essays are ranked—a scale of possibly four, six, seven, or more points. In the more common, modified forms of holistic scoring, the score ranges are anchored as well to explicit criteria that reflect the typical characteristics of each score point. These lists of criteria—variously referred to as scoring rubrics, scoring guides, or operational definitions—often are *descriptive* rather than *prescriptive*. That is, they may reflect what has been found to be true in numerous writing samples, and not what test developers deem should be true of scores at a certain level. In one of our state-mandated programs, for example, the operational definitions were developed only after the test had been administered several times so that the guide descriptions would reflect the typical writing that readers were seeing at the different score points. Similarly, the sample rubric depicted in Figure 3 was developed not to prescribe but to describe what characterized middle school essays written by students at one school in another state.

Although the principle of rank-ordering is still important in modified holistic scorings, the presence of external criteria in either operational definitions or sample papers means that essays must meet certain conditions before receiving a score. If, for example, a subset of lost essays should arrive after a large-scale writing assessment has been completed (as happened some years ago in a state-mandated testing program), the essays in that subset would not necessarily contain the full range of scores because the papers would still need to be ranked against the larger group rather than against each other in the subset; in fact, the essays might be given only lower-end scores or upper-end scores since the papers would have to meet the criteria used in the whole assessment. The subset of essays, in other words, is rank-ordered only insofar as it meets the criteria of the much larger group of essays. At our institution, we used to score some writing samples that were part of the national SAT-II writing exam. The range finders and sample papers were sent from Educational Testing Service in order for us to be anchored to a much larger scoring scale than might be the case if our small batch of essays should be rank-ordered or scored alone.

Often the external criteria are described in rubrics; at other times, they are implicitly conveyed through the existence of representative sample papers—typically, range finders or anchors—from a previous scoring. For example, when we score essays for our state-mandated

Scores	Holistic Scoring Scale
6 Extremely Proficient	Papers receiving scores of *6* generally have abundant, good details. The papers show style and thought, and often there is a strong sense of the writer. These papers have few errors, as the writers seem in command of sentence structure and mechanics.
5 Proficient	The *5* papers are also detailed and developed with some sense of the writer showing through. The writers seem to understand sentence construction although problems with grammar and spelling can begin to arise.
4 Moderately Proficient	The *4* papers usually have a thesis developed in some significant way with support, although some papers begin to lose focus, and they are not as detailed as the *5*'s and *6*'s. Usually there is a sense of sentence construction even though it is not too sophisticated. Sometimes paragraph problems begin to appear.
3 Slightly Deficient	The *3* papers provide a clear picture of the subject *or* a sense of the writer, but they are developed with generalities. Grammatical, spelling, and sentence errors begin to dominate the papers.
2 Deficient	The *2* papers either have very limited and weak development and some grammatical/mechanical errors, *or* they attempt some development and are full of errors.
1 Seriously Deficient	The *1* papers are extremely short with virtually no development at all. (In a few instances, *1*'s may be given for off-topic papers in which students did not understand the topic at all.)

Figure 3. Holistic guide for timed essays.

exams, we have written descriptors of each score point for each type of exam. The descriptors convey how the elements of thesis, organization, development, and coherence typically appear for each score point; they also discuss what grammatical and mechanical qualities papers at each score are likely to have. These descriptors accompany our range finders and sample papers that depict how the papers look when the criteria are applied to specific papers on specific topics. In contrast, when we scored our smaller set of developmental essays, we did not have explicitly stated operational definitions or scoring criteria; rather, our anchor papers and range finders from the previous years served to provide us with continuity and anchor us to a consistent scale. In holistic scoring, both the scoring rubric and the sample range finders from previous administrations serve to provide continuity from one scoring to the next.

As an illustration of holistic scoring—two impromptu essays written in fifty minutes by first-year student Jaime Montalvo at the beginning and at the end of his participation in our developmental college writing program—are presented below. When these essays were coded and intermingled as part of a programwide holistic scoring, the first essay received a summed score of 5 (out of a total of 8 points possible from two readers), and the second essay received a summed score of 7 out of 8 possible points. Despite some surface errors on the second essay, the second essay is stronger and more informative than the first, reflecting a development with specifics that the early essay completely lacks. In fact, as noted earlier in the chapter on topics, this student interpreted the topic for the pre-essay much more generically than we as topic writers had intended.

Pre-Essay: Writing in the Content Area, Summer 1995

Topic: A book, movie, or television program that made you think.

When I go and see a movie or a television program that really made me think, I tend to wonder why and how it did so. If it's a topic on which I know little of, then I go ahead and do research towards that topic to feel more comfortable talking about it to my friends and/or family members.

When I come across a program like that I stop and wonder why. What was it about that program that touched my heart of mind. In most cases it's because that topic ment a lot to me. I could relate to the topic through personal experience or through my friends and family. Also I feel as if you do see a program that touches you deep down inside, then that could change the way you view it for probably the rest of your life. You would always take it into consideration when it comes up again, and could influence the minds of many other people just through talking about it.

Now I don't have a particular movie or television program in mind, but whenever I see one dealing with the topics of starvation in third-world countries, the A. I. D. epidemic, or medical breakthroughs, that's when I stop and realize what kind of world we live in. We are all striving for a technological advancement to find the cure for a specific disease, the solution to the hunger problem all over the world, or anything to help make this world a better place to live in without all the worries.

As my personal opinion, I feel as though everyone should take a time-out and watch a movie or television program that could just possibly touch our heart enough to make us go out and try to influence our peers about the topic. That way you could get a group of people working together to help find the perfect answer to that specific question or problem.

Post-Essay: Writing in the Content Area, December 1995

Topic: a game that is intellectually challenging.

A game that is intellectually challenging is the game of golf. There are many rules you must learn before you can master the game. Not only understanding and knowing the rules is a key part of the game, but also the different kinds of strategies and approaches you must learn as well. Too many people believe that golf involves the simple task of swinging a club to hit the ball as far as you can. Then when your close enough to the hole, you simply putt the ball in the hole. The people who think that is the key to golf, they are far away from the reality.

In the game of golf, a player can have as many as fifteen different clubs. The player must know which club to use for the best results. If the player happens to chose the wrong club, then he or she may become disgusted with the results of their shot. Each club is diagnosed for a different purpose in the game. There are clubs to play the short game, the middle-range game, or the long game. It all depends on the type of player you are, when it comes down to choosing your club. All of this has to go into consideration when preparing for a shot off the tee, from the sand, in the rough, short or thick, from the water, or even from behind a tree.

There are many options a golf player can choose from when it comes to playing the better game. Should he or she go for everything on his or her first shot from every new hole?, or should they play the safe game and go for par or take what they get?

Every shot a golfer attempts requires deep consentration and perfect form. If the player messes that up in any way, then that player will more than likely hate his or her shot. Every player must also block out distractions surrounding him or her. These distractions could be animals making noises, people talking, golf-carts around the course, the weather, and anything else that could possibly distract a person, including emotional distractions. When a golfer plays the game he or she is only thinking of six things. Those are the ball, the clubs, the hole, how many strokes they have, and the strategy and approach of every shot.

With all of these things that need to be taken into consideration when playing golf, you can understand why this sport is so intellectually challenging. Anything that frustrates a golf player could really mess up his or her game completely. There are many other sports that fall into the same category as golf as far as being intellectually challenging, but I believe that golf has to be one of the hardest and longest sports to master.

It is important to recognize that unless a reader is very familiar with the scale being used and has been anchored to that scale through sample papers and criteria, the reader cannot assign a score to a paper out of context. Several years ago as an expert witness on holistic scoring in a court case, I was asked to read the essay written by the plaintiff to determine if a fair score had been given. As I was unfamiliar both with the scale used and with the other papers being scored, I knew I could not make any judgment about whether an appropriate score had been given. Similarly, instructors in our Writing Center avoid assigning holistic scores to isolated papers that students may write as practice for the state college test. Although many of the instructors have internalized the criteria from years of participation in the scorings, they do not want to assign a score out of context and perhaps mislead the student. Rather, they resort to the more analytic approach of discussing what the strengths and weaknesses are in the individual essay.

Scoring Scale

The scale that is chosen for any holistic scoring depends on the testing program and its purposes. Sometimes a four-point scale is used, although a six-point scale is more typical when finer distinctions are sought or when some provisions are desired for future growth. Occasionally, the scale may be seven points or more. Godshalk, Swineford, and Coffman (1966), who are among the original proponents of holistic scoring, recommend an even-point scale so that readers do not tend to settle on the midpoint but instead decide specifically whether a paper is upper-half or lower-half. Regardless of the breadth of the scoring scale, each scoring point is aligned across a continuum and represents a range of essays. Thus, a score of 2 encompasses those papers that are high 2s, low 2s, and middle 2s. A paper receiving a 2, or any other score, contains *to varying degrees* the characteristics of that particular score point. It is precisely the variations within any score point that present the challenge for any reader and that account for the adjacent scores that may arise. Thus, whereas one reader might consider a paper to be a high 2, another reader might consider the same paper to be more of a low 3. And both readers might be right!

In most holistic scorings, two readers score each paper. They assign their scores independently, without knowledge of the other reader's score. (Codes may be assigned to readers at each table, or the score from one reader may be bandaged before the paper is given to a subsequent reader.) Clerks spiral or arrange the packets of essays for second readings in such a way as to avoid having the same two readers paired against each other for many papers; thus, a packet of papers given to a second reader will contain essays scored by several different readers. Similarly, papers that are read in the morning by one reader are likely to be read in the afternoon by another reader so that time of day does not adversely affect the scores.

Holistic Scoring Procedures

Sample Selection

The procedures used for most formal holistic scorings follow those set forth by the Educational Testing Service. A scoring begins when a small group of experienced scorers—usually the chief reader and three or four associates—assemble to select sample papers that will serve as the training models. The model papers fall into two batches: One batch consists of the "range finders"—approximately eight papers (when a six-point scoring scale is being used) that are particularly representative of each of the six scoring points and that anchor the readers to the scoring scale. (The range finders must be chosen with special care, as the best 6 paper or the worst 1 cannot be used as range finders; otherwise, few other papers would be likely to receive either the highest or the lowest scores. Moreover, problem papers—such as those containing second-language difficulties—may be included as samples but not usually as range finders.) The second batch consists of "samples"—papers that will be used throughout a scoring session for continuous training and that sometimes include special papers for group discussion.

The sample selectors start by reading and independently scoring the range finders from the previous scoring, an important step to ensure a continuity of standards from one scoring to the next. To read the group of previous range finders, the selectors read all eight papers at once, rank-ordering them from best to worst and then assigning a score to each paper; they use the full range of scores, and assign some scores more than once. Once the chief readers' scores on the old range finders are tallied, the chief readers each select, score, and sometimes annotate twelve to fifteen papers from a large group of current essays. When the chief readers have read and independently scored each other's packets, the results are tallied. Those papers on which there is strong agreement and which best exemplify the various scoring points are chosen as range finders. Additional papers with good agreement are chosen as the samples. The model papers are then assigned codes and prepared for duplication.

Table Leaders' Meeting

Table leaders, who are experienced scorers chosen to work closely with about five scorers at their individual tables, meet with the chief readers at a table leaders' meeting held the day before the actual scoring session. At this meeting, the table leaders also begin by scoring independently the range finders from the previous scoring. Once the scores are publicly tallied and reviewed, the table leaders then score the current range finders. Just as the chief readers do, they rank-order the range finders from best to worst and assign a score, using the full range of scores. Their scores are publicly tallied, and thus the chief readers can see how well their selections of prospective range finders will hold up. If the table leaders have agreed with most of the selections, then many of the range finders will remain for the scoring of actual papers. For any papers on which there is disagreement, however, the chief readers know that new anchor papers representative of those scoring points will need to be chosen. Subsequently, the sample papers are introduced, usually in pairs of two or three. At this point, the table leaders are not explicitly rank-ordering papers; rather, they are assigning scores to papers by employing the criteria they have internalized for each scoring point. In this manner the table leaders work through all the samples, discussing as the need arises any papers on which they strongly disagree with the chief readers' scores. At the end of the table leaders' meeting, certain papers are chosen to be the substitutes for problematic range finders; these substitutes are papers that table leaders feel comfortable discussing with their readers.

Such disagreements and changes are an important part of the process, for in this model of holistic scoring, papers and scores are not arbitrarily imposed upon readers. Rather, as Edward White (1985) stresses, holistic scorers function in much the same way as "interpretive communities" of readers do—by coming together to form "an assenting community that feels a sense of ownership of the standards and the process" (p. 164). This consensus model is especially likely to be found in those large-scale assessments in which teachers and college instructors meet to evaluate special exams.

Scoring Session

The scoring session begins with general comments made by the chief reader, who (1) reminds all participants of the conditions under which students wrote the tests, (2) reviews the new topics, (3) urges readers to read quickly but completely, refraining from reexamining any parts, (4) stresses to readers the importance of scoring with the group's standards, rather than with their own, (5) emphasizes the importance of seeking help from the table leader and of overlooking superficial qualities, such as handwriting and length, and (6) informs readers of the logistical proceedings for the scoring days.

Then, like the sample selection and the table leaders' meeting, the actual scoring session begins with readers scoring range finders from the previous session—again for the purpose of anchoring everyone to the scoring scale. Once the responses are publicly tallied—so readers can see where their individual scores are in relation to those of their peers— the new range finders are introduced. After the range finders are rank-ordered, scored, and publicly tallied, readers have an opportunity to discuss their scores with their table leaders. With the framework of range finders complete, pairs of samples are subsequently introduced so that readers can practice assigning scores on individual papers. In this manner, the group members reach agreement with one another. Throughout the scoring, similar sets of samples are introduced after breaks and after lunch so that readers are continuously reminded of the group standards and can avoid an inadvertent upward drift. Periodic uses of check readings, whereby a chief reader, a table leader, and a reader independently score the same papers, further ensure that participants are scoring alike. By these means, the interrater reliability—or consistency of agreement among readers—is increased, and students are assured that the scorers of their exams are reading as closely alike, and hence as fairly, as possible.

Discrepancies

Despite the most extensive of training sessions and despite the best of readers' intentions, the human dimension in scoring means that disagreements about scores are bound to occur. Some of those disagreements occur accidentally: That is, a reader's attention may begin to wander after lunch or if the room becomes too warm, and then the reader may overreward or penalize a given essay. Or, alternately, because a reader may be strongly affected by some element, such as the conclusion, she or he may forget and overreward a problematic essay that manages to end with some flair. In such a situation, the table leader, who frequently circulates around the table to reread essays that the five or six readers at the table have already scored, may identify this problem and help to prevent the reader from drifting. Sometimes, however, such scoring slips are not caught, and discrepant scores between the two readers may result. At other times, these discrepant scores occur because of the nature of the paper itself. That is, papers may contain a real dichotomy of form and content: an essay may contain thoughtful content yet be riddled by errors in structure and usage; alternately, it may avoid mechanical errors yet be shallow and simplistic. Such papers are always difficult to score, and one reader may reward the content, while the other reader may penalize the same paper for its problems, with the result that discrepant scores arise. Or a paper may take a truly unconventional approach, which is rewarded by one reader and penalized by another.

Such discrepancies—often called "splits"—usually cover, on a six-point scale, two points of difference. The reader who is rewarding the content may give the essay a 4, whereas the second reader, who is bothered by the errors, may give the same paper a 2. Although splits are often considered to result if scores are two points apart, they are sometimes defined to include scores that are adjacent rather than identical, and on still other scoring scales they may be as far apart as three points. (A number of factors determine which discrepancies will be called splits. If the scale is narrow, such as the four-point scale used in Vermont's portfolio program, anything other than identical agreement may be viewed as a split. If other factors are present, such as the merging of multiple-choice results with the students' performance on essays in the SAT-II exams, splits may not be recognized until scores are at least three points apart.) Such splits are resolved in a number of ways, but most methods entail having a third reader—usually a table leader or a chief reader—read and score the essay. In some programs, the third score may then replace the score viewed as the more discrepant of the two; in other programs, all three scores are averaged.

The Advantages and Limitations of Holistic Scoring

Holistic scoring has the advantage of allowing large numbers of essays to be scored quickly. Because raters read quickly, assigning a single score to each essay, they are able to score relatively large numbers of essays in a short period of time. For programs with thousands of essays to be scored, such speed is a distinct advantage. An obvious corollary of speed is the reduced cost. Even though large-scale holistic scorings are labor-intensive and hence very costly, they remain less expensive than most other scoring approaches would be.

More important is the theoretical basis. Holistic scoring encompasses all aspects of writing in its evaluation: unlike primary trait scoring that targets certain rhetorical elements for evaluation, unlike analytic scoring that examines individual rhetorical and grammatical elements, and unlike T-unit analysis that assesses sentence structure according to formulas, holistic scoring refers to the whole of an essay. To Edward White (1985), this theoretical and practical emphasis on the whole is the great benefit of holistic scoring. Thus he writes:

> Holistic scoring is important for reasons beyond measurement, for reasons that return us to the nature of writing and to the importance of the study of writing itself. It is in our writing that we see ourselves thinking, and we ask our students to write so that they

can think more clearly, learn more quickly, and develop more fully. Writing, like reading, is an exercise for the whole mind, including its most creative, individual, and imaginative faculties. The rapid growth of holistic scoring in grading reflects this view of reading and writing as activities not describable through an inventory of their parts, and such scoring serves as a direct expression of that view: By maintaining that writing must be seen as a whole and that the evaluating of writing cannot be split into a sequence of objective activities, holistic scoring reinforces the vision of reading and writing as intensely individual activities involving the full self. (p. 32)

When experienced readers are used in a holistic scoring, and when extensive training and monitoring are provided, the agreement among raters—known as the interrater reliability—is often quite high. However, according to researchers Cherry and Meyer (1993), the reported agreement rates may be misleading. They argue that, too often, advocates of holistic scoring either disregard splits when they report scoring-agreement rates or fail to report the statistical procedures used in calculating the agreement rates (p. 116). While reporting problems certainly may exist, reader agreement rates are, *in formal holistic scorings,* often quite strong, particularly if the scoring scale is fairly restricted, as in a six-point scale. If broader scales are used and readers are asked to make increasingly finer distinctions among score levels, the agreement is not likely to be as high.

Although interrater reliability rates are often satisfactory in a holistic scoring, they are, as Cherry and Meyer (1993) explain, not as important as the *score* or the *instrument* reliability rate, which is usually much lower. In fact, Breland and his colleagues (1987) call the score reliability the "Achilles Heel" of writing assessment. Defining instrument reliability as "the reliability of the writing assessment as a whole," Cherry and Meyer (1993) note, "Instrument reliability is concerned with the consistency of assessments across successive administrations of a test. It necessarily takes into account all three sources of error—students, test, and scoring" (p. 114). In their view, instrument reliability plays a central role in determining the reliability of evaluations on which decisions are based regarding students' writing ability. Because of the potentially serious implications, Cherry and Meyer suggest that more attention be focused on instrument reliability, as opposed to interrater reliability alone. As they explain, "Regardless of how consistently raters assign scores to written texts, if the writing prompt (the test) is faulty or if examinees do not respond consistently to it, the holistic scores will not reliably reflect writing ability. In order to obtain accurate estimates of the reliability of holistic assessment, all three sources of measurement error—student, test, and scoring procedure—must be taken into account" (p. 115).

Criticisms of Holistic Scoring

As noted in Chapter 5, some critics, including Davida Charney (1984), have interpreted the need for training as indicative of the problems readers have in adhering to a certain set of criteria, problems seemingly corroborated by those studies that have found such superficial features as handwriting or spelling to be influential in the holistic scores assigned. Thus, Charney concludes, "Holistic ratings should not be ruled out as a method of evaluating writing ability, but those who use such ratings must seriously consider the question of the validity of the scores that result" (p. 79).

Holistic scoring is sometimes criticized for the elements that evaluators focus upon when making their judgments. One doctoral candidate, Carl Stach (1987), who studied the holistic scores assigned by three college professors to the essays of 140 first-year college students, found that the only real predictors of holistic scores were mechanics and appearance; this finding was in contrast to what the teachers said the principles of good writing entailed. In Stach's view, the implications of such findings are "that scorers in holistic procedures (and perhaps teachers in general) aspire to grade essays differently than they actually do, and that they hope to be qualitatively better graders than they are, overlooking, or 'seeing beyond,' mechanics and appearance" (p. 113). Other studies (Barritt, Stock, & Clark, 1986; Freedman, 1984) have found that readers are influenced by the expectations they bring to their evaluation task. For example, in one study, faculty members who met periodically to discuss both how they evaluated student placement essays and why disagreements occurred concluded that their judgments had been affected by their expectations of what first-year college students' writing would look like (Barritt et al., 1986, p. 320).

A number of other studies have explored the elements that influence the writing evaluation. While content and organization have been found in some studies to be influential in the writing judgments many evaluators make, other studies have suggested that length, as well as vocabulary and mechanics, may also contribute to judgments of writing quality. Yet, as Brian Huot (1993) cautions, many of these studies did not approximate the actual procedures of holistic scorings but instead used some other methodology that might affect the results (p. 217).

In addition to criticizing holistic scoring for the elements on which holistic evaluations are made, opponents of holistic scoring object to the idea of making readers agree; specifically, they believe that efforts to achieve agreement force an unnatural reading of a text. For example, Barritt et al. (1986) dispute the need to have consistency of judgment, suggesting instead that it is more important to accept and understand the basis behind disagreements. Similarly, William Smith (1993) points out that disagreements are bound to occur even among trained scorers, just as they occur among such other groups as "trained literature specialists" and "trained critics" (p. 198).

Peter Elbow (1986) likewise expresses reservations about an evaluation model that requires agreement among judges. In his view, not only may the need for agreement result in an overemphasis on such measurable surface features as grammar and spelling, but also it requires readers to suspend their own judgments in favor of other standards. For Elbow, "descriptive perceptions" (p. 255)—even when they conflict—provide a more valuable learning experience than do those evaluations which merely rank or measure.

In contrast to Charney and other critics, some educators and researchers suggest that the kind of reading required in a holistic scoring is a valid one. Edward White (1993), for example, in an essay depicting the historic growth—and value—of holistic scoring, notes:

> To the atomization of education, [holistic scoring] brought a sense of connection, unity, wholeness; to the bureaucratic machinery of fill-in-the-bubble testing, it brought human writers and human readers; to a true-false world of memorized answers to simplified questions, it brought the possibility of complexity; to socially biased correctness, it brought critical thinking. On behalf of students, it had the human decency to ask them what they thought as well as what they had memorized; on behalf of teachers, it asked them to make complex community judgments as well as to give grades. (p. 88)

In addition, White stresses the importance of the sense of community that has been fostered by the holistic scorings, a unifying sense that has given rise to discussions of what good writing is and of ways to improve the teaching of writing.

Brian Huot (1993), in a study that sought to address the *validity*, rather than the reliability alone, of holistic scorings, found that the very training procedures entailed in holistic scorings not only assisted readers in making their evaluations of essays but actually freed the readers to engage in a fuller response to the essays they scored. As noted in Chapter 5, Huot's study compared the responses made by four expert holistic scorers to those made by four novice scorers as they rated expository and persuasive essays written by first-year college students.

All raters were experienced English teachers. He found that both groups of raters valued similar criteria, with both experienced and novice scorers responding through their comments to content and organization most often. But he found that the experienced readers, unlike their novice counterparts, made many varied comments that were not related to the evaluation task at all. Noting that "not only did the expert rater group interact more personally with student texts, but the expert raters were also able to create meaning beyond their roles as evaluators, constructing a reading that reflected a wider sense of student writing" (p. 219), Huot suggests that the scoring guide freed, rather than constrained, readers to respond beyond an evaluative stance. The results of his study lead him to conclude cautiously that perhaps "holistic scoring practices may be a sound and valid measure of directly assessing student writing" (p. 228).

In a subsequent study replicating Huot's work with a different group of scorers, Pula and Huot (1993) found again that, far from interfering with the scorers' ability to evaluate the placement essays, the holistic scoring rubric and procedures appeared to enable scorers to engage personally with the essays. Finding as well that both the novice and the expert scorers rated content and organization most highly, the researchers suggest that the reading and writing experiences which scorers typically share, in addition to the scorers' educational background and English teaching careers, contribute at once to the similarities and the differences in the scores assigned. That is, extended interviews with the scorers revealed that the raters' enjoyment of reading, their own problems in writing, and their interest in "how writing works" influenced their rating practices, as did their course work, teaching experiences, and previous scoring experiences (pp. 248–253). Moreover, the small discourse community that the holistic training and scoring procedures generally create is, in the view of the researchers, valuable because it "permits raters to work as a group, achieving rating consensus, but at the same time retaining the individual and personal nature of their reading, which is so important to any description of the fluent reading process" (p. 260). Although the conclusions of Pula and Huot pertain to the scoring of placement essays, their findings suggest that the evaluative process of holistic scoring does not interfere with a full and valid reader response to a text. Thus, even though the reader response ends in a single score, studies suggest that experienced and trained holistic readers are fully engaged with the texts they are evaluating despite the speed and supposed unnaturalness of the reading situation.

In another study exploring the construct validity of holistic scoring from the perspective of English as a Second/Foreign Language,

Michael Janopoulos (1993) sought to determine whether ESL composition teachers, most of whom are trained to look beyond students' errors to their ideas—that is, to students' "communicative competence" in writing (p. 305)—would be able to do so under the time pressures of a holistic scoring session. According to Janopoulos, "communicative competence, in its simplest meaning, is the ability to communicate one's intended message to the appropriate audience" (p. 310). Janopoulos trained ESL composition teachers first to score English essays written by foreign-language graduate students, and then, without warning, he asked the scorers to write what they recalled of essays he had selected to represent very different levels of writing quality. The scorers recalled in more detail those essays that were better written, thereby showing that meaning or the comprehension of ideas, and not correctness, was a key factor in the scorers' reading process. This finding held true with other scorers in a second experiment even when the essays were much closer in quality. Again the readers showed in their recalls that they retained more of the essay that had been independently ranked as higher in quality than they retained of the second essay.

Speculating that the time constraints of the holistic scoring process may encourage readers to pay attention to particular elements while disregarding others, Janopoulos concludes that "holistic scoring of FL [foreign language] writing proficiency by trained raters possesses construct validity when the construct being measured is communicative competence" (p. 318).

Holistic Scoring in the Classroom

Teachers at both the secondary and college levels have found holistic scoring a useful technique in different subject areas to help students develop their self-assessment skills and improve their revisions. In one middle school assignment, for example, teacher Chris Paulis (1985) and his class together developed a scoring rubric that reflected five levels of achievement in meeting a particular assignment. Once the rubric was composed, students practiced using it in discussing model papers projected on an overhead. Then students gathered in groups to assign a level to each other's papers; with the information provided by their peers, students revised their papers. The students again rated the revised drafts against the standards of the rubric, and the teacher also used the rubric to evaluate the papers. When the group gave the same score as did the teacher, the paper received an additional point in order to emphasize, as the teacher noted, "the importance of evaluating writing based on its effectiveness, rather than on personal bias or whim" (p. 59).

At the college level, instructors Westcott and Gardner (1984) have their classes discuss the quality of selected student essays and the scores that the essays should receive. In the developmental classes, first-year writers start by ranking sample paragraphs and then explain the reasons for their rankings. Students' reactions to the paragraphs serve as a point of departure for a fuller discussion of writing elements. In the view of these instructors, holistic scoring not only has helped to demystify what makes good writing but also has made students think more closely about their own papers.

Certainly, holistic scoring can never provide students with the detailed or diagnostic feedback that analytic scoring can. However, as the work of these teachers indicates, holistic scoring can serve as an important way of enabling students to improve their self-assessment skills by understanding the criteria against which their work is evaluated.

Summary

Holistic scoring has been used increasingly as a means to evaluate writing in large-scale assessments both because of the speed with which the papers can be read and because of the substantial interreader reliability rate that can be achieved with ongoing training. These practical reasons notwithstanding, holistic scoring also receives support because of the holistic theory on which it is based and because of the discussions it has fostered—among scorers and students alike—about what constitutes good writing. The training and scoring sessions integral to holistic scoring have created, in effect, what scholars such as Edward White or Brian Huot and Judith Pula might call immediate or intact discourse communities of their own. Although questions have been raised about the validity of holistic scoring because of the training that is necessary, several studies have suggested that the holistic scoring procedures do not interfere with—*and, in fact, may even encourage*—a full reader response to the text. Furthermore, in a variety of subject areas and at various school levels, holistic scoring guides have come to serve as a meaningful way of helping students both develop their own assessment skills and improve the quality of their revisions.

7 Primary Trait Scoring

Whenever we read newspaper accounts of how well or how poorly students are doing in writing nationwide, the reports are usually based on assessments that used primary trait scoring. This technique is a specialized form of holistic scoring that was developed more than twenty years ago by the National Assessment of Educational Progress (NAEP) to determine, through samplings, how well the nation's students can perform in writing. Precisely because this approach forms the basis of national reports on writing assessment, the purpose of this chapter is to familiarize teachers with the principles and procedures of primary trait scoring.

Origins of Primary Trait Scoring

Although primary trait scoring uses procedures comparable to those of holistic scoring, the emphases of and philosophies behind the two approaches differ substantially. In fact, primary trait scoring was developed in response to the limitations of holistic scoring. That is, as researcher Ina Mullis (1980) points out, NAEP wanted to develop a scoring system that would (1) provide more information than the overall, relative score of holistic scoring reveals, based as the latter is on the idea of rank-ordering one selection against another, and (2) through the precision of the guide, enable the scoring to be replicated in a way that the generic scoring guide of holistic scoring does not permit (pp. 2–4).

In an essay on the development of primary trait scoring, Richard Lloyd-Jones (1977) makes the following comparison between holistic and primary trait scoring:

> The methods perfected by ETS [Educational Testing Service] assume that excellence in one sample of one mode of writing predicts excellence in other modes—that is, good writing is good writing. Some allowance is made for 'having a bad day' or other problems of the test situation. In contrast, the Primary Trait System developed under the auspices of NAEP assumes that the writer of a good technical report may not be able to produce an excellent persuasive letter to a city council. A precise description or census of

writing skills is far richer in information if the observations are categorized according to the purpose of the prose. The goal of Primary Trait Scoring is to define precisely what segment of discourse will be evaluated (e.g., presenting rational persuasion between social equals in a formal situation), and to train readers to render holistic judgments accordingly. The chief steps in using the Primary Trait Scoring System are to define the universe of discourse, to devise exercises which sample that universe precisely, to ensure cooperation of the writers, to devise workable scoring guides, and to use the guides. (p. 37)

Lloyd-Jones, together with Carl Klaus and other colleagues, devised a theoretical model from which primary trait scoring is derived. Their model, generally depicted as a triangle, highlights the role of purpose and audience in three main types of writing—explanatory, expressive, and persuasive. As Lloyd-Jones explains, explanatory discourse is "subject oriented," expressive discourse is "discourser oriented," and persuasive discourse is "audience oriented." Whereas persuasive writing attempts to convince the *reader*, expressive writing focuses on the *writer*, and explanatory writing is concerned with the *subject matter* itself (Lloyd-Jones, 1977, pp. 37–39).

Primary trait scoring is unusual in being grounded in a theoretical framework of this nature as other evaluation approaches are not (Fuller, 1985, p. 44). Primary trait scoring is also distinctive, as Faigley and his colleagues point out, in being entirely criterion-based, rather than both criterion-based and norm-referenced the way that holistic scoring is. That is, in primary trait scoring, a writer's success at a particular task is measured against specific criteria and has nothing to do with the set of papers of which it may be a part (Faigley, Cherry, Jolliffe, & Skinner, 1985, p. 106). Holistic scoring usually includes an explicit set of criteria against which papers are being evaluated, but the holistic score on a given paper also represents a rank-ordering, referring to where the individual paper stands in relation to other papers in the set.

Elements in a Primary Trait Scoring

Writing Tasks

Although topics for most writing assessments generally undergo extensive field testing, the development of the writing tasks used with primary trait scoring is particularly challenging because the exercises are so specific to each testing situation. As both Lloyd-Jones (1977) and Ina Mullis (1980) acknowledge, designing writing tasks with specific constraints that still remain accessible to all students is difficult, especially in large-scale assessments where students do not have the benefits of classroom discussion. At the same time, the specificity of the writing task—such as a problem in the school cafeteria versus a generic problem—is supposed to make evaluation easier (Lloyd-Jones, p. 42; Mullis, p. 14).

Scoring Guides

The development of the specific components of the guide is, along with the exercise itself, an essential component of primary trait scoring. This approach to scoring recognizes that different forms of discourse place different demands upon writers and that the generic scoring guide used in holistic scoring is not suitable for writings composed in different domains. Rather, specific scoring guides must be developed in the specific writing domain being tested—whether the domain is narrative, explanatory, persuasive, or expressive. The guide must take into consideration the purpose and the audience, in addition to the task itself. Audience, as Mullis explains, is particularly central to primary trait scoring:

> The rationale underlying primary trait scoring is that writing is done in terms of an audience and can be judged in view of its effects upon that audience. Particular writing tasks require particular approaches if they are to be successful. The approach used by the writer to reach and affect his audience will be the most important—the primary—trait of a piece of writing. (p. 8)

According to Lloyd-Jones (1977), a scoring guide must contain several elements, including the task itself, the primary trait being evaluated, expectations of how the students might respond, a discussion of how the task and the primary trait are linked, the descriptions of the score points, and sample papers with discussions (p. 45). Thus, the development both of the task and of the guide is a critical part of primary trait scoring.

Primary Traits

The guide for each task identifies the primary trait and provides a rationale as to what the task intends to accomplish in terms of a specific audience and purpose. The primary trait is not the same as a rhetorical mode; Mullis (1980) notes, for example, that there can be different primary traits when expressive tasks have different purposes (p. 18). Rather, the trait represents the overriding features that enable the writer to meet the purpose of the particular writing task.

Sample Guide for an Expressive Task

In Ina Mullis' (1980) discussion of the NAEP scoring guide developed for one expressive task that involves a picture of a boat in which children are playing, the primary trait is labeled "Elaborated expression of a point of view through entry into an imaginative situation." Specifically, the writing task asks students to imagine they are one of the children in the boat or standing nearby and to explain to a friend clearly and with feeling what is happening. The guide lists as the lowest score—i.e., a 1—"No entry into the imaginary world of the picture." A 2 is given for "Entry into the imaginary world of the picture," and a 3 is assigned to papers that reveal "Good entry into the imaginary world of the picture." The highest score, a 4, is reserved for papers that show "Emotive and consistent entry into the imaginary world of the picture" (pp. 30–31).

In this exercise, several "secondary trait categories" are scored separately on scales that range from three points for "point of view" and four points for "tense" to two points for "Fantasy" and "Insights." Used as part of a national study a number of years ago, this task and guide enabled NAEP to determine how well nine-year-olds, thirteen-year-olds, and seventeen-year-olds could perform on this task.

Sample Scoring for an Informative Task

For each type of writing task, the primary traits differ. In one primary trait scoring we conducted, two informative tasks were being assessed. Although the primary trait in each case entailed evaluation and analysis, the scoring guides contained targeted elements for evaluation that were specific to each writing task. The primary trait scoring guide for one task is cited in Figure 4.

Significantly, even though the primary trait may well include several elements—e.g., summary, analysis, support—other features of a paper that are not directly tied to the primary trait do not factor into the single, culminating evaluative score. In fact, Lee Odell (1981) views this focus on a primary trait to the exclusion of all others as problematic in that the guide makes no allowances either for other elements or for an unusual approach a student might take. To overcome these restrictions, Odell suggests using a broad sample of papers on which to base the guide and turning over to a scoring leader any papers with unusual approaches (p. 125).

Secondary Traits

Ina Mullis (1980) notes in her discussion of primary trait scoring that the number and type of traits considered are limited only by the test

Favorite Story
W000410
Age Class: 2, 3
Informative—Analysis

Scoring Guide

Primary Trait: Substantiation of evaluation through analysis.

Scoring Rationale: The task asks the respondents to tell why they like a favorite story; thus, they should explain their reasons or criteria for liking that story. Plot summary can be viewed as minimal support for certain criteria; however, the best papers should consider such aspects as setting, plot development, characters, meaning, believability.

0: No response.

1: *Unsatisfactory analysis.* Some of the responses identify a favorite story, but give only circular reasons for liking it, such as "I liked it because it was good." Or their reasons may be broad, sweeping generalizations or personal assertions that could apply to almost any story. (It was . . . exciting, interesting . . . or it had a good plot.) Or they may indicate that they do not have a favorite story or otherwise avoid the analytic task.

2: *Minimal analysis.* These papers summarize or discuss the story and/or they may show some evidence of beginning the analytic task by giving one or more brief criteria for liking the story. They fail, however, to develop any of the reasons and just list them.

3: *Adequate analysis.* These responses may summarize or discuss the story but they must give at least one criterion or generalization elaborated with some evidence or support. They may be uneven or unbalanced, with some parts handled well and others not so well.

4: *Elaborated analysis.* These papers present a cohesive, elaborated analysis of the features of the story and reason(s) for liking it. These papers offer either an extended, unified elaboration of one criterion or generalization *or* an interrelated list of moderately elaborated criteria or generalizations.

9: Illegible, totally off-task, or "I don't know."

Note: These are some of the strategies for supporting reasons for an evaluation:

- bringing up personal experience
- mentioning personal preference or taste
- giving evidence or examples from the story being evaluated
- emphasizing the uniqueness of the story
- expressing personal engagement or identification

Figure 4. Primary trait scoring guide from the National Assessment of Educational Progress.

makers' "imagination, zeal, and resources." She stresses that "evaluating a paper for its primary trait does not preclude describing other features of the paper. These features may be selected because they complement the primary trait or are qualities that are considered important in any piece of writing" (pp. 18–19). According to Mullis, the secondary traits can be assessed during the primary trait scoring by the original scorers or afterward by other readers; they can, moreover, be evaluated on a variety of different scales, including a simple, dichotomous scale of "no" and "yes." Indeed, NAEP includes in its periodic reports on writing a *separate* assessment of students' control of grammar and mechanics obtained through a detailed analysis of a random sample of papers.

In our own scoring, no such mechanism existed for the consideration of secondary traits—especially those of mechanics and grammar. As several papers we encountered had severe problems with mechanics and sentence structure, several scorers had difficulty focusing solely on the primary trait in these papers and disregarding students' performance in other areas. Deborah Fuller (1985) notes a similar finding in her case study of primary trait scoring: after examining the exact nature of the papers used in the scorings, transcribing the group discussions that followed, and conducting interviews with the scorers, she observed that several scorers mentioned having to learn "to put concern for secondary traits in the background" (p. 295) and thinking that their colleagues might have had a harder time than they themselves did in overlooking the secondary traits. Fuller's study of the papers suggests that if readers had in fact been affected by secondary traits, the influence probably would have been most evident in the upper-half papers, resulting in a slightly lower score than the evaluation of the primary trait alone might have given (pp. 283–284). (Presumably, the impact of secondary traits would not lower any further those papers receiving 1s or 2s.) Because mechanics are overlooked in primary trait scoring, Lee Odell suggests supplementing the primary trait scoring with some other means of tabulating errors.

Scoring Scale

The scoring scale depicted on the guide conveys the possible range of responses the task will generate. A scale of four points is often used to indicate whether the writer has performed the task to an unsatisfactory degree, a minimal degree, a satisfactory degree, or an elaborated degree; other score points, such as *0, 8,* or *9,* are included to enable scorers to deal with papers that are illegible, completely off task, or, in some other way, seriously deficient.

Complexity of Using Guides

The development of the guide and task is usually time-consuming; in fact, noting the time required for trial runs with both the exercise and the sample guides, Lloyd-Jones (1977) cautions that "in terms of convenience for the tester, Primary Trait Scoring is more difficult than other methods" (p. 46). However, in Lloyd-Jones's view, once the specific guide is developed, then it can be used readily for evaluation by "presumably any bright and verbal person" (p. 45). Notwithstanding Lloyd-Jones's optimism, the guides can be, even with all their specificity, challenging to apply in actual scoring situations. Deborah Fuller (1985), for example, takes issue with Lloyd-Jones. Recounting her interviews with the scorers and the transcribed group discussions of sample papers, she adds a cautionary note:

> The use of a scoring guide to rate papers is much more complex than a simple, objective interaction between rater and paper. Instead, evaluation is a complex transaction involving raters' use of varying strategies including re-visioning the papers for the others and negotiating trade-offs to persuade one another, an awareness of the other rater's preferences, and the readers' interpretation of both the text and the scoring guide. (pp. 211–212)

Procedures Used in Primary Trait Scorings

Our own experiences two years ago with a primary trait scoring corroborated the complexity noted by Fuller. The purpose of our scoring was to evaluate writing samples composed by secondary school students for a special educational-improvement project underway at a major private university in the Northeast. The topics used by the students had been released by NAEP, and the topic-specific guides—as well as half of the samples used for training—had also been developed and/or used by NAEP previously. Thus, we were concerned not with the development of the task or guide but rather with the application of the guide to papers written by students in the special project.

Although separate scorings were held on separate days for each of the two topics used in the evaluation—a practice that differed from our holistic scorings in which topics are intermingled—our scoring was formal and followed many of the same procedures used in a typical, structured holistic scoring. There were three tables of five scorers each, with a table leader supervising each table. The scorers were secondary or college English teachers; all were highly experienced at holistic scoring, but virtually none had previous experience with primary trait scoring.

A heavy emphasis therefore was placed upon training and upon understanding the guide.

Table leaders met beforehand to review the guides and to score the sample papers sent from NAEP; these papers became the anchor samples. Then the table leaders selected and independently scored a series of papers written by the students in the special project. They exchanged the papers among each other until every paper had received four independent scores. These papers served as additional training samples.

At the scoring itself, the readers reviewed the guide and then scored the anchor samples from NAEP and the additional forty samples chosen from the group of papers being assessed. During the training period, readers discussed with the table leaders and the chief reader any problems they experienced in applying the guide to particular papers. Despite the specificity of the guide—which for each topic attempted to anticipate any possible occurrences—the scorers still raised questions as to how something should be interpreted or what score would be most appropriate in a particular instance. In line with Fuller's findings, these questions underscored the complexity of using the guides.

After becoming thoroughly familiar with the guide and with the sample papers, the scorers rated the actual papers, using the basic four-point scale of primary trait scoring. (Other numbers on the scale were reserved for illegible, off-topic, or off-task papers.) Each paper was read twice; the score of the first reader was bandaged to ensure the independence of the second score. First readings were also spiraled among several different packets for second readings so that no two readers would be paired constantly against one another. Table leaders monitored the readers throughout, checking the scores assigned to papers selected at random from each scorer's packets; samples were presented, and a formal check reading was also conducted in which each reader, table leader, and chief reader independently scored the same essay to determine how well everyone agreed. The resulting interrater reliability rates, while adequate for the purpose of the evaluation, were lower than the reliability rates usually obtained by NAEP. The lower correlations were another indication of the complexity of interpreting the guides, especially those guides composed by others.

Issues of Reliability and Validity

In Lloyd-Jones's view (1977), the sharp focus and the clarity that primary trait scoring brings to writing assessment strengthen its validity.

Acknowledging that "Primary Trait Scoring also depends to some extent on the face authority of the readers, but even more on the competence of the people who make the exercises and the guides," he adds that "a user of the test can easily examine just what the testers thought they were examining. The test thus gains credibility in its openness. Not the authority of the reader but the persuasiveness of the scoring guide becomes the issue" (pp. 46–47). In her dissertation comparing primary trait scoring to a more general criteria scale used by the 1979 National Council of Teachers of English Achievement Awards in Writing Program, Patricia Gilbert (1980) also views the specific nature of the scoring guide as an advantage; she concludes that the scoring guides of primary trait scoring have content validity in that they clearly specify not only the task but also the actual elements by which writers' success at fulfilling the task can be assessed (pp. 93–94).

From her case study of primary trait scoring, Fuller (1985) likewise concludes that this scoring approach does, in fact, determine "the effectiveness of a composition on a reader" (p. 284). The presence of "highly conventional papers" among the lowest scores, as well as "unconventional papers" among the highest scores confirmed for her the validity of the guide; the differences she found among reader responses when the same papers were scored two years apart further suggested to her that readers were actually reading the papers in the sense that their responses to the texts were shaped by their new experiences.

With thorough training in using the primary trait scoring guides, readers can achieve high interreader consistency. The .90+ interrater reliability rate often obtained in NAEP scorings has led Ina Mullis (1980) to conclude that for the purpose of measuring a group performance at a certain time, one reader may suffice—even though, she cautions, two readers are recommended. Moreover, she stresses that any measurement of individual students necessitates having at least two readers and as many writing samples as possible (p. 23). (In the scoring we conducted, reader scores had to be identical to signify agreement between readers; any discrepant scores—that is, any nonidentical scores—were not refereed. Instead, the first reader's score was considered the appropriate one, and the second reader's score—if not identical—became factored into the reader reliability rate.)

Adaptations and Implications for Teaching

To accommodate its changing assessments, NAEP has made some adaptations in its primary trait scoring procedures in recent years.

For example, in a 1990 pilot portfolio study, NAEP asked each participating school to have its fourth- and eighth-grade students submit one sample of their best writing. Because the papers submitted to NAEP were done for a variety of assignments, a team of teachers developed domain-specific, rather than task-specific, scoring guides to address the informative, narrative, and persuasive samples. Six scoring levels were used, rather than the four often used with specific tasks; moreover, because the six-point scale typically requires finer levels of discrimination, the adjacent agreement rate was reported as well as the identical agreement rate (see Gentile, 1992, pp. 24–27).

Primary Trait Scoring in the Classroom

Because of the focused nature of this evaluation method, primary trait scoring can provide much more information than holistic scoring can about students' success or failure at fulfilling the purpose and addressing the audience of the *specific* writing task. In this respect, Lee Odell (1981) seems accurate in noting that "primary trait scoring seems especially useful for combining diagnosis and evaluation" in that the exact nature of students' problems—and probable solutions—will then become apparent (pp. 127, 130).

In addition, the guide's specificity—which enables scorings to be replicated and topics to be reused—offers schools and school districts a means of assessing school programs and exploring student growth. In fact, Mullis stresses that one benefit of the primary trait scoring approach, along with NAEP guides and exercises, is its usefulness for schools and districts (p. 26). Patricia Gilbert (1980) also emphasizes that such guides and exercises would enable classroom teachers to show students what is effective or ineffective about their essays; however, she acknowledges that unless a topic is accessible enough to be reusable with a number of students, individual teachers would undoubtedly find it too time-consuming to develop guides for specific assignments and undergo training in their use (pp. 99–100).

To illustrate how primary trait scoring guides might work for a classroom, instructor Caroline Dennis and I devised a primary trait scoring guide (shown in Figure 5) for one assignment in her developmental Reading and Writing in the Disciplines course linked to anthropology. Two responses to the computer lab assignment are presented below; the first essay, written by first-year student G, received a 3 out of a possible four points on the primary trait scale; the second essay, written by first-year student T, received the top score of 4.

Define the term **adaptation** in the context of anthropology. Then describe the results of adaptation in one of the cultures you have studied this term. Be sure to include physical adaptation as well as that of tools, shelter, agriculture, clothing, etc.

Primary Trait
The primary trait in this informational piece of writing is to reveal by means of an appropriate application an understanding of the concept of **adaptation** as used in anthropology.

0 No response.

1 *Unsatisfactory analysis.* The writer of the essay does not make any applications. Or the essay applies one or two aspects of the culture but omits others entirely.

2 *Minimal analysis.* The essay reflects some understanding of application, but the use of weak examples suggests the understanding is limited.

3 *Adequate analysis.* The essay indicates an understanding of adaptation through its variety of examples. However, the examples lack detail and are presented more as a listing than as a full discussion.

4 *Elaborated analysis.* The essay reflects a strong understanding of adaptation through detailed examples that apply to personal experience, as well as to a culture discussed in the textbook.

Figure 5. A sample primary trait guide for a class assignment.

Essay by Student G: Computer Lab Assignment Receiving a Primary Trait Score of 3

The purpose of Anthropology is to have knowledge about how different cultures live within their environment and how they produce products in order to live within their boundaries. In Anthropology this is described as adaptation. Adaptation according to Professor M. is the behavioral and physical adjustments to the environment.

An example of adaptation would be Nanook and his people who lived east of Hudson's Bay, in Arctic Canada. In order for Nanook and his people to survive the extreme cold weather they had to adapt to it by having a special diet, specially made double-layered clothing with waterproof sealskin boots, and snow goggles in order to protect their eyes. For their homes, the Eskimos had either Igloos or tents depend on the time of season. The Eskimos also had their on type of weapons in order to survive in such conditions. The weapons that they used were nets, hooks, and harpoons for fishing and for hunting they had traps, spears, and harpoons with lines to catch their prey.

Another good example of adaptation would be the people from the Andes mountains. The global conditions of the Andes mountains are high altitude, the dryness of the desert and the wetness of the Amazon Rainforest. When the Spanish first tried to conquer the Incas they were not use to condition of anoxia, which is the decrease of oxygen at low barometric pressure. Anoxia impacts all life forms. The Incas who inhabit this region are use to this condition which explains the fact that the Spanish took sixty years to reproduce an offspring. Another group of people from this region is the people from Tiwanaku, who throughout time created their own agriculture products, for example, potatoes. That is what gives the income to live and survive in those conditions.

Therefore, I have to the best of my knowledge defined the word adaptation in the context of Anthropology. I have also included specific examples that helped me understand the concept of adaptation. From personal experience I had to adapt to the way of college life, which is to learn how to write papers, learn how to study for exams all over without memorization, and being on my own. So no matter, what adaptation is all around us but we probably have not notice.

Essay by Student T: Computer Lab Assignment Receiving a Primary Trait Score of 4

I woke up one day and realized where I was. I stood there in the middle of the floor in my very own, and very small bedroom. For the first time in my life I had my own room with my own closet. Of course at first I was very excited to finally be on my own. Now, seven months later since I have arrived in Gainesville, I can admit that I have fully adapted to my new surroundings. Adaptation is the physical and psychological adjustments to an environment. Adaptation is part of everyone's lives. At one time or another, you have to adapt to certain conditions. Sometimes adaptation can be very minor such as sweating when it is hot outside and shivering when it is cold. On the other hand, adaptation can be a way of life.

The people of the Andes mountains are adapted to extreme conditions. It would be impossible for an average human to live like the Inca did. The Inca have adapted to the extreme dryness of their region. Their engineering feet of canals, which till this day still baffles scholars, was their form of adapting to the dryness. Another feet was the way the Inca harvested. Due to the mountainous feature of their land, it was impossible to grow many types of food. The Inca carved plateaus along the mountains in order to grow certain types of food.

Another problem with food as well as the well-being of the people was the lack of oxygen. The land in the Andes was so elevated that the oxygen ran thin. This prevented many types of food to grow. So, the Andes harvested over thirty types of potatoes that were able to grow in thin air. The lack of oxygen not only hindered harvesting, it affected the Inca's bodies directly. Anoxia is what would happen to any average human if they stayed in the Andes for an extended period of time. The Inca adapted by growing larger lungs in order to breathe.

Just like the Inca, I had to adapt to my new surroundings. Growing up in south Florida, I was accustomed to humidity and extreme heat. I was also adapted to the hectic life that is lived in Miami. Every were you go there are sirens, traffic, and overall stress. Since I have arrived in Gainesville, I have noticed that I have less stress in my life. I do not need to drive everywhere, instead I can walk since everything is nearby. The people are very different. Not everyone is rude and loud.

The most I have had to adapt to though is the weather. It can get very cold in Gainesville by my standards. I never had to worry about sweaters until now.

Everyone goes through some sort of adaptation in their lives wether it be large or small. Though life for the Inca was normal to them, we see it as a great example of adaptation to severe conditions. My case is obviously minute compared to the Inca but for me, it is my case of adaptation.

Summary

Primary trait scoring is based on the idea that different modes of discourse place different demands on the writer in terms of purpose and audience. Writing tasks, therefore, require careful development, as do the scoring guides, which are tailored as much as possible to the specific writing task, audience, and goal. The specificity of the guides means that scorings can be replicated quite closely; it also means that this approach can provide diagnostic information not available with holistic scoring.

At the same time, the source of this scoring method's strengths is also the source of its weaknesses. That is, developing specific guides for specific tasks can be very time-consuming. Moreover, while secondary traits can be included, the primary trait of each task remains virtually the overriding focus of the evaluation.

In my own experience, primary trait scoring emphasizes depth over breadth. By scoring the two informative tasks for the special program, the readers and I were able to derive a clear picture of *exactly how* the students in the program justified or explained the positions they took. At the same time, the scoring guides we used overlooked other qualities of the students' writing, and, in our particular assignment, there were no additional provisions made for determining those qualities. Thus, we had an in-depth picture of the key trait the tasks were assessing, but we had no picture of other elements of students' writing. If a school or district seeks such in-depth information about students' performance in a particular discourse form, then primary trait scoring is valuable. If, on the other hand, broader information is sought, then primary trait scoring would not be appropriate unless provisions were made for evaluating secondary traits as well.

8 Analytic Scoring

The image of red-spattered papers has diminished during the past few years with the emphasis on multiple drafting and peer collaboration throughout the writing process. Yet feedback remains important to students, and with classes still large at most school levels, many teachers use written comments rather than individual conferences to provide that feedback. In this respect, some version of analytic scoring continues to be a common means by which teachers evaluate their students' classroom writing. However, analytic scoring should not be equated with the practice of simply marking errors; rather, it implies examining the particular— or at least salient—features of compositions in terms of their audience and purpose and commenting upon the students' effectiveness in handling these features. A teacher may congratulate a student on good content while commenting on the weak sentence structure or pointing out ways in which the organization could be improved. Through such analysis, teachers often hope to provide the guidance necessary for students to write more effectively.

Theoretical Background of Analytic Scoring

Despite its adaptations in the classroom, analytic scoring is criticized by some researchers for the very theory on which it is based. Edward White (1985), for example, is strongly opposed to what he calls "analytic reductionism" (p. 35). In the first edition of his writing assessment text, he suggests that "in ways parallel to multiple-choice testing, analytic scoring imagines a model of writing that is neatly sequential and comfortably segmented" (p. 30), and he disputes the implicit belief that skills added together make good writing. Rather, he states, "the lack of agreement on subskills in the profession suggests that writing remains more than the sum of its parts and that the analytic theory that seeks to define and add up the subskills is fundamentally flawed" (p. 123).

A similar view is suggested by Lloyd-Jones (1977), who also categorizes analytic rating scales as one of the "atomistic methods" used to assess writing. Although such scales seem more complex in *appearing* to address the elements of entire compositions, Lloyd-Jones cautions that the categories used for measuring the elements are not only arbitrary but also removed from the larger context of the composition (pp. 35–36).

Like Lloyd-Jones, Faigley and his colleagues (1985) indicate that the categories isolated for analytic scoring may be difficult to define; they note, moreover, that a guide or scale developed for one type of writing may not be applicable to other types. They suggest that analytic scoring, like holistic scoring, is norm-referenced rather than criterion-referenced in that analytic scoring uses a "continuum of relative quality" to reflect levels of quality in various elements of student writing instead of defining specific criteria or traits as primary trait scoring does (pp. 104–106).

Despite these criticisms, analytic scoring has its adherents, too. Peter Elbow (1993), for example, argues against the ranking that holistic scoring involves and instead supports the type of evaluation that entails "looking hard and thoughtfully at a piece of writing in order to make distinctions as to the quality of different features or dimensions" (p. 191). In the course of doing so, Elbow believes, readers may be forced to acknowledge the individuality of their responses and to take into consideration the fuller context within which the piece has been written.

Liz Hamp-Lyons (1995) also argues on behalf of analytic scoring, a form of which she labels as "'multiple trait scoring.'" In her view, teachers who gather to discuss the various writing traits that will comprise a multiple trait instrument retain the sense of community valued by holistic scoring proponents; yet, at the same time, unlike holistic scorers, participants must clearly identify what they consider good writing to be and explain the reasons for their choices (p. 454). As Hamp-Lyons notes, the differences in viewpoints toward analytic scoring represent serious philosophical distinctions in how writing is viewed: acknowledging, for example, the frequent use of holistic scoring in many large assessments, she observes that multiple trait scoring, unlike holistic scoring, is, nevertheless, more reflective of those viewpoints that emphasize the complexity of writing.

The nature of writing—that is, the question of whether writing is "a holistic or an atomistic entity"—formed the basis for a study by Kyle Perkins and Sheila Brutten (1990). Examining the compositions of 110 ESL basic writers to determine the degree of interrelationship among the five elements of content, organization, vocabulary, language use, and mechanics, Perkins and Brutten sought to identify whether some elements of writing served as virtual "prerequisites" for the mastery of other elements. The students' in-class descriptive essays were scored by two trained readers using the ESL Composition Profile devised by Jacobs and his colleagues; agreement between the two readers was high.

Perkins and Brutten found that only one "prerequisite relationship" appeared to be statistically significant; that is, at the 50 percent mastery level, effectiveness in organization seemed necessary for effectiveness in language use. In addition, correlation tests indicated that all the elements were, at a statistically significant level, interrelated. Concluding that "for this sample of ESL composition students, writing ability was learned as a whole rather than as a series of separate components" (p. 81), the researchers endorse those current instructional approaches that emphasize writing not "as a set of sequential, separate tasks" but "as a holistic gestalt with a focus on meaning, function, and purpose" (p. 83). Perkins and Brutten limit their conclusion to the sample of students whose writing was observed. Nevertheless, while the interrelationships they identify do, in fact, underscore the links among all the skills, it should also be noted that the Composition Profile they used to evaluate the students' papers is not the same as a typical holistic scoring in which the score is derived from a single overall impression. Rather, each paper was read five different times holistically for the different aspects of the writing (p. 78), thereby approximating some analytic ratings.

Variations in Analytic Scales

Just as the theory behind analytic scoring is both berated and applauded, so, too, the analytic scales used in such scorings vary enormously in terms of extensiveness and rating levels. One of the most noted scales is that developed by Paul Diederich from his earlier work on the factors that influence readers; after trying the instrument in several high schools over a period of years and after consulting with teachers, Diederich developed a scale of eight factors, with double weighting given to "ideas" and "organization" (Faigley et al., 1985, p. 105). The scale is reprinted in Figure 6.

A different analytic scale, which was devised by Hoetker and Brossell (see Writing Assessment Specialists, 1990) as part of a pilot project for large-scale assessment purposes, isolated eight different elements that would provide feedback to students who had failed the holistically scored essay component of the then-state-mandated competency test for college sophomores. Figure 7 lists the eight elements of this scale, seven of which were rated in the students' version as *good, acceptable, needs improvement,* or *unsatisfactory;* the first element, thesis, was rated as either *thesis* or *no thesis.* The students' version contained descriptions of each quality.

Institutions were to be sent additional information that indicated the number and percentage of students who had received the various rating levels on each area. A pilot test of this analytic scale was subsequently conducted to determine the feasibility of using analytic scoring to provide additional feedback to students and their schools about areas of strength and weakness. The actual scale was never fully implemented.

	Low		*Middle*		*High*
Ideas	2	4	6	8	10
Organization	2	4	6	8	10
Wording	1	2	3	4	5
Flavor	1	2	3	4	5
Usage	1	2	3	4	5
Punctuation	1	2	3	4	5
Spelling	1	2	3	4	5
Handwriting	1	2	3	4	5

Figure 6. Diederich's analytic scale. From *Assessing Writers' Knowledge and Processes of Composing,* by Lester Faigley, Roger Cherry, David Jolliffe, and Anna Skinner, 1985, Norwood, NJ: Ablex. © 1985 by Ablex. Reprinted with permission.

Individual Student Analysis Version

1. THESIS. The presence or absence of a central idea or purpose.

2. FOCUS. How well the writer attends to the thesis.

3. ORGANIZATION. How effectively the writer carries out a plan for developing the essay; how well the essay is put together.

4. DETAILS. How well the writer uses examples, arguments, and explanations to support general statements and conclusions.

5. DICTION AND VOCABULARY. How effectively, economically, and accurately the writer uses words.

6. SENTENCES AND SYNTAX. How accurately and effectively the writer shapes and uses sentences.

7. GRAMMAR AND MECHANICS. How consistently the writer follows the rules and conventions of standard written English in regard to grammar, usage, spelling, punctuation, and capitalization.

8. CONTENT. How successfully the essay conveys an impression of thoughtfulness, authoritativeness, and competence.

Figure 7. Condensation of analytic scale from Writing Assessment Specialists (1990). Elements 2 through 8 are rated as *Good, Acceptable, Needs Improvement,* or *Unsatisfactory.* © 1990 by the Florida Department of Education, Tallahassee, Florida. All rights reserved. Used with permission.

Several years ago, as part of another pilot study in which portfolios from diverse secondary school English classes were evaluated on an analytic scale to determine the feasibility of using portfolios on a large scale, we devised a comprehensive analytic scoring guide against which raters could evaluate the six different entries in the portfolios. The guide addressed major rhetorical elements—thesis, organization, development, and content—as well as word choice, sentence structure, usage, punctuation, and spelling. In addition, the writer's knowledge of the writing process was examined, as were the writer's reflective skills. Bonus points were awarded for creativity, originality, humor, and voice. A scale of one to four was used for each element.

Analytic Scales for Classroom Use

Various analytic scales have been devised for classroom use or other instructional purposes. Unlike the scales used for large, external assessments wherein comparability is important, classroom scales can be adapted readily to suit the particular assignment. Peter Elbow, for example, whose grid is reproduced in Figure 8, notes that he changes the criteria in accordance with the writing task. Moreover, in a paper "From Grades to Grids: Responding to Writing by Criteria," Elbow indicates that he sometimes uses four levels, rather than three, and that he may write on his computer minor or extensive comments beside the criteria

Strong	OK	Weak	
			Content, insights, thinking, grappling with topic
			Genuine revision, substantive changes, not just editing
			Organization, structure, guiding the reader
			Language: syntax, sentences, wording, voice
			Mechanics: spelling, grammar, punctuation, proofreading
			Overall (note: this is not a sum of the other scores)

Figure 8. Peter Elbow's grid. From "Ranking, Evaluating, and Liking: Sorting Out Three Forms of Judgment," by Peter Elbow, 1993, *College English*, 55, p. 195. © 1993 by NCTE. Reprinted with permission of the author.

he is stressing. In Elbow's view, the grids help students understand the reader's perspective much more than a single grade ever could (personal communication, spring 1996).

An essay analysis chart has been used in the writing program at Boise State University to help students who have failed a competency essay recognize where they need to improve. As discussed by Richard Leahy (1992), the analysis sheet lists specific statements depicting strengths and weaknesses in four broad categories: Focus/Ideas, Development/Organization, Style, and Correctness. The instructor can check where appropriate and make comments or suggestions at the end. The scale is provided in Figure 9.

FOCUS/IDEAS

Strengths

_____ The essay follows the assignment and answers both parts.
_____ The essay really says something. It gives the impression that the writer is going somewhere with the idea.
_____ The main idea is carried forward by succession of relevant supporting ideas.
_____ The writing shows an unusual or surprising perspective on the subject.

Weaknesses

_____ The essay does not clearly address the assigned topic.
_____ The essay does not answer both parts of the assignment.
_____ The essay (or part of it) seems to be mainly filling paper rather than really saying something.
_____ The reader must get past the introduction before knowing where the essay is going.
_____ Lack of supporting ideas creates a bare-bones, unsatisfying effect.

DEVELOPMENT/ORGANIZATION

Strengths

_____ Details and examples are appropriate and clearly related to the ideas they support.
_____ The idea in each paragraph is finished out before the paper goes on to the next paragraph.
_____ The essay has a clear order that is easy to follow.
_____ Paragraph divisions clearly indicate changes in topic.

(continued on next page)

Figure 9. Boise State University grid. From "Competency Testing and the Writing Center," by Richard Leahy, 1992, *WPA: Writing Program Administration, 15* (3), spring 1992. © 1992 by *WPA: Writing Program Administration.* Reprinted with permission.

Weaknesses

_____ The development is inconsistent; parts of the paper are fully developed while other parts are skimpy.

_____ Details and examples are not really specific.

_____ Some paragraphs end before their ideas have been finished out.

_____ Haphazard organization makes the essay hard to follow.

_____ Too many paragraph divisions

or

_____ Too few paragraph divisions make the supporting parts of the essay hard to distinguish from one another.

STYLE

Strengths

_____ Sentences are varied in length and structure.

_____ Important words and ideas get clear emphasis.

_____ Word choices are accurate.

_____ Word choices are appropriate to the context, not too casual and not pompous or too formal.

Weaknesses

_____ All sentences tend to have the same length and pattern.

_____ Sentences tend to be short and choppy.

_____ Sentences tend to be long and stringy, with parts not clearly related to each other.

_____ Some word choices are unclear or inaccurate.

_____ Some word choices are too casual or too formal for the context.

CORRECTNESS

Strengths

_____ Instructions have been followed (write in ink, skip every other line, etc.).

_____ There are no errors (or very few) to distract the reader.

_____ The handwriting is easy to read.

Weaknesses

_____ Instructions have not been followed (write in ink, skip every other line, etc.).

_____ The reader is distracted by: Sentence-level errors (fragments, run-ons, comma splices, subject-verb agreement, confused sentence structures, etc.).

_____ Punctuation errors

_____ Spelling errors

Figure 9. *(Continued)*

A sample application of two of these analytic scales follows. The impromptu essay below was written in fifty minutes on the topic "Important Skills for Beginning College Students" by college junior Michael Grant. Figure 10 presents a scoring of the essay by Martin

Simpson, an instructor in our program, using Peter Elbow's grid; Figure 11 presents Simpson's scoring of the essay using the Boise State University Analytic Scale.

Impromptu Essay by Michael Grant

For any student attending college for the first time there are three major skills that they must master for a successful college career, Time Management, Study Skills, and Money Management. If these three things are taken care of college will not only be fun, but a successful venture as well. These three ideas would cover any problem that a new student would encounter at college. Each one will assist in a wide array of situations.

First and most important is time management. Without time management the young students world will tumble down around them. There are always things to do places to go and people to see, and most students are not familiar with having so many choices. Balancing their time between their social life, their scholastic life, and their personal life is many times more difficult than it is in highschool. This is mainly because everything is new. If you have never had a college class you don't know how much time you need to study for them or how much sleep you need to get through a day. You are not use to being around 30,000 new people your age with the same interest as you. How much time do you spend on the phone with your friends back home or your faimily? College is practically a whole new world, and being able to spread yourself out to what you need to do and what you want to do becomes a very important skill.

Speaking of things you need to do, that is where study skills become important. A students ability to study and study efficiently is highly important but often overlooked. For many students High School was a breeze and studying was not a neccessity. This leaves many new students at a loss when they come to college, and classes are more difficult. The time it takes to study increases if the students skills are not hoaned, interfering with social and personal time. Needless to say, if they don't study well they will not pass their classes and flunk out anyway. Failing school is a waste of money and a waste of time.

Wasting money is the third trap that new students encounter. You get credit cards in the mail every day, and your on your own with your Financial Aid. There is no mother or father. You pay your own bills, food, clothes etc. What you spend your money on is very important. Pay for housing or get a new stereo, pay fees or get new tires for my car? Students are responsible for themselves and must be prepared to except the challenge.

The best way to meet and beat that challenge is to manage your time well, manage your money well, and study properly. If these things are done college will seem as easy as highschool but more fun.

The same analytic scales were applied to the impromptu essay presented below; the essay was composed by Christopher Sprecker in the

Strong	OK	Weak	
	X		Content, insights, thinking, grappling with topic
			Genuine revision, substantive changes, not just editing
X			Organization, structure, guiding the reader
		X	Language: syntax, sentences, wording, voice
		X	Mechanics: spelling, grammar, punctuation, proofreading
	X		Overall (note: this is not a sum of the other scores)

Figure 10. Application of Peter Elbow's grid to essay by Michael Grant. Grid reproduced from "Ranking, Evaluating, and Liking: Sorting Out Three Forms of Judgment," by Peter Elbow, 1993, *College English, 55,* p. 195. © 1993 by NCTE. Reprinted with permission of the author.

FOCUS/IDEAS

Strengths

  __X__ The essay follows the assignment and answers both parts.
  _____ The essay really says something. It gives the impression that the writer is going somewhere with the idea.
  __X__ The main idea is carried forward by succession of relevant supporting ideas.
  _____ The writing shows an unusual or surprising perspective on the subject.

Weaknesses

  _____ The essay does not clearly address the assigned topic.
  _____ The essay does not answer both parts of the assignment.
  __X__ The essay (or part of it) seems to be mainly filling paper rather than really saying something.
  _____ The reader must get past the introduction before knowing where the essay is going.
  _____ Lack of supporting ideas creates a bare-bones, unsatisfying effect.

(continued on next page)

Figure 11. Application of Boise State University grid to essay by Michael Grant. Grid reproduced from "Competency Testing and the Writing Center," by Richard Leahy, 1992, *WPA: Writing Program Administration, 15* (3), spring 1992. © 1992 by *WPA: Writing Program Administration.* Reprinted with permission.

DEVELOPMENT/ORGANIZATION

Strengths

_____ Details and examples are appropriate and clearly related to the ideas they support.

__X__ The idea in each paragraph is finished out before the paper goes on to the next paragraph.

__X__ The essay has a clear order that is easy to follow.

__X__ Paragraph divisions clearly indicate changes in topic.

Weaknesses

_____ The development is inconsistent; parts of the paper are fully developed while other parts are skimpy.

__X__ Details and examples are not really specific.

_____ Some paragraphs end before their ideas have been finished out.

_____ Haphazard organization makes the essay hard to follow.

_____ Too many paragraph divisions

or

_____ Too few paragraph divisions make the supporting parts of the essay hard to distinguish from one another.

STYLE

Strengths

__X__ Sentences are varied in length and structure.

_____ Important words and ideas get clear emphasis.

_____ Word choices are accurate.

_____ Word choices are appropriate to the context, not too casual and not pompous or too formal.

Weaknesses

_____ All sentences tend to have the same length and pattern.

_____ Sentences tend to be short and choppy.

_____ Sentences tend to be long and stringy, with parts not clearly related to each other.

__X__ Some word choices are unclear or inaccurate.

_____ Some word choices are too casual or too formal for the context.

CORRECTNESS

Strengths

__X__ Instructions have been followed (write in ink, skip every other line, etc.).

_____ There are no errors (or very few) to distract the reader.

_N.A._ The handwriting is easy to read.

Weaknesses

_____ Instructions have not been followed (write in ink, skip every other line, etc.).

__X__ The reader is distracted by: Sentence-level errors (fragments, run-ons, comma splices, subject-verb agreement, confused sentence structures, etc.).

__X__ Punctuation errors

__X__ Spelling errors

Figure 11. *(Continued)*

computer lab for his Reading and Writing in the Disciplines class, which was taught by Martin Simpson and was linked to a history course. Figure 12 contains Martin Simpson's analytic scoring of this essay with a content-area version of Peter Elbow's grid, and Figure 13 contains his analytic scoring of the essay with the scale from Boise State University.

Impromptu Essay by Christopher Sprecker

Question: Discuss the populist and progressive movements and their impact on American political history.

Politics of the late nineteenth century involve not only republicans and democrats, but the rise of the populist and progressive movements. The two movements evolve due to seprate reasons and they are most easily compared by their differences. The populist party was made up of farmers fighting to obtain rights for themselves. The progressive movement, on the other hand, was an organization of urban industrialists who were in hopes of passing reforms that would adjust the nature and direction of American society. By evaluating the opposing stances of the two groups on political issues, the differences between the movements is made obvious.

In the latter part of the century, farmers felt that politicians were not listening to them. They were suffering economically due to overproduction and the dry soil but were far from blaming themselves. For their pride it was much easier to blame the industrialists. Farmers believed the protective tariff was hurting their trade with other countries as was the gold dollar. Both of these were instated to help the infant industries which created ill feelings among the farmers towards the industrialists. The anger prompted the organization of the populist party which was not, however, successful. This radical party ironically pushed to recapture pre-Civil War society. Specifically they wanted government to take over ownership of railroads, telegraphs and other such large industries. Even more radically, they wished to see immigration stopped and a graduated income tax instated for those multi-millionaires.

In a nutshell, the progressives stood for many things in which the populists opposed. They were middle class, from the cities and ultimately better educated. Generally they excepted the world around them although they didn't like a large part of it. In hopes of altering those things they didn't like, they came up with reforms that would adjust the nature and direction of american society. Overall, the progressives were more satisfied than the populists and they wanted to go forward. This further highlights the irony of the radical populists wanting to recapture 1860. The progressives were more successful. This was due largely in part to the fact that they embraced parts of both the republican and democratic parties.

The differences are easily distinguished. It is easy to understand why the progressives brought Teddy Roosevelt and Woodrow Wilson to the presidency while the populists brought no one. The populists ultimately created chaos in which the progressives tried to bring to order.

Name: *Christopher Sprecker*			Course: *Reading and Writing in the Disciplines*
Weak	**OK**	**Strong**	
	X		Memory of course information
		X	Understanding of central concepts; ability to apply them
		X	Ability to give reasons for opinions and interpretations
	X		Writing skill
	X		Effort
_____ Distinction or A			__X__ Pass _____ Fail or U

Figure 12. Application of Peter Elbow's content-area grid to essay by Christopher Sprecker. Grid from Peter Elbow, adapted from an essay in *Embracing Contraries: Oppositions in Teaching and Learning* (p. 171), by Peter Elbow, 1986, New York, NY: Oxford University Press. Adaptation reprinted with permission of the author.

Advantages of Analytic Scoring

Despite all the variations, the analytic scales represent efforts to break writing into its elements so that students can receive feedback as to where their strengths and problems lie. The scales, most of which can be adapted for classroom use depending on the writing assignment and the teacher's goals, all share an attempt to distinguish between the elements of form and content—between larger rhetorical issues and the more surface concerns of mechanics and grammar. Because readers in an analytic scoring are not balancing together all the elements of a composition, they are able to focus on providing feedback in discrete areas. Students—especially in assessments with large stakes—are eager to receive that precise feedback. To those of our students who had failed the state-mandated essay subtest, for instance, and who consequently needed to remediate their writing skills in our Writing Center, there was little comfort in knowing that they had received a summed holistic score of 5, as opposed to their former score of 4, on their latest essay attempt; as they were still short of the 6 needed to pass, they wanted to know *why*. Because they did not receive their examination essays back, they could not evaluate their papers against a scoring rubric; thus, the students remained frustrated by the lack of information. And in those instances in which students feared they were regressing because they

---

FOCUS/IDEAS

Strengths

__X__ The essay follows the assignment and answers both parts.

__X__ The essay really says something. It gives the impression that the writer is going somewhere with the idea.

__X__ The main idea is carried forward by succession of relevant supporting ideas.

__X__ The writing shows an unusual or surprising perspective on the subject.

Weaknesses

_____ The essay does not clearly address the assigned topic.

_____ The essay does not answer both parts of the assignment.

_____ The essay (or part of it) seems to be mainly filling paper rather than really saying something.

_____ The reader must get past the introduction before knowing where the essay is going.

_____ Lack of supporting ideas creates a bare-bones, unsatisfying effect.

DEVELOPMENT/ORGANIZATION

Strengths

__X__ Details and examples are appropriate and clearly related to the ideas they support.

_____ The idea in each paragraph is finished out before the paper goes on to the next paragraph.

__X__ The essay has a clear order that is easy to follow.

__X__ Paragraph divisions clearly indicate changes in topic.

(continued on next page)

Figure 13. Second application of Boise State University grid to essay by Christopher Sprecker. Grid reproduced from "Competency Testing and the Writing Center," by Richard Leahy, 1992, *WPA: Writing Program Administration,* 15 (3), spring 1992. © 1992 by *WPA: Writing Program Administration.* Reprinted with permission.

had received a 3, for example, instead of their former score of 4, the holistic score was a cause of much distress. We solved the problem by having them write additional, timed essays within our Writing Center, essays that we could then examine analytically.

Just as classroom teachers have, through their markings and written comments, long provided a form of analytic scoring in the hope that students will gain some understanding of where the writing needs to be improved, so do analytic scorers in large-scale assessments (as well as in research studies) seek to identify where students' strengths and weaknesses lie. Portfolios in Vermont, for example, have been scored analytically for several years, with readers rating individual student entries on five key elements: purpose, organization, de-

Weaknesses

_____ The development is inconsistent; parts of the paper are fully developed while other parts are skimpy.

_____ Details and examples are not really specific.

__X__ Some paragraphs end before their ideas have been finished out.

_____ Haphazard organization makes the essay hard to follow.

_____ Too many paragraph divisions

or

_____ Too few paragraph divisions make the supporting parts of the essay hard to distinguish from one another.

STYLE

Strengths

__X__ Sentences are varied in length and structure.

_____ Important words and ideas get clear emphasis.

_____ Word choices are accurate.

__X__ Word choices are appropriate to the context, not too casual and not pompous or too formal.

Weaknesses

_____ All sentences tend to have the same length and pattern.

_____ Sentences tend to be short and choppy.

_____ Sentences tend to be long and stringy, with parts not clearly related to each other.

__X__ Some word choices are unclear or inaccurate.

_____ Some word choices are too casual or too formal for the context.

CORRECTNESS

Strengths

__X__ Instructions have been followed (write in ink, skip every other line, etc.).

_____ There are no errors (or very few) to distract the reader.

_N.A._ The handwriting is easy to read.

Weaknesses

_____ Instructions have not been followed (write in ink, skip every other line, etc.).

_____ The reader is distracted by: Sentence-level errors (fragments, run-ons, comma splices, subject-verb agreement, confused sentence structures, etc.).

_____ Punctuation errors

__X__ Spelling errors

Figure 13. *(Continued)*

tails, voice or tone, and grammar/usage/mechanics. Readers rate the portfolios on four different levels, using the descriptors "Extensively," "Frequently," "Sometimes," and "Rarely." Their guide has been revised now to include, among other features, what Geof Hewitt

(1995) calls "'the Gordian Wedge'"—a central question for each element so that instructors can initially decide between the upper-half and lower-half papers before making the final judgment. Thus, readers mentally answer "yes" or "no" to a question dealing with the clarity of focus before they assign it an appropriate score (pp. 159–160). Such analytic scores provide instructors and/or schools with information about specific features that may need extra work.

Analytic scoring as an assessment measure has the additional advantage of being more comprehensive than primary trait scoring. Whereas primary trait scoring focuses on how well writers have fulfilled the specific traits of a particular assignment according to its purpose and audience, analytic scoring goes beyond those specific features to evaluate other dimensions of the task. In an analytic scoring of an expository process essay, for example, not only would the clarity and sequence of the writer's explanation come under scrutiny, but also the structure and style used to discuss the process might be evaluated. Thus, the comprehensiveness of the feedback provided seems to be the overriding strength of analytic scoring.

Disadvantages of Analytic Scoring

But the very advantage that analytic scoring offers is also the source of its disadvantages: that is, the comprehensive scoring of each entry takes time and effort, and hence, for large-scale assessments, is apt to be much more costly. Our pilot portfolio project with secondary English classes in which teachers first scored portfolios holistically and then scored other portfolios analytically showed the holistic procedure to be far more efficient than analytic scoring—especially with portfolios. Scoring the portfolios analytically took an average of twenty minutes, with some portfolios of the Advanced Placement English classes taking well over thirty minutes. When, on the other hand, a third of the portfolios were scored holistically, scorers spent approximately five or more minutes on each portfolio, again with the portfolios of the AP students taking much longer.

In addition to the factors of time and cost, another drawback to analytic scoring is the difficulty of interpreting what the categories mean. Faigley and his colleagues (1985) note, for example, that the term "flavor" as used by Diederich in his well known rating scale is ambiguous and could be hard to distinguish from "wording" (p. 105). Such ambiguity of interpretation is not, however, the only source of difficulty. Even knowing what categories to include on an analytic scale can be challenging, as test makers try to balance the need for providing meaningful information with the need for conserving time required for the evaluative task. It becomes difficult to know, for example, whether to cluster together grammar and mechanics or development and organization; if the categories are too broad, then no real distinctions can be made and the student will not have much information from which to learn. If, on the other hand, there are too many fine discriminations to be made, not only will the task become very cumbersome, but students may be altogether turned off by the complexity of the results (reminiscent of the negative classroom grading practice of marking *every* error in a paper). Such was our feeling with the analytic scoring of our pilot portfolios discussed earlier. At the end of analytically scoring the portfolios, we were concerned that the guide—with its potential multiple points reeking of those heavily marked compositions that students tended to ignore—was undoubtedly far too detailed for students to have any interest in reflecting on the results.

Still another problem with identifying appropriate categories for analytic scales arises, according to Faigley et al. (1985), when the analytic guide is to be used on a *variety of writings*, for then those categories that are applicable to one type of writing will not necessarily be relevant to another. For example, the thesis that is so important in expository writing does not have the same significance at all in narrative or descriptive writing. Similarly, students' own voices, critical in so many types of writing, have less impact in academic writing.

But if selecting the categories beforehand is difficult, then it may be equally difficult to discern what the ratings themselves mean. These rating levels—which often include such descriptive degrees as "to some extent" versus "often," or "weak" versus "poor"—can be semantically troublesome and add to the difficulty in providing an analytic rating of multiple elements in an entry. What one reader may interpret as "good," for example, another reader may see as "very good." In fact, the need for making a series of judgment calls across a continuum ranging from "poor" to "excellent" for each essay explains why the agreement rate among analytic raters typically is not as high as it is with holistic scoring, wherein fewer decisions must be made.

Another disadvantage that arises with analytic scoring—and for that matter, with all forms of scoring—is that the final information obtained via one scoring method may not be similar to the information obtained via another, especially if distinct reading approaches have been used. For example, a student who receives a summed score of 4 (on a six-point scale) from a holistic scoring may be bewildered if an analytic scoring of the same paper subsequently indicates that the content, organization, and development of the paper are adequate and that only the one broad category of mechanics and grammar is weak. Such a student may not understand that the weakness of the latter category—because of its serious impact *on that particular essay*—may indeed serve to lower the score sufficiently to make the final holistic score less than passing. Conversely, a student with good mechanics may, nonetheless, have failed in the holistic scoring because of a lack of development, poor focus, or weak organization *in that particular paper.* As a colleague has noted, such different scoring results with the two methods do not suggest that there is a credibility problem (Dianne Buhr, personal communication, May 15, 1990) but rather illustrate the very different emphases and reading approaches of both analytic and holistic scoring methods.

An essay (see below) written by one of our entering developmental writers illustrates the variations that can result. This placement essay received a score of 4 from each of two holistic scorers, thus totaling the highest possible score of *8* on a four-point scale during a formal holistic scoring. As Figure 14 reveals, when two experienced instructors from our program scored the essay analytically several months later (albeit without common training in using the guide), their judgments differed from one another across most categories and thus reflected their individual interpretations of the levels of quality.

Placement Essay

The advantages of being the youngest child is overwhelming, but tedious nonetheless. Mothers always seem to look upon their youngest child as the "baby" which, isn't a big problem considering the attention given. However the other extreme of this spectrum is the teasing an older brother may use for his own satisfaction. Growing up as the youngest does have these advantages and disadvantages, which is why growing up the youngest is so trying at times. Just dealing with these situations may be annoying.

Firstly, the youngest child is the "baby" of the family. This means that because he or she is the youngest, the attention given by the parents is a bit greater than what the previous children received. The youngest child will be the last one to play for a little league baseball team, the last one to refuse a bath, and the last one to go away to college. The parents may feel as though they're losing a real part of their lives. For twenty-five years they've been accustomed to cleaning up after their children.

So to say the least, the youngest child receives the benefits in life. They seem to get away with what the other two or three siblings couldn't. A trip to the ice-cream parlor is a common site. While mom showers her youngest child with hugs and kisses, father goes out to play catch with his kid in the backyard. This is a parent's last chance to experience such happiness on this scale.

However, there is an opposite side to this story. Growing up the youngest, also means, big brothers release of aggression. A younger child always seem to be teased, humiliated, and demeaned. A small child looks upon an older sibling as a role model. This is why it hurts so much when big brother doesn't allow his little brother to play football with him and his friends. Also, because the youngest child is the "baby," the youngest child gets treated like a baby. A lack of respect on a mature level can cause some serious headaches.

Being a younger brother or sister is at times great. This child can get away with anything, and if not, mom can't resist those puppy-dog eyes. Being a younger child is at times horrifying. Older brothers and sisters can be so cruel. The youngest child does however, receive one more lesson. Having to endure these attacks from both sides does help in developing skills in dealing with situations. If the youngest child can learn how to take some responsibilities on his/her part and refrain from getting a hot-head, then this child can succeed. After all, success is what mother and father wants most for their little "man."

Mario Lopez

Continuum of Overall Paper	Very Good	Accept-able	Weak, Needs Work	Very Weak	Comments
1) Thoughtfulness of content	Rater 1	Rater 2			
2) Clarity of thesis		Rater 1	Rater 2		
3) Focus	Rater 1	Rater 2			
4) Structure/ organization		Rater 1	Rater 2		
5) Introduction/ conclusion	Rater 1	Rater 2			Rater 2: Thesis should be more clear
6) Unity and coherence	Rater 1				
7) Specific development of ideas		Rater 1	Rater 2		Rater 1: Would like more detail Rater 2: Paragraphs could be developed more
8) Accuracy of word choice		Rater 1	Rater 2		Rater 2: Faulty comparison 5–6 word choice errors
					(continued on next page)

Figure 14. Analytic scorings of placement essay.

Continuum of Overall Paper	Very Good	Accept-able	Weak, Needs Work	Very Weak	Comments
9) Consistency of viewpoint	Rater 1		Rater 2		Rater 2: Feels like this essay shifts from objective to autobiographical
10) Good use of readings					
11) Creativity, other	Rater 1		Rater 2		Rater 1: Nice conclusion
12) Voice	Rater 1		Rater 2		
13) Completeness of sentences	Rater 1	Rater 2			
14) Variation in sentences		Rater 1			Rater 1: Too much use of "to be" verbs
15) Verb & noun endings	Rater 1	Rater 2			
16) Subject-verb agreement		Rater 2	Rater 1		Rater 1: A few instances of errors Rater 2: 1 error
17) Pronoun use/ adverbs	Rater 1	Rater 2			
18) Parallel structure	Rater 1	Rater 2			
19) Accuracy of modifiers		Rater 1, Rater 2			
20) Accuracy of commas			Rater 1, Rater 2		
21) Punctuation		Rater 2	Rater 1		
22) Capitalization	Rater 1	Rater 2			
23) Spelling	Rater 1	Rater 2			
24) Other					

Figure 14. *(Continued)*

Summary

Precisely because of the differences in the scoring methods—differences in reading approach, emphasis, and scales—it is important to acknowledge the strengths and limitations of each method. Whether in terms of theory, of research, or of practice itself, none of the current scoring approaches alone is optimal for all situations, and thus—depending on the purpose of the assessment, the resources available, and the information or results sought—one scoring approach may be more suitable than another.

In many respects, evaluating a composition by means of the three different scoring methods discussed is similar to the processes we go through whenever we evaluate how well our car is running. If we were judging the performance of a particular car holistically, then we would, in fact, be ranking its performance against the performance of other cars in its class. It might be "trouble-free" or "super" if it were on one end of the continuum; it might be "trouble-prone" or "a lemon" if it ranked at the other end. But we would be judging it in its entirety and in relation to other cars also judged in their entirety.

If, on the other hand, we were judging the primary trait of the car, then we would evaluate in depth some component central to its purpose. We might, for example, be concerned about our brakes in winter weather. In that case, we would ask a mechanic to examine the brake fluid, brake drums, brake shoes, and brake rotors to determine the stopping performance of the car. We would not, at that moment, be very concerned with other parts of the car.

If, finally, we wanted to evaluate the car's performance analytically prior to deciding whether to keep or sell the car, then several categories of components would come under our scrutiny—including the transmission, engine, brakes, and exhaust system, perhaps even such accouterments as the horn, windshield wipers, and signal lights. Thus, any of these approaches to evaluating a car may provide valuable information, depending on the purpose behind the rating; no single approach, however, will work for all purposes. Similarly, any of the scoring methods discussed for writing assessment may provide valuable information about students' writing, but the methods are not interchangeable; rather, the theories underlying the various approaches reflect substantial differences which make a given method more or less useful depending on the kind of information one wishes to obtain.

TIPS FOR TEACHERS

Developing and Using Scoring Guides in the Classroom

Giving students the chance to work with scoring guides, whatever the rubric chosen, should help them both to see the value of writing criteria and to gain practice in assessing their own writing skills. Of course, teachers may wish to use scoring guides that others have developed rather than creating specific guides for their own classes.

Guides for Holistic Scoring

1. Teachers should first determine the qualities of writing—such as organization, development, creativity, or focus—that they both emphasize in their instruction and consider whenever they grade papers holistically.

2. Teachers can then divide a set of classroom papers into piles according to the quality of these writing elements and describe—rather than prescribe—on a continuum of four to six points how these qualities are manifested in papers from each pile, from strongest to weakest.

3. For example, a teacher may describe a 4 paper as being "effectively organized and strongly focused," whereas a 1 paper is described as "typically disjointed and unfocused." Older students can help write these descriptions, provided that the papers are anonymous.

4. Teachers can broaden or modify these descriptions to reflect other elements they emphasize in succeeding assignments.

5. Using this kind of descriptive guide, teachers can have their classes practice scoring a set of *anonymous* papers. The results of the scoring can be tallied in class, so that students know where their scores stand in relation to those of their peers.

6. Teachers can then ask their students to evaluate their own papers against the criteria. As developing self-assessment skills takes time, students often need repeated practice in using the criteria.

Guides for Primary Trait Scoring

Developing the guides for primary trait scoring will take much more precision and will need to be tailored to the particular assignment, audience, and purpose.

1. Teachers should ask their students to help identify key elements—or primary traits—in their assignments, and, using sample papers that teachers have pre-selected, they can work together on describing the levels of quality that each score point reflects.

2. For example, for a persuasive paper, teachers may decide, together with their classes, that the overriding, primary trait that distinguishes such writing is the breadth of reasons the writer uses to support his or her claims. On the basis of the sample papers collected, teachers and students can create specific descriptions of the types and numbers of reasons each score level reflects.

3. Again, students should practice using this guide on a set of sample, anonymous papers, and the results can be discussed. Then students can rate their own papers with the guide.

Guides for Analytic Scoring

1. Teachers should first determine the central elements that they wish to include in a particular guide and decide how broad or specific the guide should be. For example, will it include the broad category "mechanics and usage," or will it include several subcategories for this area?
2. Then teachers can decide the rating system they will use to evaluate each category—a verbal system, such as "excellent" or "proficient," or a numerical system to convey the range of quality. They should discuss this system thoroughly with students.
3. The students can train to use the guides by practicing on sample papers.
4. Finally, students can rate their own papers against the criteria.

9 Reliability and Validity

Sue M. Legg

This chapter addresses ways to evaluate the judgments we make about student achievement. Much has been written about the value of encouraging students to reflect on their work; the same principle applies to teachers. Teachers who reflect on their own teaching and on students' individual and collective achievements will improve the instructional process. The goal of this chapter is to provide teachers with the information they need in order to evaluate their own and other assessments in the context of the current national debate about curriculum and assessment. The discussion about how standardized tests can limit curriculum must be reconciled with the fact that without some standardization of assessments, it is impossible to tell with enough certainty what students know and are able to do with their knowledge. The challenge is to develop a broadly based assessment system that will better reflect students' achievements. Teachers skilled in the evaluation of the assessments will be in the strongest position to determine what the assessment system of the future should be.

There are techniques that help teachers make informed judgments that will withstand external scrutiny; these are the means by which the reliability and validity of decisions are established. Teachers who understand and use these tools may have some uncomfortable moments if the data do not confirm their assumptions about teaching and learning; nevertheless, when it can be shown that ratings of student achievement are replicable, stakeholders place more confidence in the scores. When the same or a parallel assessment yields similar results, the assessment is considered to be a reliable measure. It is even more important, however, that the meaning attributed to the scores can be validated. Some assessments may be intended to represent a particular type of achievement, such as skill in writing, but, in order for the scores to be valid, the content, construction, and use of the assessment must be appropriate.

The greater the consequences of the use of assessment scores, the more rigorous the process of constructing and validating assessments must be. Most teacher-made assessments can be used confidently in the classroom as informal evaluations of student work. As these assessments accumulate during a course, a teacher gains a good understanding of a student's strengths and weaknesses. Assessments must withstand a more rigorous scrutiny, however, when the stakes for students are high and it becomes necessary to compare teachers' judgments about students, to make placement decisions about students, or to evaluate the effectiveness of a course or curriculum. While in such cases measurement experts are often called upon to construct and evaluate formal assessments, teachers who understand the basic tenets of making valid and reliable assessments empower themselves in their own role as decision makers.

Our focus is on making valid assessments of students' ability to write and to evaluate the consequences of those decisions. Writing ability, however, is a theoretical construct and can be defined in many ways. Some assessments, for example, define writing narrowly as mastery of grammar and syntax or more expansively as expertise in expression using various rhetorical modes. The types of measures used define what is meant by writing ability, and valid judgments about what students know and can do are based on a compilation of evidence that "supports the appropriateness, meaningfulness, and usefulness of the specific inferences made from test scores" (American Educational Research Association, 1985). The process by which we accumulate this evidence depends upon how we intend to use the test results.

The complexity of making assessment decisions about the construct of writing ability can be illustrated by a hypothetical student's case. Suppose a student fails an essay examination for placement in Honors English. The student petitions to enroll in Honors on the basis of having earned an "A" grade in a previous English course taught at another school. How do we decide what the student can do? It is easy to assume that a student who fails an essay examination cannot write well and to credit the high course grade to grade inflation. What other explanation might there be? The answer lies in an analysis of the reliability and validity of the placement test score. There are a number of questions we can ask to structure this analysis:

Does the assessment represent the desired skills?

Does the passing standard represent the appropriate level of quality?

How much confidence can be placed in the scoring process?

What is the impact of the scores on students?

The approach to answering these questions is reviewed in the following overview of the elements that give meaning and stability to test scores.

Validity: Bringing Meaning to Test Scores

As our understanding of the impact of testing has grown, so has the framework within which we consider test validity. For many years, we were concerned primarily about the content validity of a test. That is, if we developed an examination for which the score represented mastery of a subject area, then we needed to demonstrate that the appropriate content was covered on the test. A skills analysis was done to be certain that the questions were drawn from the entire range of skills that were included in the curriculum. As long as the test questions matched the content to be covered, the test was valid. Now we recognize that, if inferences are to be made about students' cognitive abilities, it is important not only to clarify what the test covers, but also to consider alternative explanations for students' scores. A poor essay score may be related more to inadequate background knowledge, for example, than to an inability to write an argumentative essay.

Similar validity issues arise whether a single essay or a portfolio is used to evaluate student achievement. A score assigned to a single essay has limited value as an indicator of writing ability. How well a student writes on a given day depends upon the structure of the topic, the student's motivation and prior knowledge of the subject, and a myriad of other factors. Assumptions that the same student writes well across rhetorical modes may be unfounded. A student may have a gift for description but be relatively weak in analytic writing tasks. While portfolios offer a more comprehensive sample of students' work, the meaning attributed to the portfolio score is determined by how the portfolio is structured and scored. If the portfolio includes single entries representing several writing modes, then the portfolio may appear to be valid, but it too shares the limitations of the single essay. Only when the portfolio contains multiple samples from the same writing mode does it become credible. Repeated examples of skill mastery are necessary to obtain an accurate measure of achievement. For this reason, portfolios that include work drafts and revisions representing several different writing modes may have good instructional value but limited reliability and validity if used for instructional accountability.

The rigor of validity criteria should correspond with the intended use of the scores. The greater the consequences, the more evidence is called for. Samuel Messick (1989) suggests, moreover, that we must consider whether the social consequences of a test are a result of the test or a reflection of the actual phenomenon being measured. Classifying a student as inadequate on the basis of a test score may seriously misrepresent what the student is able to do. Simply because it could be demonstrated that some groups of students can score higher than other groups on a test may not be reason enough to give the test. The differences in test scores should represent observable differences in students' ability to apply their knowledge in meaningful ways.

The discussion thus far has been intended to make the case for considering the validity of assessment scores. The following sections summarize the ways that the validity of assessments scores can be established. This overview centers on Messick's (1989) consideration of the issues relating not only to the internal characteristics of assessments, e.g., their content and context, but also to their uses and consequences. These are the basic components of construct validity.

Construct Validity

Construct and content validity are similar (Cronbach, 1971). Both are used to determine whether tests measure what they are intended to measure. Construct validity is concerned with theoretical concepts such as problem solving, and content validity is defined by the content about which we wish to generalize. If we create a test consisting of problems to solve in a subject area, and the student is successful in solving those problems, then it may be argued that the student has problem-solving ability. It also may be argued, however, that the test questions were too easy, too familiar, or too limited in scope to provide evidence of real ability. Low scores may underestimate ability simply because students are unfamiliar with the format of the questions or are not properly motivated to do their best. Thus, construct validity is determined not only by examining the content of the test, but also by comparing the students' scores on related tests. A thorough validity study, moreover, includes an examination of alternative noncognitive explanations for students' scores.

The usual model for examining construct validity is the multitrait, multimethod approach described by Campbell and Fiske (1959) in which correlations between similar measures are compared to correlation of traits that should be different. For example, essay tests of writing should correlate with each other and with reading comprehension. On the other hand, if we include a measure of handwriting quality, the correlation with writing ability should be quite low. Students' handwriting is not expected to be related to their ability to express themselves in writing. Thus, in this case, the construct of writing ability is confirmed by the correlation between scores on the two essays and the lack of correlation with scores on a measure of handwriting skill.

Content Validity

Content validity involves a logical analysis of the content coverage of the assessment by subject-matter experts. It helps teachers respond to students who argue that "the test did not cover what was taught" or "I know more than the test covered." In order to deal with these concerns, test specifications are developed that provide for content validity by designating the number and format of questions on each topic and the cognitive level of the questions, i.e., whether the questions measure factual knowledge, application of knowledge, or higher-order critical thinking skills. The number of questions or points assigned to each component of a skill indicates its importance relative to the total number of points for an assessment. Two writing assessments on expository skills have quite different meanings if, for example, one places relatively more importance on tone and word usage and the other places more emphasis on supporting details.

The issue of content coverage is most easily demonstrated by comparing essay and multiple-choice tests. For a given testing period, say, fifty minutes, it is possible to ask about fifty different multiple-choice questions covering a range of topics. In the same time period, it is possible for students to respond to one or two extended essay questions, but, if decisions are to be made about the breadth of student knowledge, the preferred testing method is a multiple-choice test. Even with multiple-choice examinations, however, the number of questions representing each topic within the subject area must reflect the appropriate balance of content if the test is to be valid.

Broad content coverage in performance measures can be difficult to obtain. Just as a single essay score represents limited knowledge and understanding of a subject, so does a single research paper. Teachers overcome this obstacle by accumulating evidence over time about student competence. The validity of judgments based on a collection of evidence as a measure of content knowledge and skill would depend in part on how carefully the teacher planned assignments and tests to represent the content objectives. Scores on ill-prepared performance measures can also misrepresent what students know and can do; for example, some performance measures may require only a regurgitation of what students have memorized from lectures or texts. This information usually is forgotten quickly and may have no bearing on real learning.

Writing modes require different cognitive skills. A narrative piece represents different skills than does an argumentative one. When considering the validity of a score, the task assigned must be measured by the appropriate means. A narrative about conducting a science experiment may not provide the rigor needed to document the students' skills in observation and following procedures; a log may be more appropriate. Even if the proper task is assigned, it is possible for it to represent a different cognitive skill than the one intended. Thus, a valid assessment provides evidence that the measures used not only represent the skill but also elicit the desired behavior. In order to provide that evidence, teachers may need to turn to the professional literature to find studies that corroborate their assertions, incorporate some structured observational checklists in the assessments, and/or obtain independent expert ratings of student work.

Criterion-Related Validity

Studies of construct validity compare scores on different measures of the same ability in order to ensure that the ability has been defined correctly. The use of these scores to place students in different levels of a subject or a course, however, requires a standard against which the test score is to be judged. This standard not only defines the level of competence required, but also it must demonstrate that the skill is relevant to success in the course in which a student is to be placed. Criterion-related validity studies validate the use of scores for placement purposes. The criterion can take many forms—for example, it could be grade point average of students enrolled in the course, prior grade point average of successful students enrolled in the course, or a level of competence set by systematic observations of performance of the desired skills. There are two types of criterion-related validity studies: concurrent and predictive.

Concurrent Validity

If an assessment is used to make a current evaluation of student achievement, it can be validated by retesting the students within a short time period on an alternative assessment; this process would be defined as a concurrent validity study. This kind of study gathers evidence (test scores and performance measures) at the same time from people already selected from a class or other group. This evidence may demonstrate what students are able to do at the moment, but it will have limited use as a predictor of future behavior. Some changes occur as students mature and have other experiences upon which they can draw to improve their performance.

Concurrent validity studies have a legitimate purpose when they are used for performance assessments. In writing assessments, for example, scoring rubrics must have clear descriptors that represent actual performance for each level. Studies to establish this relationship are conducted by asking subject-matter experts to independently define elements of a scoring rubric. Confirmation by experts of essential elements in a scoring rubric—along with comparing scores for the same students on related measures—helps to establish the correspondence between what is expected and what actually occurs. Teachers can follow the same procedures in an informal way by working with other teachers to develop rubrics and to compare their students' scores on related assignments. Anomalies in scores may be an indication that the construction of the assessment warrants further review.

Predictive Validity

Predictive validity studies are conducted when students' placement test scores are compared to some future performance such as success in a subsequent course. Usually, success in the course is defined by using the final course grades or final examination scores as the criterion measure. A validity study is designed to give the placement test to all students at the beginning of the course, and the scores are compared at the end of the course to the criterion chosen. The assumption to be validated is that students whose initial scores are higher are better prepared to succeed than those with lower scores. While a reliable and valid predictor will improve placement decisions beyond the chance level, the use of placement scores must be tempered with the realization that many factors other than assessments affect the accuracy of placement decisions. For example, the course grades may not be representative of the differences in student achievement, because students with different levels of achievement may have received the same grades. In other cases, the placement test itself may not correspond closely to the demands made by the higher-level course.

Predictive validity presents some serious practical problems. Predictive validity studies collect test data—before decisions are made—on a sample of students similar to the population of applicants for a course. In a true predictive validity study, initial assignment to the course is random; some people will be selected who are expected to fail. In this way, cutoff scores are based on what all potential students can do. Once the validity is established, the cutoff scores are used to screen for those students most likely to succeed. In a highly competitive program, some teachers may object to initially admitting students who, on the basis of a test score, appear to be less qualified than others not admitted.

Selection problems are not the only concerns. Striving for accurate, stable measurement creates its own dilemmas. One of the more serious issues is restriction of range in the score scale. Restriction of range occurs when relatively few points separate the highest and lowest scores on a criterion measure (e.g., grades ranging from *A*s to *C*s). Restriction can result in reduced correlations between the predictor and the criterion (i.e., between the placement test scores and the final course grades). Reduced correlations, in turn, mean reduced accuracy in placing students in the appropriate levels. There are several occasions when it is likely that the range of scores will be too small to provide good measurement of student achievement. If the criterion is too easy or too difficult for the applicants for a course, then most students will obtain similar scores. When a performance measure is scored using a four-point scale, for example, it is not uncommon for qualitatively different levels of achievement to receive the same score. The number of points on the scale must reflect the qualitative differences in achievement. Finally, if a predictive validity study is based on the achievements of students who already are either self-selected or preselected for a course, then assessments based on this group of students will also be similar.

Mark Reckase (1993) discusses another practical problem when he states that it is difficult to derive estimates of the expected predictive validity of portfolios. First, no actual validity studies were found in the literature. Second, the predictive validity of an assessment is specific to a particular use. For example, the correlation between ACT Assessment English scores and college course grades ranges from the .10s to about .50 depending on the characteristics of the English course and the sample of students. (When there is perfect agreement between the students' ranking on two different measures, there is a correlation coefficient of 1.00. The percentage of the relationship that can be explained by a correlation is calculated by squaring the correlation coefficient. Therefore, a correlation coefficient of .10 explains only one percent of the relationship between the ACT Assessment English scores and the college grades in at least one type of English course.) Third, the magnitude of the validity coefficient is strongly related to the number of points in the criterion measure—i.e., the fewer the number of points (or the smaller the range of grades) on the criterion measure, the lower the correlation coefficient will be. Nonetheless, Reckase gives some clues to what might be expected.

One source of information about the usefulness of writing samples as predictors is the work done to determine the usefulness of an essay as part of the revision to the SAT (Bridgeman, Hale, Lewis, Pollack, & Wang, 1992). Scores on a twenty-minute writing sample correlated in the .20s with English course grades. An increase in the number of writing samples in a portfolio designed to reflect college level writing should increase the validity coefficient. Reckase concludes that "a well structured and carefully scored portfolio assessment has the potential to provide scores that meet the standards of reliability required for use with individual students" (p. 10). Portfolio scores that are derived by summing scores from individual entries (as opposed to holistically scored portfolios) can, under proper conditions, be used to differentiate among students.

Validity for Decisions

The process of establishing validity for the use of a test score, Messick argues, must take into account the consequences of the decisions about students. One approach is to evaluate the effects of tests on the accuracy of decisions. Murphy and Davidshofer (1991) cite average criterion-related validity coefficients of .27 for tests measuring various mental and other abilities used as predictors of performance. By squaring the validity coefficient, we see that the strength of the prediction accounts for only 7 percent of the variability in performance. If test scores are used to predict scores on similar tests, the validity coefficients can and should be very high. However, levels of criterion-related validity rarely exceed .6 to .7. This means that good placement tests are likely to improve placement decisions by about 50 percent over random selection of students.

The impact of placement decisions can be evaluated by comparing the percentage of students who are placed accurately with the percentage who are placed inaccurately. To do this, students with a broad range of achievement are assessed and allowed to enroll in the desired course. When students are placed in courses or programs on the basis of assessment scores, high scores on the placement measures should predict success in the course, and this result is called a true positive in

Table 1
Pass/Fail Classification Table

		Grades in Honors Course	
		Fail	Pass
Portfolio Score	Pass	False Negative .10	True Positive .65
	Fail	True Negative .20	False Positive .05
Placement Decision:		Reject	Accept

the example shown in Table 1; in contrast, a false positive result occurs when a student scores below the passing standard on the placement measures but succeeds in the course. Similarly, a true negative occurs when the student fails both the placement measures and the course, and a false negative result occurs when the student meets the passing standard on the placement test but fails the course.

Returning to the example of placing students in an honors course, suppose that the results of a portfolio assessment were to be used to place students. It is possible to evaluate the accuracy of proposed placement decisions. In this hypothetical example, the four boxes in Table 1 represent possible outcomes for a given placement cutoff score. In the first column, 10 plus 20 percent, or a total of 30 percent, of the students would not be placed in the honors course on the basis of a given placement score, and 70 percent would be placed in honors. By combining percentages, we see that 85 percent of the students were placed accurately; that is, 65 percent of the students who succeeded in the course also passed the placement test, and 20 percent of the students failed both the placement test and the course. Another 15 percent of the students either passed the placement test and failed the course (10 percent) or failed the placement test but passed the course (5 percent). The impact of different placement score cutoff levels can be evaluated in this way in order to find the level with the highest percentage of true positive scores.

Additional information is needed to make these placement decisions meaningful. If we know that most students are likely to achieve the passing standard on the placement test and there are many spaces available in the course, then random selection will lead to successful placement a high percentage of the time. If few people are expected to succeed and the number of available spaces is small, then random selection will result in many misplaced students. Taylor-Russell (1939) published a series of tables that show the combined effect of the quality of the pool of applicants and the validity of the placement score on the utility of placement tests. In general, when 50 percent of the students are expected to succeed and the placement scores have a wide range and high validity coefficients, then placement tests are useful additions to placement decisions. Higher placement scores among those students selected will also reduce placement errors.

Bias

Even if ratings are seemingly reliable and valid, there may be a differential impact of the assessment on subgroups of students. In order to examine the results of assessments for potential bias, average scores for racial/ethnic or gender groups within the same total score category are calculated for each question in the assessment. When the average score on an individual question is higher or lower for one racial/ethnic group, the question is flagged for review.

This approach can be applied to components of performance assessments. If, for example, student portfolios contained three assessments each scored on a ten-point scale, the total possible points would be thirty. The thirty points could be grouped into five-point components. If, for a given category of test takers—say, high-scoring students—the average score on one of the individual components was several points higher for men than for women, then this assessment task should be reviewed (see the second score set in Table 2). Studies of this type are a simplified version of what are called "differential item functioning" (DIF) studies, and they are used to determine if the questions are unfair or if they represent instructional or curriculum effects that disadvantage a particular group of students.

This description of the DIF procedure provides a conceptual understanding of how potential bias is evaluated. Unfortunately, there is not much research reported for DIF studies of constructed-response questions. In work done at the Educational Testing Service (ETS), however, Dorans and Schmitt (1990) noted that constructed-response questions tend to show more DIF than do multiple-choice questions. Thus, teachers should consider the possibility that their own assessments may have unintended bias for racial/gender or other groups and conduct their own informal analyses from time to time.

The fact that an assessment shows DIF in one or more components does not in itself mean that the assessment is biased against or for a particular group. It is, however, an indicator that the assessment would bear some scrutiny for causes of the discrepant scores. There are any number of reasons why DIF might occur—for example, vocabulary that

Table 2
Comparing Achievement of Males and Females
on 3 Portfolio Entries

Total Assessment	Assessment 1 (10 points)		Assessment 2 (10 points)		Assessment 3 (10 points)	
	Males	*Females*	*Males*	*Females*	*Males*	*Females*
All Students						
25–30	9	9	9	7	9	9
20–24	7	8	6	3	8	9

is unfamiliar to a group of students, or the lack of exposure to some aspect of the curriculum. While classroom assessments are not typically reviewed for DIF, an informal scrutiny of scores for racial and gender groups can provide some understanding of why students of seemingly similar ability sometimes do not achieve at the same level on certain types of assessments.

Reliability: Score Stability

Reducing measurement errors improves the stability of scores. This section gives an overview of ways to identify the amount of error and types of errors that affect our confidence in how well scores represent students' true abilities. Conditions that contribute to inconsistent ratings can be examined statistically, and this section provides an overview of generalizability studies, of measures of internal consistency, and of rater reliability, along with some discussion of reliability issues related to specific assessment situations. While most classroom teachers would not conduct these studies themselves, it is helpful to understand why they are done. In situations that have high stakes for students, district measurement specialists may conduct these analyses, and teachers need to be able to interpret the results.

The reliability of scores can be affected by many factors: topic, context of scoring, or the rater's own bias. This section talks about ways that sources of error can be identified, e.g. generalizability studies which factor out these sources of error so that it is possible to determine how much a score is affected by elements that may be considered to be separate from the measure of student competence. A "G" study would isolate effects such as topic, rater bias, and context (perhaps time of day).

Generalizability Theory

The theory of generalizability (Cronbach, 1971) helps to focus our attention on the conditions under which the scores should be similar or different. With generalizability studies, it is possible to determine how much of the difference in assigned scores is due to raters who scored too high or too low. Depending upon how the generalizability study is structured, it is also possible to identify sources of rater error due to other factors of interest such as the choice of topic, the classrooms or schools assessed, or local scoring conditions.

In a generalizability study of the consistency between ratings collected over time for a state assessment, Anne Fitzpatrick et al. (1994)

compared the results of having the same sets of papers scored by different raters in different years across grade levels. Correlations across grades for all content areas except writing equalled or exceeded .73. Only in the eighth grade did the correlation for writing samples in the first year reach .72. During the second year, the correlation among the eighth-grade writing samples fell to .57, which was representative of the correlations for writing in the other grades. In other words, the two sets of raters had a relatively low level of agreement on the quality of the same papers. The authors recommend research into the sources of error in rating, particularly the error associated with scores for students who are in the same grade level but at different levels of achievement. Raters could have agreed, for example, upon scores for low- and high-achieving students but disagreed about scores for students in the middle of the range. The authors also suggest examining the relationship between rater consistency and the type of scoring rule used. Some rubrics may refer to observable qualities in students' responses, such as grammar and syntax; other rubrics, for more abstract qualities such as analytical reasoning, may be more difficult to score reliably.

The Fitzpatrick study is only one of many studies that reinforce the need to consider the impact of the tasks—and the way in which they are scored—on the evaluation of student achievement. While Koretz, Stecher, Klein, and McCaffrey (1994) cite an example of direct writing assessments in which reliable ratings were obtained (the example is Dunbar, Koretz, & Hoover, 1991), they also describe how failure to adequately train raters and standardize the portfolio tasks can invalidate an assessment.

Rater reliability is one component of a generalizability study that is often calculated when a more comprehensive study is not feasible. An understanding of rater reliability is especially important when teachers come together to rate a group of papers. Some teachers may tend to rate the same qualities in different ways or generally give higher or lower ratings than other teachers. Agreement among raters can be deceptive, and examples of how differences in ratings can be masked are shown below. Rater reliability of essay scores is estimated in two ways: coefficient Alpha and interrater agreement.

Alpha

Alpha coefficients are used to estimate the internal consistency of the ratings assigned to essay examinations. Internal consistency of ratings is defined as the degree of similarity of ratings given to a set of papers by more than one rater. When the ratings demonstrate a high level of internal consistency, there is agreement between raters on the scores awarded at all points of the score scale. To demonstrate this point, if two readers assign scores from one to six points, Alpha can be used to calculate the average difference between the scores assigned by each reader. Those differences are compared to the average difference between scores when the two sets of scores are combined as a single set. That is, if the readers R1 and R2 have read the same four papers and assigned scores as shown in Table 3, then their average ratings would be the same, but the impact on individual students would be quite different; rater two would give two students higher scores and two students lower scores.

Both raters tend to see the papers as similar; in each set of papers, three are scored alike and one is different. Scores are higher on average, however, for rater two. Thus, the range of scores is increased to scores from 1 to 4 when the scores are combined, instead of a range of 2 to 4 for rater one and a range of 1 to 3 for rater two. The resulting Alpha coefficient would be lowered to reflect the differences in rating by the two readers.

Interrater Agreement

In a review of reliability studies of performance measures, Dunbar et al. (1991) found that rater reliabilities can be quite variable depending upon the scoring procedures and the number of points on the scale. While rater reliability can be improved, Dunbar reports that there is considerable evidence to show that score reliabilities tend to be quite low due to the inconsistency of student performance on tasks, even those tasks in the same domain. This section focuses on evaluating sources of disagreement in ratings. It is recognized that, even if a high level of rater agreement is obtained on one assessment, ratings on a subsequent similar assessment might be quite different.

Rater errors fall into three categories: (1) halo errors, (2) leniency errors, and (3) range restriction errors (Murphy & Davidshofer, 1991). Halo errors occur when a reader is favorably influenced by the quality of one paper when reading subsequent essays. Leniency errors represent

Table 3
Comparing Rater Scores for Reliability

Rater 1 Scores:	4, 2, 2, 2: mean score = 2.5, standard deviation = .87
Rater 2 Scores:	3, 1, 3, 3: mean score = 2.5, standard deviation = .87
Combined ratings:	4, 2, 2, 2, 3, 1, 3, 3: mean score = 2.5, standard deviation = 1.69

a tendency to assign ratings that are too high or too low. Range restriction errors occur when readers tend to avoid giving papers either low or high scores. These errors all have an impact on the percentage of agreement between raters when they read the same set of papers. High rater agreement can be obtained for the wrong reasons; if all raters assign only ratings in the middle of the range, say, ratings of 2s or 3s on a four-point scale, there would be high agreement. These scores would not be reliable estimates of student achievement because the quality of writing in each score category would vary widely.

Comparisons of average ratings can also be misleading because two raters may appear to be consistent if their average ratings are calculated over a set of papers, yet, when one looks at the individual ratings, they are quite different. Consider two sets of scores: for set A, the scores are *3, 3, 3,* and *3;* for set B, the scores are *1, 6, 2,* and *3.* The average score for set A is, of course, three; the average for set B is also three. Clearly, then, average scores are not a good indicator of score reliability. To increase confidence in the evaluation of students' level of achievement, we need multiple measures, each of which is scored reliably. The combination of scores of similar assessments will give a more consistent picture of students' abilities. This approach to estimating reliability is termed "composite score reliability."

Composite Score Reliability

The reliability of a composite score is a way to measure whether estimates of achievement are consistent when a score is calculated by combining scores from several subsections of an assessment. As long as the scores represent the same skills, then combining more scores produces higher composite reliability. This is true as long as each of the scores for the individual subtests is also reliable.

Even if the content and skills are defined adequately for an assessment of student achievement, a single example of student work is insufficient to make fair and accurate statements about a student's level of development. Anyone can have a bad day. How much evidence is needed is a matter of judgment. Mark Reckase (1993) demonstrated that it would require five similar entries in a portfolio in order to achieve stable score estimates of student achievement. Basically, this means that it would take five essays of the same type to approximate the score consistency that a single well-constructed multiple-choice test would have. A portfolio-based assessment system that is to be used for statewide accountability would have to demonstrate the same level of reliability as equivalent multiple-choice examinations.

The average of five separate ratings on the same or similar essay topics should be a good estimate of student ability, though Reckase shows that eight writing samples would be needed to achieve a composite reliability of .85, the criterion established for most nationally normed achievement tests. The problem is that while most portfolios require at least five writing samples, they generally are not drawn from the same rhetorical mode. In fact, to do so would severely limit how representative of general writing achievement the portfolio would be. We all understand that writing skill in one mode, like exposition, does not necessarily predict skill in other writing modes. Yet, to obtain good estimates of writing ability in each rhetorical mode, Reckase shows that five to eight pieces would be needed for each mode. The point is that if the stakes for students are high, the portfolio should conform to these criteria.

The Reliability of Judgments about Improvement in Student Achievement

Up to this point, we have considered the meaning and stability of the judgments we make about achievement by individual students. We may also be interested to know how much confidence we can have in making decisions about how much improvement a class has made. Common sense tells us that if we assess students at the beginning and end of a course, we should know whether or not there has been any change in achievement; since we know that we need valid and reliable assessments, we need only to compare the average class scores for the two assessments. Not so. The following section gives an overview of two issues that must be taken into account when we make group comparisons: (1) equating the assessments to adjust for unequal difficulty, and (2) estimating the reliability of gains in students' scores over time.

Equating Assessments

Comparing results from one assessment with results from another requires that the assessments be equated in some way. Without equating for unequal difficulty in the test, differences in scores could be attributed either to the students or to the test. While there are a number of statistical techniques for estimating the congruence between score scales on similar assessment instruments, the details of these procedures are beyond the scope of this chapter. Teachers typically do not equate classroom assessments. With a sufficient number of informal assessments, the teacher can get a good understanding of what students know and can do. However, when assessments are used for course evaluation or for accountability purposes, there are approaches that teachers can use to determine whether reported changes in achievement across time are due to the raters, the assessments, or the students' achievement. Robert Linn (1993) has described models for calibrating assessments by embedding anchor items from national assessments into local assessments. Embedding prescored items from one assessment into another allows the scores given to the same topics to be compared. The second approach to equating is to use external scoring teams to score local assessments.

Embedding anchor papers from a previous assessment to be scored with the current papers enables comparisons to be made of the average ratings on the anchor set of papers on the two occasions. If the average ratings on the embedded anchor items were different on the two administrations, then the difference in achievement of the students over the time period may be due to changes in the raters, not changes in the students. Teachers may want to adjust scores based on the difference between the average scores for the embedded essays from the first and second administrations. Skaggs and Lissitz (1995) recommend this type of mean equating as long as the writing prompts are designed to be very similar and the rater reliability is high.

If it is not possible to embed similar essays in a subsequent assessment, it may be possible to use an external team of raters to score a local assessment. This can be accomplished by exchanging papers with a team of teachers from another school or district. A well-trained external team may be able to provide the consistency in rating that may be difficult to obtain when teachers rate assessments of their own students. Correlations of ratings by external teams on two occasions for high school writing assessments in the Linn study were quite high at .81. Correlations of this magnitude are only partially reassuring. On a six-point scale, for instance, a one-point difference is an important difference, and one-point differences would be common even with highly reliable scores.

Reliability of Gain Scores

On those occasions in which we may be interested in evaluating how much student achievement has improved, the reliability of the difference in scores between tests or occasions becomes important. When scores on tests differ, the difference between scores may be due to real differences in achievement or to instability in the scores. The higher the reliability of the scores of each test, the greater confidence we can have in the difference between them. Even if the individual test scores show high reliability, however, more information is needed to make good decisions about student achievement. When the same students are tested on two occasions, the lowest scores tend to increase and the highest scores tend to decline, a phenomenon known as regression toward the mean. Decisions about individual student gains are therefore problematic. The issue is particularly relevant when we evaluate our own students' progress. It would be easy to believe that we did more to help the lowest-achieving students at the expense of the highest-achieving students, when in fact the change was due to a statistical phenomenon.

Confidence in the difference between scores obtained on two occasions, such as pretest and posttest results for a course, can be enhanced if students are randomly divided between experimental and control groups. One group is taught under a new instructional method, and the other is taught in a traditional way. In this manner it is possible to track how much change is due to the new instructional method and how much change would have occurred anyway. Even with controlled studies, however, scores for the lowest-achieving students tend to increase and scores for the highest-scoring students decrease. Thus, studies on achievement gains for students in remedial programs tend to show improvement while scores for students in gifted programs may not. Learning in both groups may have shown improvement, but the change in statistical rankings is obscured by regression toward the mean. The importance of this statistical phenomenon in practical school settings is explained by John Hills (1993).

Summary

Factors that contribute to the valid interpretation of assessment scores are complex and interrelated. In determining the content to be assessed, care must be taken to assure that it represents the skills that students are expected to achieve. Appropriate content coverage alone is an insufficient guide to constructing good assessments. It is important to carefully plan the format of the questions, their level of difficulty, and the context in which the assessment is given. The construction of assessments must also be congruent with their intended use. If assessments are to be used in selecting students for a course or a program, then the issues and practical problems inherent in criterion-related validity studies must be considered. Even the decision rules that emanate from criterion-validity studies must be weighed not only for the accuracy of the decisions that are made, but also for their potential impact on students.

It is possible to have seemingly reliable and valid measures that have a differential impact on small subgroups of students. There are many ways to evaluate DIF, but generally the approaches tend to categorize students in similar overall ability groups and then examine how students from different racial, cultural, or gender groups within the same ability groups fare on the individual topics or questions in the assessment.

Any assessment that will have a significant effect on students must be both valid and reliable. Yet, these two concepts are sometimes at odds with one another. It is possible to develop sufficiently complex assessments that will adequately represent a cognitive skill, but the very diversity needed to represent the skill may nullify any chance to replicate the assessment. It is difficult to have confidence in assessment results that cannot be replicated. There are, however, some approaches to evaluate the sources of errors in assessment scores. Generalizability studies that isolate the errors attributed to raters or to the context of the assessment improve the reliability of assessment scores. In addition, by combining several similar measures, both the reliability and the validity of an assessment are enhanced.

Finally, this chapter has addressed the issues involved in making valid and reliable judgments about the improvement of student achievement over time. Some methods have been reviewed for evaluating the differences in achievement on different measures of the same construct. Even with equivalent scores on repeated measures, uncertainty remains about the reliability of the difference between the scores. Students' scores may have improved, but, without a tightly controlled experimental design, it may be impossible to determine whether or not the increase was real or was a chance occurrence.

These are the tools that teachers can use to evaluate assessments of student progress. The bottom line is that a variety of assessments is needed in order to represent knowledge, and it must be possible to replicate the results if we are to have confidence in the scores. Time, money, and common sense tell us that we cannot make every assessment meet all of the criteria discussed in this chapter. Nor should we. The informal assessments that teachers make every day provide valuable information to improve teaching and learning. Incorporating some of the concepts presented in this chapter can improve informal assessments. Once in a while, however, when the consequences to students are great, we need to go beyond informal assessments. When these occasions arise, understanding the "tools of the trade" will help to ensure that the assessments that are proposed for our schools, our state, or our nation provide the kind of information that we need.

10 Writing Assessment in the Disciplines

With the growth of the writing-across-the-curriculum movement has come an interest in writing as a learning tool in diverse disciplines. Certainly, interest in writing in subject areas has existed for many years, to which most people's experiences with essay exams, book reports, or laboratory reports can testify. However, the growing use of portfolios and other forms of performance assessment in mathematics, science, history, and various subjects reveals the increased value being placed on writing as a tool for learning and for assessment.

The purpose of this chapter is to provide a brief review of the ways in which writing serves as a bridge to various disciplines by either formally or informally enhancing students' mastery of subject-area content. Because similarities and differences exist between writing as it is used in English classes and as it is employed in other subject areas, English teachers and teachers from different disciplines have much to share with one another. Certainly, the value of such collaboration was illustrated for us when a group of five Alachua County teachers from elementary, middle, and high school worked with a consultant and with us at the university in a portfolio training program that spanned seven months. The teachers, half of whom focused on science and half of whom focused on English, met with us periodically to plan, initiate, implement, and assess portfolios within their classes. The project culminated in a notebook of materials entitled *A Framework for Training Teachers in Portfolio Assessment* produced by the Florida Department of Education (see Legg et al., 1994) as well as a two-day workshop to train other interested teachers in the county. As the English and science groups met each month (either separately or together) to discuss the portfolio procedures and contents or the assessment strategies, the similarities and differences in what we were all trying to do at various levels in different subject areas became readily apparent. Whereas the English teachers could focus on the processes, skills, and modes that were entailed in students' writing for the portfolios, the science teachers had to focus on ensuring that students' written portfolio entries reflected an understanding of scientific content. Whereas the quality of writing was an important factor in the

English teachers' group assessment of the seventh-grade English class portfolios, the quality of writing was less significant—albeit still important—in the science teachers' group assessment of eighth-grade science portfolios. For the science teachers, who needed to evaluate their students' portfolios for the scientific language, scientific representations, and scientific method—as well as organization and creativity in scientific thought—writing quality was simply represented by the overall category of mechanics.

The collaborative project thus illustrated both underlying commonalities and differences in the way writing is perceived and valued across disciplines. Writing is central to English, both as a vehicle for expression and as a focus for literary appreciation and thought; it is, in effect, an end in itself. In some content-area disciplines, on the other hand, writing is not the end, but the means to an end—an end that includes the understanding of subject matter and the expression, at once oral and written, of that understanding. These differences are important to remember, for the writing encouraged in English classes is not necessarily the same as that valued in other subjects. The passive voice so rejected in English classes may be essential in science writing, for example, where the "doer" is less important than the deed itself; similarly, the element of voice valued in the student writing of English classes is, in the sciences, far less important than precision of language and specificity of procedures. The different expectations which specific disciplines have in terms of style, format, and language conventions can be illustrated vividly by one workshop activity advocated by Susan McLeod, in which English participants evaluate the rhetorical structure of an article (or articles) written for the social sciences or other disciplines (see McLeod, 1996). Different expectations also encompass the types of writing required by the various disciplines, including reaction papers in the humanities, proposals in social sciences, laboratory reports in the sciences, or problem-solving case studies in business and the social sciences (see Kirszner, Jusawalla, & Mandell, 1990).

But to stress the differences is not to ignore the similarities, for, as Kirszner, Jusawalla, and Mandell also indicate, there are common assignments as well: book reviews, summaries, letters, journals, narratives, and research papers seemingly appear in most subject areas. Moreover, once content-area teachers have decided upon their course objectives and have designed appropriate writing assignments, Tchudi and Yates (1983) encourage teachers to have their students work in stages that closely resemble the recursive stages of the writing process identified by Flower and Hayes (1981) and common in most writing workshops. The following sections will explore the differences and similarities between, on one hand, writing and its assessment in English classes, and, on the other hand, content-area writing and its assessment (both internal and external).

Using Writing to Learn in the Disciplines

Writing across the curriculum is comprised of several strands, one of which is the writing-to-learn movement. In this strand, writing becomes a way for students to come to terms with an unfamiliar discipline by writing about their personal concerns, observations, experiences, or questions regarding the new field (Young, 1994). To this end, teachers often employ learning logs or journals as a means of enabling their students to grapple in personal or expressive ways with the content of their subjects. These writing-to-learn activities serve as building blocks for students both in their understanding of content material and in their ability to express that understanding; they resemble the prewriting processes students are encouraged to undertake in their English writing classes. The journals allow students to reflect upon their learning experiences and to become personally engaged with the subject matter. Because, as Margot Soven (1996) points out, journals serve as "histories of evolving thought," they are often written in the first person and are not usually revised (pp. 22–23). Moreover, teachers usually do not grade journals, preferring instead to put check marks in the journal and to comment occasionally on an important idea or passage.

Although many instructors seem pleased with their students' learning as reflected through the journals and logs, others have found it necessary to provide more focus for their students' journal writing by providing some directives or specific questions. Indeed, Sandra Stotsky (1995) observes that there has been little empirical support for the idea that writing in journals will necessarily improve students' performance in their learning of different content areas, although she acknowledges that the exact nature of the journals used for the studies she has examined remains unknown. Stotsky cautions that even though using personal experience may indeed help students understand abstractions, "concept development may not take place if students do not move from personal experience to focus on the concept and, instead, continue to mesh personal experience with the concept or end up focusing chiefly on personal experience" (p. 769).

Other writing-to-learn techniques employed by teachers in various disciplines include assigning summary writing, reflective writing, and open-ended questions on quizzes. Lynn Hancock (1995), for example, writes of mathematics classes in which students are given open-ended questions as a way of experimenting with new approaches to problems; in some cases, students are also given the chance to revise early drafts of their answers to these problems by reflecting on feedback they receive from their instructors. Students help develop and use scoring rubrics, and thus both instruction and learning are sustained throughout the assessment stage.

Summary writing is another approach used by many instructors from different disciplines to foster active learning and critical thinking on students' part. Noting that empirical studies support the worth of such activities, Stotsky (1995) points out that summaries and note taking "generally focus students' attention on what is in the text rather than on what they can bring to it from personal experience" (p. 769).

Sally Radmacher and Elizabeth Latosi-Sawin (1995) report on the success of Latosi-Sawin's version of a summary method that is called "read/rank/review" in helping to increase psychology students' comprehension. In this pilot study, students first wrote sample summaries, which the teacher ranked on a four-point scale according to the extent of the revision needed; then students examined a sample summary rated a 4 and a sample summary given a 1 to consider the criteria for summary writing. Finally, students compared two summaries with middle scores and explained why they ranked one summary as better than the other. Students who participated in the summary writing performed significantly better on the final exam than those students who did not write summaries.

An earlier study by Phillip Horton, Robert Fronk, and Raymond Walton (1985) explored the extent to which writing summaries of college chemistry lectures would help first-year students and sophomores in one class perform better on their examinations. Students in the treatment group earned extra points by writing summaries on eight different lectures during a three-week period. The instructor then would clarify any misconceptions that appeared in the summaries prior to the examinations. Results showed that members of the treatment group performed significantly better than their peers did on the examinations. More important, 82 percent of the students said that the summaries had helped them better understand the course material, and 73 percent thought summaries should be required in the future.

Other variations on writing-to-learn activities include asking students to write notes to their peers with questions about course material and, in turn, to respond to their fellow students' questions (see Young, 1994). Assignments of this nature help students both to understand the content-area material better themselves and to communicate their knowledge to others.

Any assessment of these writing-to-learn activities is, as with prewriting or similar strategies in English classes, likely to be for internal classroom purposes only. However, such writing activities do function as a foundation, serving not only as a vehicle for enabling students to master content material but also as a precursor for portfolios or for the written portions of other types of performance assessment.

An illustration of an important writing-to-learn activity is provided by the work of first-year college student Gaidi Hartage (see below). He wrote this paper for Caroline Dennis's Reading and Writing in the Disciplines class linked to an anthropology class he was taking at the same time. In this pilot course targeted for developmental students at our university, students met in small writing classes and did extensive writing that was tied to a variety of subject-area courses. This particular writing assignment asked students to write a paper that synthesized the lecture notes with their readings and a film. Because synthesis is a difficult—albeit critical—skill for many students, the writing assignment provided a concrete way for Gaidi to practice integrating the subject matter from three different types of sources. Figure 15 contains a sample of Gaidi's lecture notes on which he based the paper, and Figure 16 represents his partially completed self-assessment guide.

Writing-to-Learn Exercise by Gaidi Hartage

The emergence of independent civilizations without diffusion was known to North and South America. Dr. M., an Anthropology professor at the University of Florida, and also a well known Archaeologist has explained through lecture the characteristics of an emerging civilization, and the meaning of a civilization. Dr. M. uses the Inca civilization as an example of an emerging civilization. V. Gordon Childe's characteristics to the meaning of civilization was also introduced through Dr. M.'s lecture.

Gordon Childe a British prehistoric and archaeologist introduced the characteristics that make up civilization. He believed civilizations possess some type of Social Stratification. This power was to be controlled by the Elites. The Elites are people of a small group who possess the power control people of a civilization. The Elites are made up of Egalitarian or Stratified Societies. Stratified Societies obtain leadership or power through inherited status and power of force. Egalitarian Societies have no inherited status of power, leadership is based on achievement and respect. Labor specialization was needed in a civilization. These people specialized in a specific field such as artistry craftsmanship and architecture. These people were responsible for building monumental works. Monumental works show a symbol of power and reinforces social stratification. Childe also believed record keeping was necessary

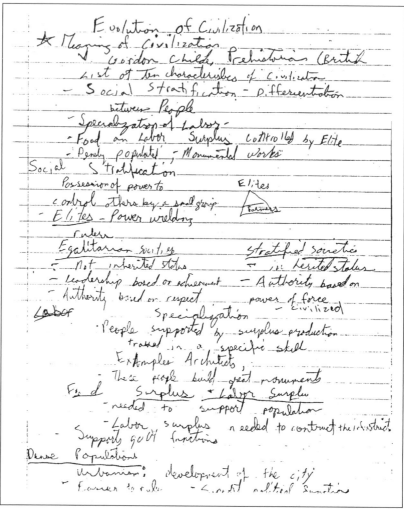

Figure 15. Sample of Gaidi's classroom notes.

to organize surplus and taxation. The Inca civilization organized records through colorful strings, this system was called Quipo, archaeologists still are trying to translate the knots and variety of strings used to keep records.

The Inca civilization in South America was independently aroused without diffusion. Emerging civilization contain some of the same factors. Racists explanations are a key factor in a civilization (Dr. M. Nov. 18, 96). Samuel Morton's skull testing was an example of racial explanations in a civilization. Diffusionist explanations attempt to explain the existence of a civilization in inferior races and climates. Thor Heyerdahl and Grafton Elliot Smith made attempts to explain the diffusion of Egyptians into the Americas. Smith believed civilizations emerged from Egypt and spread around the world, this belief was called Heliocentrism. Heyerdahl believed that Egyptians traveled across the Atlantic and spread civilization in the Americas. Unilinear Evolution which states some cultures are halted due to their inability to invent, is also a factor of an emerging civilization. This factor of natural selection made Europeans superior because of their ability to use their environment (Nov. 18, 96). This also justified eradictation of the Indians.

Self-Assessment Guide for Synthesis Exercise

1. What do you see as the purpose of your paper?

   The explanation of Childe's explanation of a civilization and how civilizations emerge

2. Who is the main audience for your paper?

   Anthropology students

3. How have you tried to attract your reader's interest?

   Yes

4. Have you provided a strong thesis statement that gives a focus to your paper? If so, underline the thesis. If not, re-word the thesis.

   (Not done)

5. Does each paragraph treat a separate idea? If so, put a check in the right-hand margin.

   (Not done)

6. Have you developed your paper with specific examples? Starting with the number 1, put a number beside each specific example in the margin.

   (Not done)

7. How have you concluded your paper?

   How the Inca's film showed the Inca's as an emerging civilization

Check your paper over carefully for any grammar or mechanical errors by reading each sentence separately.

8. Are all your sentences complete?   _____

9. Have you avoided any run-ons or comma splices?   _____

10. Is your punctuation accurate?   _____

11. Is your word choice accurate?   _____

12. Is your sentence structure clear?   _____

Figure 16. Self-assessment exercise.

The video Time's Lost Civilization: Inca Secrets of the Ancestors was used to coincide with Dr. M's class lecture. This film gave a look at how the Inca civilization emerged as a civilization. The film showed how the Inca lived before and after European contact. The Inca had environmentally and culturally adapted to the Andean environment. The Inca had a variety of different crops and showed an importance in ancestor veneration. Much of the Inca's identity was lost during contact and conquest of the Europeans.

Gaidi Hartage
Autumn 1996

Portfolios in the Content Areas

From their writing-to-learn assignments, students may select some entries to submit for their subject-area or interdisciplinary portfolios. Such portfolios, which often include research papers, laboratory reports, case analyses, and reflective essays, are becoming more common as teachers of various disciplines, like their counterparts in English, endorse the possibilities that portfolios offer. In fact, teachers across the board see the inherent link between assessment and instruction as an overriding advantage of portfolios. Teachers also endorse the individuality and self-responsibility that portfolios foster: portfolios help students gain increased mastery of content materials over time; provide opportunities for students to express concepts creatively as well as apply them; and prompt students to reflect about their growing understanding of content.

In general, content-area portfolios are still used mostly for internal classroom assessment purposes, although there are notable exceptions. For example, mathematics portfolios have been used for external assessment purposes in Kentucky and Vermont, and, in 1993, science portfolios were introduced on a pilot basis as an optional part of California's Golden State Science Examinations. Some school systems have chosen interdisciplinary portfolios as a partial requirement for graduation; in these districts, students may present their portfolios to a panel of teachers and administrators. One college requires its history majors to submit portfolios that contain graded work done over several terms; the reflective essay asks students to reflect upon their development as history majors (see McCandless, 1994).

Types of Entries

Teachers in content areas face the challenge of providing for sufficient portfolio coverage of both the content and the processes entailed by their specific fields of study. One question that science or history teachers may face, for example, is what to emphasize in the portfolios—the skills their science and history students need or the students' actual understanding of specific science and history content. Will the emphasis of the portfolio be, for instance, on works that demonstrate an analysis and synthesis of historical evidence, or will it be on works that reflect understanding of a particular historical period? (See McCandless, 1994.) Similarly, will the science portfolios focus on science processes such as formulating questions and making predictions and observations, or will they emphasize knowledge strands, such as energy or force and motion? (See Legg et al., 1994.) Although portfolio contents are typically aligned with course objectives, determining the type(s) of entries to be included remains a particular challenge if the portfolios are to reflect the concepts, outcomes, skills, and processes central to the subject area.

As is true for writing portfolios, the exact nature of the portfolios in content areas varies according to the subject and the purpose of the portfolio program. Papers written in response to questions or to problems are among the most common entries, and reflective essays or letters play a major role in most portfolio requirements. But some portfolios contain photographs, videos, audiotapes, computer disks, and models (Hinojosa, 1993). Moreover, while portfolios typically are required to include cover sheets (with thorough explanations about the entries), reflective letters, and evidence of best work, some content-area portfolios also require group work, learning logs, drafts showing revision, or problems and assignments that need additional work or improvement.

The potentially broad scope of requirements used in content-area portfolios is shown in the following specifications of entries for the interdisciplinary portfolios of an International Baccalaureate Program in San Diego:

> 1) a process for solving a problem; 2) evidence used to prove a point; 3) observation of an event with conclusions drawn from observations; 4) effective expression of an idea in writing; 5) best work so far; 6) a group effort; 7) something new that was learned; 8) hard work including revision and reworking; 9) something creative; 10) something the student would like to work on again; and 11) at least one work from each class (English, mathematics, physics, and world history). (Storms, 1990, p. 3)

Growing Mastery of Content

Essential to most content-area portfolios is the idea that students should be able to demonstrate a growing understanding of the principles of the field and to communicate that understanding. This strand of the writing-across-the-curriculum movement focuses on helping students learn to write according to the conventions of a particular discipline; in this strand, models of writing assignments in specific disciplines are often included to aid students. For example, instructors in one college history department have long designed writing assignments that contain a "model of analysis" so that their students learn to evaluate evidence and write interpretive essays of historical moments (Mcclymer and Moynihan, 1977). More recently, researchers Charney and Carlson (1995) undertook a study with college psychology students to explore the importance of models in helping the students to write the research methods section of two experiments that the students observed on videotape. Finding that the use of models, while not automatically improving students' writing, has an effect on the elements of content and organization (p. 111), the researchers conclude that "model texts are a rich resource that may prove useful to writers in different ways at different stages of their development" (p. 116).

Because content-area teachers strongly emphasize the need for students to increase their comprehension of subject matter, the notion of revising or "updating" drafts in a portfolio assumes a special significance. According to science teacher Robin McGlohn (1991), who periodically asks her middle school students to compose answers to questions such as "What is energy?" and then update their responses, the value of her two-semester portfolio lies in requiring students to work over a sustained period of time on improving both the content and the form of their responses (p. 7). Teachers in other subject areas also view as a strength the idea of students struggling over time to clarify their thoughts about questions, such as that posed by Nanette Seago to her middle schoolers: "What is mathematics?" For such teachers, portfolios are valuable because they give "opportunities to learn what students *know* about content areas, to assess curriculum needs, and to become cognizant of how students are actually thinking" (see Carson, 1991, p. 6).

Demonstrating how students' comprehension of material has increased, therefore, is critical to most content-area portfolios. (In that vein, one of the Alachua County science teachers with whom we worked on the portfolio project asked her middle school students to submit two laboratory entries to their portfolios over a six-month period so that she could know whether students had improved in their understanding of what such procedures entailed.) In addition, because the inclusion of drafts in most portfolios reveals the processes involved, students' misunderstandings also become readily apparent (the Mathematics Portfolio Project, 1990, p. 2). A glance at the benchmark papers for the Vermont Mathematics Portfolio Project (1991) confirms this benefit of portfolios: through an explicit comparison of sample student responses in which students indicated *why* they made the choices they did, Vermont educators were able to identify and analyze where individual students had gone astray in interpreting the given scenario or problem to be solved.

Creativity and Individuality of Portfolios

Particularly important in the use of science portfolios is the fact that portfolios give students a chance to be creative. According to middle school science teacher Robin L. H. Freedman (1993), "When students articulate what they understand in a drawing, story, or poem, they are reinforcing the factual content being presented. In the creative mode, students must use both sides of the brain, connecting the analytical to the creative side, a process that facilitates learning" (p. 6). Freedman asks middle school students to respond to open-ended questions with what she labels "'creative essays'" that synthesize factual material with a creative approach. Freedman cites the following sample question:

> You are part of an interplanetary expedition. Your job is to analyze the soil of the planet you have arrived at to determine if plants from Earth can survive in the new environment. What will you do? What tests will you perform? How will you protect yourself and your crew from contamination while you are conducting your experiments? How will you know your tests are valid? (1993, p. 6)

Creativity is also important in the portfolios for California's Golden State Examinations in Science, where students are required to submit a portfolio entry that treats a scientific concept or theme in some creative form—whether art, music, or poetry. As a result, students express their understandings of scientific material through diverse means including board games, videos, and haikus (Martin, Miller, & Delgado, 1993, p. 12). Similarly, in the collaborative portfolio assessment project we undertook with five teachers from county schools, Sarah Martin encouraged her fourth-grade students to submit a narrative piece for their science portfolios.

Such efforts to make room for creativity in science are important, for as Robert Yager and Alan McCormack (1989) note, "Most view a science program as something to be done to students to help them learn given information. Little formal attention has been given in science programs to the development of students' imagination and creative thinking. And yet creativity in terms of questions, possible explanations, and testing ideas is central to science" (p. 46).

Evaluating Content-Area Writing

The issue of evaluation, which can be troublesome under the best of conditions, is especially problematic with content-area writings. Certainly, teachers expect to evaluate the content in these portfolios or performance assessments, but they may be less clear as to the role that writing quality might play in these evaluations. While overall writing quality is a prominent factor in the writing portfolios of English classes, it is an underlying issue in content-area portfolios and performance assessments—and one that often creates ambivalence.

Teachers have tried various approaches in dealing with the issues of mechanics and overall writing quality. One science teacher wrote, "Let it be understood that a science teacher is not an English teacher. We are not there to grade grammar and usage. Our responsibility is to give our students another place to practice their writing skills and to demonstrate their conceptual understanding of science" (R. Freedman, 1993, p. 17). Another science teacher, Robin McGlohn (1991), enlisted the help of ninth-grade English teachers in her pilot use of portfolios in order to determine how the entries in the science portfolios compared to the same students' written performance in their English classes. Not only were her students impressed with the idea that their English teachers would be reviewing the science portfolios, but the English teachers were also impressed with the quality of work they saw their students performing in another subject area (McGlohn, p. 6). Still other teachers, such as the science teachers involved in the collaborative project with us, include mechanics as a category to factor into their scores, while some college instructors stress the idea of "professionalism" or "presentation" to convey the need for their students to produce quality written work. Margot Soven (1996), who encourages the development of a "limited set of criteria" tailored to each assignment, observes that the general criteria should remind students that grammar, usage, and mechanics will still be important even though content will be emphasized most (pp. 15–16).

Evaluation is an area in which English teachers can be of particular help to content-area teachers—not by actually evaluating the portfolios or the written performance explanations that may accompany experiments or other performances, but by sharing with content-area teachers strategies that have worked in English classes. For example, English teachers can show how designing careful assignments for a specific audience and clear purpose can encourage better student writing, just as guiding students through prewriting stages can result in stronger drafts. Moreover, English teachers can share with their science colleagues the value of peer editing or of minilectures in which format and stylistic matters are addressed. They can also show how targeting key errors is more effective than marking everything and, similarly, how conducting brief conferences during the writing process works better than commenting at length once the work is done. Through these approaches, English teachers can convey the way in which writing evaluation has shifted from marking every error to emphasizing, first, how the writing task can be undertaken, and subsequently, what a student has done well. As Tchudi and Yates (1983) note, "It is important to emphasize that students learn both writing and subject matter best when they *succeed* at what they have set out to do and when someone helps them understand why they have succeeded" (p. 68).

For large classes or for external evaluations, such as state- or district-wide assessments, scoring rubrics—either analytic or holistic—may be used in content areas. The complexity of these rubrics underscores the difficulties of reflecting mastery of content, processes, and conventions of various disciplines. For example, the portfolios piloted with the Golden State Examinations were given eight scores each—on a scale from 0 to 4—for the three entries that dealt with problem solving, creativity, and understanding and for the five "unifying qualities" that included revision and collaboration. The portfolios were scored separately by the classroom teachers and then by an external, trained scorer.

The document *Grade Eight Benchmarks* for the Vermont Mathematics Portfolio Project likewise includes, on a four-point scale, three "mathematics communication criteria" (language, representation, and presentation) together with four problem-solving criteria ("understanding of the task," "approaches/procedures," "decisions along the way," and "outcomes of activities") (1991, p. 1).

Two science teachers participating in our portfolio project, Bob Howland and Sarah Martin, devised similar rubrics for their science portfolios, with Bob's targeted toward the secondary level and Sarah's toward the elementary level. As depicted in Figure 17, their rubrics covered six basic categories, including "organization, mechanics, scientific language, scientific representations, scientific method, and creativity"; the categories were rated on a six-point scale from "far below grade level" to "far above grade level" (see Legg et al., 1994, pp. 65–66).

Some content-area portfolio programs use a holistic scoring approach just as some writing portfolio programs do. For example, the Kentucky mathematics portfolios are scored holistically, with an overall score—"novice," "apprentice," "proficient," and "distinguished"—characterizing a student's performance in problem solving, reasoning, mathematical communication, and understanding. Tom Hinojosa

	1	2	3	4	5	6
Categories to Consider…	Organization Planned, logical, sequential, & focused	Mechanics Spelling, punctuation, capitalization, grammar, & usage	Scientific Language Scientific vocabulary, symbols, & equations (when appropriate)	Scientific Representations Charts, tables, graphs, models, diagrams & equations, explanations of data	Scientific Method Purpose, hypothesis, methods & materials, data & conclusion, (when appropriate) problem-solving strategies	Creativity New perspectives in science

DESCRIPTION OF LEVEL

LEVEL	
6	Far above grade level. Very minor flaws. Logical interpretations and explanations which are effectively communicated. Demonstrates inspired thought, logical and focused planning, accurate use of language, terminology, and effectively displays information or data.
5	Well above grade level. Minor flaws. Uses focused interpretations and explanations which are displayed mostly in a precise, accurate, and complete manner. Generally correct use of terminology and language. Scientific processes used appropriately when applicable.
4	Grade level to slightly above. Few major flaws and some minor flaws. Interpretations and explanations logical and mostly clear. Generally correct use of language, terminology, and scientific representations of data. Demonstrates some thought and some research.
3	Grade level to slightly below. Some major and minor flaws. Interpretations and explanations of data somewhat clear. Demonstrates minimal thought and research. Moderate to mediocre in application skills and in use of language and terminology. System for display of data or information not always clear or effective.
2	Well below grade level. Some major and many minor flaws. Minimal organization, incomplete displays of information. Crucial information left out. Data represented in disorganized manner. Minimal problem solving strategies and incomplete understanding of concepts. Mediocre in application skills, logic, focus, and use of terminology and language.
1	Far below grade level. Many major and minor flaws. Absence of thought, research or use of language. Disorganized, inaccurate, or poorly displayed information. Misunderstanding of tasks. Lack of problem solving strategies. No evidence of understanding of concepts. Poor in application skills, logic, focus, or use of language.

Note: Depending on the nature of the writing assignment, it is probable that not all of the criteria described will apply all the time. When designing a writing assignment, determine which criteria will be used for assessment.

Figure 17. Science portfolio assessment guide for elementary school by Robert Howland, Santa Fe High School, Alachua, Florida, and Sarah Martin, Norton Elementary School, Gainesville, Florida. From *A Framework for Training Teachers in Portfolio Assessment*, by S. Legg et al. © 1994 by the Florida Department of Education, Tallahassee, FL. All rights reserved. Used with permission.

(1993) advocates evaluating science portfolios holistically—"assessing the overall approach the student showed in his or her work in terms of conceptual understanding, performance, and application" (p. 17).

Holistic scoring has been, in the view of college science professor M. L. Rodgers (1995), instrumental in enabling him to ask students to write six laboratory reports in a large chemistry course. His scoring rubric evaluates, on a six-point scale, students' mastery of scientific content and the writing qualities of focus, appearance, content, and structure. He shares the rubric with his students when he makes the assignments, and he has successfully trained student assistants to help him with the grading. He uses time saved in grading the reports to provide workshop consultations with students while they prepare their first drafts (p. 120).

Performance Assessment

In addition to traditional tests, some content areas use portfolios and other types of performance assessment to measure their students' understanding of a subject. Richard Stiggins (1987) describes performance assessment in the following manner:

> Performance assessments call upon the examinee to demonstrate specific skills and competencies, that is, to apply the skills and knowledge they have mastered. The demonstration can take place during the normal course of everyday events (e.g., during normal classroom life) or in response to specific structured exercises provided by the examiners. Regardless, the examinee's task is to construct an original response, which the examiner observes and evaluates. (p. 34)

Researchers have urged caution in using performance assessments for accountability purposes rather than for instructional purposes because of the time and resources entailed and because of the scoring issues involved (Shavelson, Baxter, and Pine, 1992). In Kentucky, however, science, social studies, and humanities have all been evaluated at certain grade levels by performance assessment. Students typically gather in a library, where they are grouped randomly and given an assignment or an experiment to complete together, using materials often provided in kits. Once the students gather the information, they write individual responses to questions regarding the task; these responses may then be scored by an external scoring program. Written responses in these performance assessments thus serve as the means by which students reveal their individual understanding of subject-area content as demonstrated collaboratively through hands-on problem solving.

Summary

Writing plays an increasingly pivotal role in content areas, where it helps students write to learn and learn to write in specific disciplines. Portfolios, in particular, form the building blocks of writing in many content areas, as students reveal their efforts to move from what Art Young (1994) calls private discourse across the bridge of classroom discourse to public discourse. Through the informal logs and journals, the multiple drafts and revisions, the feedback from teachers, the formal entries modeled after the writings of a discipline, and students' reflections about how they have improved their understanding of a field, portfolios reveal students' progress in moving from writing to learn about a particular discipline to writing to communicate their knowledge to others.

Used primarily for instructional purposes within classrooms, portfolios and other types of performance assessment are undertaken for some external purposes as well, such as program evaluation or graduation requirements. Increasingly, scoring rubrics with sample assignments are being designed for various subject areas in order to illustrate for students the criteria on which they will be assessed.

Because writing in the content areas is both similar to and different from writing in English classes, English teachers and their colleagues in other fields have much to gain from working with one another on writing and its assessment.

11 Issues of Equity
in Writing Assessment

Because language lies at the very core of human experience, writing assessment, which is predicated largely on the expectation that students will write in Standard Written English and on the premise that they have indeed had opportunities to practice their writing in Standard English, can give rise to issues of equity for virtually anyone, depending on that individual's previous experiences and background. Assessment can be especially problematic for those groups of students for whom Standard English is either a second dialect or a second language; who have a different cultural background or certain learning disabilities; or who have had little formal instruction in composition or few actual chances to practice composing in Standard English.

The purpose of this chapter is to determine the impact of writing assessment on those students by exploring the nature of the problems and inequities. The problems appear to stem from five major sources: (1) the language barriers themselves; (2) different cultural expectations for the writing modes; (3) writing tasks that are inaccessible or personally objectionable; (4) inexperience in writing in the modes being assessed; and (5) scoring approaches that factor in students' errors.

Language Barriers

Among the problems encountered as a result of language barriers are the need to shift from conversational dialect to the language required for academic writing; unfamiliarity with the requirements of certain writing modes; and the time constraints imposed by most assessment situations. In the case of those students who speak Black English and for whom Standard English is a second dialect, the similarities between first and second dialects may, as the ESL educator Ilona Leki suggests, make it difficult for students to change dialects (1992, p. 29), especially when they must proofread or perform other editing tasks in a timed writing assessment. Certainly, some of this difficulty is evident in large-scale scorings when we encounter essays in which students have carefully appeared to tack on "ed" or "s" to the ends of some words and omitted the same necessary endings from others. If students become prematurely concerned about correcting errors or changing dialects, they can, as the work of Sondra Perl (1978) has shown, experience a blocking of their larger composing processes—especially, as we might surmise, during the stress of a testing situation. Nor do the potential problems of novice writers lie solely with sentence-level language errors. The language problems may be broader in scope, centering, as David Bartholomae (1985) points out, on many students' unfamiliarity with the more formal language required by their university or other academic community. Students may have what Bartholomae calls "a more fragmentary record of the comings and goings of academic discourse . . . the key words without the complete statements within which they are already operating" (p. 160). These students' inexperience in academic writing, combined with second-dialect problems, may thus give them particular difficulty when undertaking writing assessments.

Research by Arnetha Ball (1992) also points to the unfamiliarity of written expository discourse as one source of difficulty for some African Americans. Ball notes that African American expository vernacular patterns typically rely on what she calls "circumlocution, narrative interspersion, and recursion." The first approach entails linking a series of anecdotes to a topic developed implicitly by association. The second approach, narrative interspersion, signifies the use of a narrative to carry an expository theme; and the third approach, recursion, involves repeating the same idea with different images (pp. 509–510). For her study, Ball first instructed high school students and fifth and sixth graders from several urban classrooms in the organizational patterns typically used in academic writing, as well as those used in conversational situations; she then asked students to identify the patterns and to indicate their preferences. She found that students of *all ethnic backgrounds* preferred to use the vernacular patterns of organization in their conversations. However, the African American high school students clearly preferred using the vernacular patterns in academic writing as well. The results corroborated findings of an earlier study by Ball in which 71 percent of the twenty African American students she surveyed in inner cities indicated that "they had to change their words and language use in order to produce academically successful compositions" (p. 517). While her study is small, it suggests that for some African American students, using Standard Written English in an expository assignment requires them to change dialect codes during the proofreading process and to alter their organizational patterns during the composing process as well.

Many students for whom English is a second language may also be inexperienced in composing in Standard English. Leki (1992) points out that ESL writers often struggle with word order problems and with a very limited vocabulary; when they have to focus on these language problems, students may be less able to concentrate on the larger issue of planning their essays. Leki further notes that inexperienced ESL writers (like many other inexperienced writers) have difficulty in "knowing where their writing is going and keeping larger chunks of meaning in mind as they write" (p. 78). For ESL students, in particular, many of whom have not yet learned to think in English, the problem of time constraints in direct writing assessment exacerbates their language difficulties. (Certainly, our own experience with one young woman from China illustrated this issue. Mai worked very hard in our Writing Center to gain the skills necessary to pass the essay portion of our mandated state examination; however, even though as a "retake" she was entitled to double time—two hours—her practice sessions with us clearly indicated that she needed still more time to enable her to plan fully, to write her essay painstakingly, and to do some limited proofreading and revising.)

Time constraints can also aggravate the language problems that some students with learning disabilities experience in direct writing assessments. Graham, Harris, MacArthur, and Schwartz (1991) stress the importance of a writing workshop approach, with practice, feedback, and time provided. They attribute the writing problems that students with learning disabilities often experience both to the interference that the physical act of producing text has on the composing process and to the students' lack of understanding of the writing process and of appropriate approaches to use (pp. 312–314). For these students, the tasks of planning, composing, and revising papers may already be burdensome, and the testing constraints of direct writing assessments are exceedingly difficult—even when unlimited time may be provided.

Many years ago, one student who had learning disabilities worked in our Writing Center to improve his skills sufficiently to pass the essay subtest of the state-mandated assessment. Although this student was a successful junior, he had a terrible time dealing with the constraints of the direct writing assessment. His papers were short, undeveloped, riddled with misspellings of ordinary words, and very difficult to read because of ill-formed letters. We worked with him extensively, yet he continued to fail. Finally, he was allowed to compose the essay on a word processor, and then he passed.

In some writing assessment programs, students with learning disabilities are routinely given the opportunity to use word processors, thereby making their revising and spelling tasks easier. However, as Graham and his colleagues acknowledge, research on the effect of word processing on students with learning disabilities has been limited. In recognition of the particular burden that assessment can place on these students, some institutions grant waivers for particular subtests.

Cultural Assumptions about Rhetoric

The very rhetorical expectations of the cultures that students come from may also vary. Leki (1992) notes, for example, that "students from different cultures construe their rhetorical role differently" (p. 66), and she calls attention to the various rhetorical conventions that different cultures value. Whereas English-speaking cultures value explicitness of explanations and relationships, East Asian countries may emphasize indirectness. Whereas the English culture emphasizes specific examples, the Spanish culture may prefer generalizations and extensive introductions (pp. 94–100). Leki cautions, therefore, that "because they have learned different rhetorical conventions and because they may not yet have developed a sense of their U.S. audience's requirements, ESL writers may produce writing which violates the expectations of native speakers of English" (p. 102).

Roxanne Mountford (in press) also calls attention to the limitations of a too-narrow conception of academic writing, pointing out that the emphasis on one type of academic writing—the thesis with points given in support—reflects a certain world view and conception of knowledge to which many cultures and subcultures do not subscribe. She states that "although cultural anthropology has again and again shown that cultural difference underlies schisms between European American and African American patterns of speech and writing, and between men's and women's speech patterns in many American subcultures, our academic policies—particularly on writing—have largely worked to ignore or erase such differences" (in press). In Mountford's view, the cost has been enormous in terms of the "misunderstanding and underappreciation "that many groups have experienced.

Ethnographic research by Marcia Farr (1993) further illustrates the implications of some differences. As Farr emphasizes, "The multiplicity of discourse styles that fill many classrooms . . . can represent particular ways of reasoning, of viewing the world, and of using language" (p. 7). To underscore her point, Farr analyzed the discourse characteristics of two persuasive oral speeches made by a Mexican American and by a Mexican immigrant in different political meetings; the speeches showed not only how the oral styles differed from the written styles of English essays but also how highly valued those oral styles were in their respective communities. Farr stresses the importance of recognizing that different discourse patterns may convey reasoning and that the essay standards by which we judge something as illogical do not necessarily apply to other means of communication which may be based on different cultural assumptions (p. 32).

Different cultural assumptions may also be important to recognize as a contributing factor to plagiarism, an issue that arises occasionally regarding entries completed for portfolio assessments. Leki (1992) explains, for example, that what appears as plagiarism in the academic culture of the United States may result from different assumptions that some ESL students hold regarding the importance of collaborating with one another and the unimportance of demonstrating either originality or individual ownership of ideas in writing (pp. 71–72).

Writing Tasks That Are Inaccessible or Personally Objectionable

As was noted in Chapter 3, writing assignments can have an enormous impact on assessments. For example, many ESL writers, as well as some native speakers of English, may be quite troubled by a topic in a writing assessment that asks them to reveal something about themselves. Indeed, Leki (1992) emphasizes that the personal essay so valued in American composition classes may be unfamiliar to students for whom English is a second language. According to Leki, so uncomfortable do some ESL students become when asked to write on a personal topic that they may even make up an experience instead. Students from disadvantaged backgrounds may also find personal topics embarrassing, overly emotional, negative, or otherwise problematic. In one study by Haviland and Clark (1992) of college students at the basic writing level, one-third of the students indicated that, when writing essay examinations, they preferred a nonpersonal topic to a personal one because they liked to distance themselves from the assigned topic (p. 49).

If the personal topic is troublesome to some students, other writing assessment topics requiring general knowledge can also, as Chapter 3 has shown, make a writing task difficult. Even when topics are heavily field-tested, their problematic side for certain students may not be immediately revealed. Indeed, topics which appear to be accessible may actually be puzzling to some test takers; we have found that topics dealing with fads or with values, for example, present difficulties for ESL students. Even topics dealing with something as supposedly commonplace as computers will not necessarily be accessible to disadvantaged students. Darling-Hammond (1994) notes her concern that "the selection of tasks [for performance-based assessments] will rest on cultural and other referents" that may not be accessible to all test takers (p. 17). In a similar vein, Roberta Camp (1993) stresses that "we will need to think and observe carefully, for example, to determine whether the writing performance required for our new assessments are equally appropriate for students drawing on different cultural and linguistic experiences" (p. 68).

One inadvertent consequence of the topic or mode emphasized in both instruction and assessment may be gender inequities. In a large-scale study of eighth-grade writers by Englehard, Gordon, and Gabrielson (1992), for example, female students in the Georgia state assessment did better in analytically scored essays than did males in all three modes (narrative, descriptive, and expository) and on all three types of tasks (general knowledge, imagined experience, and personal experience). In fact, those writing tasks that were based on direct experiences received the highest ratings (p. 326)—an interesting finding in view of some problems associated with personal experience topics. Not only were gender differences greater with the narrative mode than with the expository or the descriptive mode, but also they were most substantial with those topics requiring personal experience (p. 331). In particular, the female students performed better than their male counterparts on the three domains of sentence formation, usage, and mechanics. The gender distinctions were less noticeable in the domains of content/organization and style. Sandra Stotsky (1995), also noting that female students in the National Assessment of Educational Progress (NAEP) have performed better than males at all levels, suggests that an overemphasis on personal experience topics, along with the narrative mode to which such topics often give rise, may negatively affect both boys and girls. First, personal topics may minimize the type of "informational writing, in science and technology especially," that has appeal for boys; second, frequent use of personal topics may direct girls away from an interest in science and technology (p. 765).

Instruction in the Modes

As research, theory, and practice have all shown, writing instruction is—like writing practice—critical for good assessment results. Researchers Engelhard, Gordon, and Gabrielson (1992) found in their large-scale study of eighth-grade writers that narrative essays averaged the highest ratings, descriptive papers the next highest, and expository the lowest. They stress that "the ability to succeed in a writing task is likely to be, at least in part, a function of the opportunity to learn how to do that kind of writing" (p. 331). In a study of seventh-grade writing noted previously, Pamela Kegley (1986) found that only 31 percent of the persuasive papers were considered adequate, in contrast to 56 percent of the narrative papers. Because the students in her study were carefully matched as to race and previous language scores, Kegley attributed the differences to the mode of discourse, noting that modes cannot be viewed as interchangeable in assessments. The significance of providing instruction and practice in different modes of writing is also stressed by Ruth and Murphy (1988), who point out that the writing performance of students in one state exam has varied whenever students encounter a change in the mode of discourse being assessed—at least until they have had a chance to practice the new mode (p. 80). Studies done by the National Assessment of Educational Progress over the years have shown similar variations in the results obtained depending on the writing modes assessed. Clearly, then, the extent and quality of the instruction and practice that students receive in the modes of writing on which they are assessed can influence how well they perform on assessments. If students' school experiences have not included opportunities for such instruction and practice, inequities can arise.

Darling-Hammond (1994) points out that students from disadvantaged backgrounds often have been placed in lower tracks in school and have been subjected to remedial programs that emphasize only discrete, low-level cognitive skills. Furthermore, in schools staffed by what Darling-Hammond describes as "a disproportionate share of those teachers who are inexperienced, unprepared, and underqualified," students' instruction may consist of isolated grammar exercises, and they may receive little information about the composing process and little chance to do much actual writing themselves (p. 15). Like Darling-Hammond, Marcia Farr (1993) also expresses concern about inequality, noting that weakest groups often are not taught the "essayist literacy" reflected in the rhetorical requirements of most writing assessments (p. 12).

Scoring Approaches

Finally, the language problems of ESL or second-dialect speakers of English may receive a different emphasis depending on the scoring approach used for the writing assessment. In primary trait scoring, control of the language is often not considered vital to the writing task being evaluated; while sentence structure and grammar might be evaluated as *secondary* traits, they often are not rated as part of the *primary* trait. In analytic scoring, on the other hand, the severity of a student's language problems may or may not be fully identified, depending on the weight assigned to each element in the particular scale used. Finally, in holistic scoring, control of the language blends with other elements of writing to contribute to the overall impression. Whereas minor or occasional errors are not likely to mar a paper that has strong content and development, severe sentence-level errors or syntax problems that interfere with the communication of meaning are apt to result in a lower holistic score.

The effect that holistic scoring may have on ESL writers and on basic writers has arisen as a concern in two articles. Exploring why holistic raters typically demonstrate a strong agreement about the lowest scores they assign, Richard Haswell (1988) suggests that holistic scorers have tended to oversimplify the bottom papers. Haswell believes that raters, influenced by the errors riddling such papers, may overlook the logical organization, original voice, and "verbal wit" that may be present, and he warns that "high concordance on low holistic scores looks awfully like stereotyping" (p. 314).

In a study discussed in some depth in Chapter 7, Michael Janopoulos (1993) found that, even in a holistic scoring context, trained ESL composition teachers paid attention to the meaning—the "communicative competence"—of essays written by students for whom English was a second or foreign language. Because communicative competence stresses looking beyond the errors of form and emphasizing content (p. 310), Janopoulos believes that scorers who have taught ESL composition are perhaps the most suited for holistically rating the communicative competence of ESL students. While noting that form cannot be separated from content, Janopoulos stresses that trained ESL composition teacher-scorers can "identify unconventional text organization" even in the timed constraints of a scoring and, moreover, that they may have different expectations from other raters (p. 321).

However, as discussed in Chapter 5, the training and monitoring procedures of a formal scoring help holistic scorers to evaluate writing through a common lens so that an individual scorer neither penalizes nor rewards students unduly. Indeed, the development of a consensus among readers who assent to and adopt the criteria as their own has been noted by Edward White (1985) as a vital part of the training process.

Equity Issues and Standards

To acknowledge potential difficulties that some groups may experience with writing assessment is not, however, to suggest that external writing assessment be eliminated or that standards be ignored. Even though the notion of standards is sometimes controversial, high standards remain a goal that most schools—as well as state governments and the nation—strive toward. However, standards combined with assessment alone will not suffice to overhaul schools; as Wolf and Reardon (1996) point out, standards must be part of a "coherent system suffused by the conviction that high achievement is widely attainable" (p. 6). What must be done, the educators urge, is to foster a "steadily more demanding curriculum" in which "mastery is actually taught, not merely called for" (p. 11). They urge teachers to examine students' development and learning patterns over time and to sequence their learning in such a way that all students can see thinking taking place, can take advantage of the opportunities, and can perform well on the assessments and meet the standards. Wolf and Reardon remind readers that "if the standards or new forms of assessment, like portfolios, are to be tools for redistributing opportunities to learn," then students must understand, grapple with, and apply the standards (p. 14).

Wolf and Reardon believe that standards, learning, and assessment should be integrally and deeply linked. Without content and performance standards to aim toward, the type of learning advocated by Wolf and Reardon would be less likely to occur, and schools would be less likely to provide the curriculum, faculty, and resources necessary for meeting the delivery standards. In a similar vein, Albert Shanker (1996), critiquing the *Standards for the English Language Arts,* observes that "though they talk a great deal about offering equal opportunities to all students, in discarding the idea of standards, they also throw out the best hope of getting some kind of equity among our widely disparate English curriculums."

As we have seen, most writing assessments presume the need for Standard Written English and for certain rhetorical approaches. Making students explicitly aware of these expectations thus becomes important. Standard Written English remains, rightly or wrongly, the "dress code" of academic and most other formal means of communication—including the business world and the Internet; it is what Rei Noguchi (1991) refers to as the "suit and dress shoes" way of writing. Stressing the importance of acquainting students with standard written grammar forms, Noguchi states: "It is not that jeans and sneakers are intrinsically wrong and that a suit and dress shoes are intrinsically right. . . . Rather, different situations call for different styles. The choice of style (or dialect, as the case may be) is no less significant in language, particularly in writing, where the nature of the medium heightens the assumption that addressers have taken the time to refine their message to meet the needs and expectations of the addressees" (p. 30).

To be certain, one could argue, as Tom Fox (1993) does, that mastering the language or standards of the academy has *not* ensured the expected academic or economic access for minorities or ESL speakers (p. 41). Nevertheless, enabling students to master Standard English will, in Noguchi's view, prevent linguistic features from serving as an excuse for those in power who might block the progress of specific groups of people (pp. 29–30).

It is important, therefore, that teachers help students gain flexibility in adapting this written code which is necessary for many situations. While acknowledging and valuing different cultural expectations and different language codes, teachers can help students determine when, where, and how their written language codes may need to be switched; teachers can, moreover, clarify where and how the rhetorical expectations of various cultures differ. Students who understand these differences will be in a stronger position to make informed choices when necessary.

As different ways of writing become more common, the rhetorical expectations of English-speaking cultures may eventually allow for more flexibility or diversity. Until that acceptance occurs, teachers can incorporate curriculum practices that establish, as Arnetha Ball suggests, "bridges between patterns used in students' home discourse communities and those required for school success" (1992, p. 525). While objecting to the bridge metaphor itself with its one-way implication, Carol Severino (1992) similarly advocates curriculum practices that help students link "home and school literacies, an acknowledgment of the common ground between the two" (p. 9). Such linkings, as well as the explicit articulation of ways in which dialects and rhetorical expectations differ, can help all students succeed at meeting the standards.

Summary

Because of the close link between writing assessment and students' language experiences at home and at school, issues of equity must be recognized and carefully considered. In the case of internal classroom assessments, teachers can compensate for, or be sensitive to, any inequities that may arise within writing assignments they make and portfolios they score. On the other hand, the more formalized external writing assessments, with their frequent time constraints and other restrictions and their culturally embedded topics and rhetorical expectations, may place at a disadvantage some students for whom Standard English is either a second language or a second dialect, as well as some students with learning disabilities. Other students at a disadvantage may include those who have not had much instruction or practice in the modes being assessed; additionally, the scoring approach used in the evaluation may or may not highlight students' particular weaknesses.

Indeed, possible hardships imposed by timed writings may serve as a strong justification for using portfolios rather than single timed-writing assessments in that portfolios enable students to work for a longer time on their writing, engaging in revision of language problems and addressing topics that may be meaningful to them. At the same time, because technical issues, time, and costs all work against using portfolio assessment on a large scale, timed essays appear likely to predominate in external writing assessments. Therefore, teachers need to become more involved in the design and review of topics for external assessments, in the scorings themselves, and especially in those English instructional practices that will enable students to experiment with the types of writing on which they are being assessed and to gain practice in composing fluently in Standard Written English.

12 Future Directions

The future directions of writing assessment are difficult to predict. Because of conflicting trends in assessment, the rippled glass analogy with which this text began may be just as applicable a comparison on which to end. In many states writing assessment is buffeted by political changes—by ever-increasing expectations, the reality of funding constraints, and demands for accountability. Writing assessment seems particularly vulnerable—not only because scoring methods are subjective (and expensive), but also because the writing itself is so *visible.* An individual's mistakes on a mathematics test may not warrant public notice, but a letter to an editor with errors will surely attract negative attention—and much public speculation about what it means to write well.

The purpose of this chapter is to explore trends in writing assessment and to consider how teachers can become involved.

Computers in Scorings

Recent computer developments hint at the possibility of drastic—and certainly controversial—changes in future scoring procedures. Page and Petersen (1995), for example, stress the potential use of computers in large-scale essay scorings. They report an experiment in which their computer program, Project Essay Grade, examined length, sentence structure, and other variables and then accurately predicted the average judgments of six human scorers on three hundred essays. In the researchers' view, such computer scorings would offer the advantage of scoring essays more rapidly, more inexpensively, and more accurately than two human judges scoring each essay. Acknowledging that "for the early years of such computer ratings, it makes sense to use at least one human rater for each essay," they argue that "while the computer might provide more accurate assessment than any single human rater, a human rating could still head off certain kinds of error and could even offer some reassurance that human standards would still be involved, especially in judging offbeat essays" (p. 562). How readily English teachers—or the general public, for that matter—will accept the notion of having computers "read" and evaluate essays remains to be seen.

Evidence of such controversy appears in the response of Kathryn Fitzgerald (1994) to a study by Emil Roy (1993). Roy explored the validity of a computerized system, which he called the Structured Decision System (SDS), in grading placement examinations at Utah. His computer system tallied paper length, high syllable averages, and low percentages of unique words. When he compared the four different placement levels to which his program had assigned forty-six students with the placement level first assigned on the basis of holistic scores, he found that 65 percent tallied with the original scores. He was further able to account for other apparent discrepancies by including in his "SDS sorting algorithm" the number of words per sentence for placement in advanced writing courses and the range of possible prepositions for placement in remedial writing. In Roy's view, computerized scoring is stronger than holistic scoring for several reasons: "since it ignores content, exams never trigger reader bias; and no slippage of rating accuracy results from prolonged reader fatigue or boredom" (p. 49).

It is precisely the lack of attention to content in Roy's computerized scoring system that troubles Kathryn Fitzgerald (1994). While acknowledging his responsible use of procedures, Fitzgerald expresses her concern about the implications of his findings, which run counter to current theories emphasizing the varying criteria necessary for different types and purposes of writing. Her concern arises from her own experience in holistically scoring the same placement exams Roy used: For the purpose of Utah's program, scorers pay particular attention to students' ability to move inductively from specific to general and to examine issues from different perspectives (p. 7). In other words, cognitive development, as expressed through the content of the students' writing—a content the computer totally ignores—is critical for the placement purposes of that particular writing program. Moreover, noting that Roy needed to make "ad hoc adjustments" to his computer program to account for discrepancies, Fitzgerald points out that he was "addressing a problem that human readers constantly confront—that few essays perfectly fit the profile of a single placement category, even when described holistically. Human readers must constantly weigh the importance of one feature of a text against another, a process that a computerized system is forced to quantify" (p. 15). She expresses concern that the cost efficiency of a computerized scoring system might lead administrators to overlook the importance of writing as a "rhetorical act inseparable from its content, contexts, and purposes" (p. 17).

Purposes in Assessment

This emphasis on computerized scoring stands in clear opposition to other trends that emphasize the need for more sensitive, humane assessments or for new assessment models altogether. To this end, a number of educators suggest that the *purposes* behind the assessment be reconsidered. For example, Linda Darling-Hammond (1994) calls for altering the very purposes of assessment so that it serves as the basis for carefully examining the learning context rather than for ranking, comparing, and sorting students and schools (p. 7). Other educators have also stressed that the main purpose of assessment should be to enhance learning rather than to serve the functions of gatekeeping or accountability. Stressing that "informed observations" of young students' reading performances are far preferable to reading tests, for example, Peter Johnston (1987), like Darling-Hammond, argues that assessment should not be used for norm-referenced, comparative purposes, but rather to improve "optimal learning for all" (p. 335). In a similar vein, the Assessment Committee of the College Conference on Composition and Communication (CCCC) emphasizes that "writing assessment is useful primarily as a means of improving learning" (1995, p. 432).

Context of the Assessment

Importance of Context for Examinees

In addition to rethinking the purpose behind writing assessment, a number of educators suggest changing the very nature of the assessments themselves. Increasingly emphasized is the importance of having a contextualized assessment—an assessment that is integrally linked to instruction and to the specific purposes of the examination, rather than decontextualized the way standardized multiple-choice tests are often perceived as being. Wolf and Reardon (1996) suggest that assessment should be embedded within the curriculum, and the CCCC Assessment Committee (1995) argues that assessments should engage the interest of examinees in such a way that students can best demonstrate their proficiency. Such context-based assessment can, the Committee notes, help to avoid misrepresenting the abilities of students of color. Roberta Camp also foretells valuable changes that may occur in proposed uses for assessment as schools undergo restructuring. Citing the work of Catherine Keech-Lucas, Camp (1993) finds promising those new assessment models labeled "ecological"—that is, assessments which not only consider "the whole environment of the learner" but also influence that environment positively by providing in-depth information to all concerned (p. 67).

The idea of linking effective instructional practice to large-scale assessment lies at the heart of a study undertaken by Gearhart, Herman, Novak, and Wolf (1995) in which the researchers explored whether a narrative rubric that had successfully helped elementary teachers guide the classroom writing of their students would also have the potential to work if applied to a large-scale writing assessment. The analytic rubric, called *Writing What You Read* (WWYR), highlighted those elements essential to narratives—theme, character, setting, plot, and communication; the rubric also provided for a single holistic evaluation for overall effectiveness.

The five scorers who used the WWYR scale to evaluate a set of papers from a suburban school judged the scale to be instructionally effective; in addition, they viewed three of the five analytic elements as effective for large-scale assessment. In subsequent interviews, scorers suggested possible revisions for two or three of the analytic elements, and they expressed concern about how much training might be entailed if the scale were transferred to a large-scale assessment; the researchers found, moreover, that the scale might not be able to indicate "a technically sound profile of students' strengths and weaknesses" (p. 238). While acknowledging the challenge of providing a rubric that effectively meets both classroom needs and large-scale assessment purposes, the researchers nevertheless express optimism that an analytic scale similar to their WWYR rubric might serve as an alternative to holistic scoring and better link the context of classroom instruction with large-scale assessment. Their concern with extending the benefits of a successful classroom rubric to external assessment perhaps resembles the way that effective classroom portfolios, begun as an instructional tool, have also been adopted as an external assessment measure.

Importance of Context for Evaluators

In addition to influencing the performance of examinees, context is believed to play a critical role for evaluators. Pat Belanoff (1991) observes that "in real-world reading, we always judge for a reason, within a context, according to the purposes a writer sets up. Thus, the only decisions we *can* make are contextual" (p. 60). In a similar vein, the CCCC Committee (1995) acknowledges the "socially contextualized" nature of evaluative reading, stressing that a local "community of interpreters" can, in fact, be effective and fair in their evaluation (p. 432).

The role that context plays for evaluators becomes the point of speculation for Michael Allen (1995), who writes of his pilot study in which seven educators from diverse geographic areas and colleges evaluated portfolios that had been written for college programs (where students knew scorers other than their teachers would be reading their work) and for individual classrooms (where students knew their teacher would be grading their work). Allen found that the clarity of the program rubrics enabled readers to agree to a surprising extent on the scores they assigned to portfolios from each other's portfolio programs—even when they did not endorse the philosophy or practices of the particular portfolio program. The readers agreed to a lesser extent on the scores they gave to portfolios that came from individual classrooms, a circumstance that Allen attributed to the "more personal and pedagogical context—a 'hidden rubric'" of the classroom (p. 83). To Allen, the issues raised by his initial study were whether "context, in the form of a well-articulated rubric, make[s] for expert readers, or are expert readers needed in order for the local context to be understood?" (p. 82). Even the e-mail evaluation sessions Allen subsequently established as an informal means of continuing the evaluations became a form of community.

Certainly, in our experience the sense of community that develops over time in holistic scorings—whether informal or formal—is a real asset. The sense of community, collegiality, and commitment was one of the greatest benefits of the holistic scorings that brought teachers together from throughout Florida three times a year to score essays for a state-mandated college test. In these sessions, college and secondary instructors from diverse sections of the state bonded as they shared viewpoints and interpretations of writing during the formal training with samples, during the one-on-one conferences between table leaders and readers, and during the informal talks at break times. A similar sense of community was visible as well whenever the instructors in our Writing Center program met at the end of the term to score essays or portfolios as part of the overall developmental program evaluation. Because these instructors had been working with a common syllabus and meeting together biweekly throughout the semester, the unity was, in one sense, not surprising. However, the earnestness and good will with which they undertook the task highlighted the value and fairness that can result when, as the CCCC Committee endorses, local communities of scorers rate essays.

Dynamic Assessment

The move toward more context-based assessment is aligned with the trends toward dynamic assessments that measure processes as well as products and that extend over a period of time rather than assessing single events. As Roberta Camp (1993) suggests, performance assessment and portfolios reflect these directions. Performance assessment requires students to reason through *how* a problem might be solved, while portfolios, through their multiple drafts, indicate what stages of change and improvement the student's work has undergone over time. In fact, because portfolios allow students to demonstrate their ability to write in a variety of modes for different audiences, portfolios are, in the view of the CCCC Assessment Committee (1995), apt to foster better classroom practices and to give students a true picture of what good writing means. Moreover, as discussed in Chapter 4, the reflective component of most portfolio programs has been instrumental in helping students learn to assess their own strengths and weaknesses, and self-assessment is surely a key instructional goal.

Still other trends include reexamining such terms of test theory as validity. Camp (1993) stresses the importance of defining validity broadly enough so that the value of the assessment is understood not only in terms of how well it measures what it intends to measure, but also in terms of how it is used—namely, the inferences that are made about the students and the consequences those inferences have on instruction (p. 61). Because assessment drives instruction, the CCCC Committee likewise emphasizes the value of having assessment demonstrate "systemic validity" by fostering sound instructional practices in the teaching and evaluation of writing.

Assessment Knowledge and the Role of Faculty

While endorsing the value of these new trends, Richard Stiggins (1995) cautions that no single assessment approach can serve the variety of purposes for which assessment is used. He argues instead that a balanced approach to assessment is necessary, a balance that acknowledges the importance of traditional, as well as performance-based, assessments. Only through an improved understanding of assessment, he stresses, can educators support using various assessment approaches to meet such different instructional goals as ascertaining students' grasp of content material, ability to reason, mastery of certain skills, or ability to apply knowledge by creating an effective product (pp. 241–242).

Finally, the involvement of faculty is viewed as increasingly important in assessment issues. Peter Johnston (1987) emphasizes the value of training teachers to become sensitive observers of their students' performances, while Richard Stiggins argues on behalf of having teachers, as well as administrators, enhance their knowledge of assessment issues. Roberta Camp (1993) also believes that teachers will be further involved in formulating writing assessments (p. 71). In a similar vein, the CCCC Assessment Committee (1995) encourages faculty to become informed about writing assessment and to participate in all stages of its use (p. 435).

Such knowledgeable participation by teachers is critical if they are to influence the future directions that writing assessment takes. Teachers often view external writing assessment with some distrust, feeling that their own performance in the classroom is, along with their students' performance, on the line. Certainly, that has been the case with those of us who teach in the Writing Center at the university. One of our non-credit programs has entailed providing individualized writing assistance to students who have repeatedly failed the essay portion of a state examination. After working with students individually over a semester or two, we are intensely concerned with their results. We are elated when they pass, and we are disturbed when some do not. We may recognize and acknowledge to one another a particular student's severe language problems or difficulties with essay development, but, when a student fails, we also reflect on our own teaching, wondering to ourselves what we might have done differently to help that student.

The same ambivalence toward external writing assessment arises when those of us who taught the developmental classes in the Writing Center met to score portfolios or essays for program evaluation. Although the portfolios were selected through random sampling, we found ourselves hoping that the portfolios chosen from our classes would be those of our best students. The consequences were not personally serious for us if our students did not perform well, but ultimately there was no way to avoid the sense of responsibility that we felt for our students' "surrogate" performance on writing samples or portfolios that were externally scored.

Precisely because teachers often feel the pressure—either real or imaginary—of accountability, it is essential that they become involved in external writing assessments. Their involvement can take several forms: With the firsthand knowledge of students that comes from close observation, teachers can be influential in designing effective, accessible, and fair topics in direct writing assessments; similarly, they can participate in the field testing and external reviews of topics already developed. Knowledgeable as well about the limitations of direct writing assessments, teachers can encourage assessment committees to provide students with extra time, opportunities to discuss topics, and access to dictionaries or other resources. Moreover, they can include some opportunities within their classrooms to enable their students to practice writing and revising under timed constraints. They can adopt portfolios in their own classes and work at finding ways to close the gap between internal and external portfolio assessments.

Teachers can also, if possible, participate in external writing assessments (of either portfolios or single samples) and thereby familiarize themselves with the scoring criteria and with group discussions of good writing. Even if they cannot participate in such scorings, they can still make themselves familiar with scoring procedures and with the criteria so that they can conduct smaller scorings in their schools, creating their own local communities of scorers and establishing some ownership in the process. Through these means they can share with their students and their colleagues the criteria on which papers are graded in external assessments. Given the many standards for good writing, such familiarity with the criteria is critical for all concerned.

Moreover, while recognizing the limitations of most scoring approaches—whether holistic, analytic, or primary trait—teachers can nonetheless push strongly for *human scorers* so that computers, with their mechanical counting of syllables and words, do not become substitutes for the human interchange between writer and reader that lies at the heart of communication.

Teachers can, through local school or district committees, serve as a bridge between the public and their state assessment departments, explaining to parents the goals and emphases of the instructional writing program while, at the same time, discussing with assessment officials ways in which writing instruction and writing assessment may become more closely aligned. By understanding the complexities of writing assessment—appreciating both the technical limitations and the instructional strengths of portfolios, for example—teachers can become a powerful force for communicating what the ideal of writing assessment should be.

Summary

Hence, the directive of the CCCC Assessment Committee for faculty to become involved seems a fitting point on which to end the main body of this monograph. The central purpose of this text has been, after all, to enhance teachers' understanding of assessment issues so that they can become increasingly involved in those external writing assessments that often have an impact—direct or indirect—in their classrooms.

As this chapter underscores, the issues are complex, and tension often exists between the possibility of new directions that writing assessment can take and the reality of what actually occurs. While the ideal form of writing assessment remains one that is dynamic, equitable, instructionally effective, technically sound, and context-based, this ideal is far from being fully realized. But despite the problems in developing forms that meet these ideals—despite the ripples that still appear in the glass of writing assessment—writing assessment is likely to continue to play a role in the restructuring of the nation's schools. That is as it should be, for writing as a fundamental conveyor of language and critical thought continues even in this age of multimedia to reflect much of who we are and what we teach in our classrooms. The ideal form of writing assessment may remain elusive, but its ultimate goal of improving all students' learning is surely worth striving to attain.

Postlude: In My View

In this text I have tried to present a balanced perspective on writing assessment—the strengths and weaknesses of each assessment approach; the advantages and limitations of the scoring methods; technical efforts to link numbers with words; the impact of writing assessment in other disciplines; and, most seriously, the issues of equity that writing assessment raises. My purpose in attempting this balance is so that you as an individual teacher-reader can be informed about the complexities of writing assessment and make your own decisions and contributions to your school based on that knowledge.

Now I would like to offer my own critical reflections about writing assessment based on my experiences as a teacher and as one who has been involved in all phases of writing assessment for many years.

Impact of Writing Assessment

I do not view writing assessment with the hostility or dismay that many people seem to feel, nor am I troubled by the notion of having numerical scores assigned to the essays or portfolios that students write—scores that may then be used for comparative purposes across classes or schools. Scores are, for me, simply symbolic shortcuts—in much the same way that letter grades are—for the ideal narrative evaluations of students' writing.

Indeed, I think the increased attention to writing assessment in many places and at many levels has had positive results over the past few years. I think of one local elementary school that, since implementing a fourth-grade writing assessment, has increased its writing scores substantially despite its large number of economically disadvantaged students. When asked how that increase was achieved, the principal replied that a whole culture of writing had been established in the school, with students immersed in many kinds of writing and for many purposes. Perhaps that culture would have been established anyway without the impetus of a state-mandated writing assessment, but there can be no arguing that those children have benefitted far more from such an emphasis on writing than mere scores can ever convey.

Contextual Assessment

I believe that local context is important in writing assessment, both for the test takers and for the scorers, who must understand the purposes of the writing and the backgrounds of the writers (see Huot, 1996). However, I also think that writing assessment is no less meaningful and no less valid when it is removed from a local context. If one of the central purposes of writing is communication, and that is certainly the case given the growing emphasis on global communication, then it follows that writing can be assessed in more than just local contexts. Indeed the possibility of permanence that writing offers, as opposed to most forms of electronic communication, argues for a broader view of writing assessment than adherents of contextual assessment imply.

My own experiences support this broader view. I have participated in far too many scorings—including analytic, holistic, and primary trait scorings, both of portfolios and of single samples—to think that assessment of writing can be meaningful *only* if it is grounded in a local context. When a group of us in Florida holistically scored essays written by middle school youngsters in Tennessee, we did not need to know the full dimensions of their writing project to score their essays holistically in a compassionate and effective way; similarly, we did not need to know the full scope of the project in a school district in the Northeast that resulted in our scoring, on a primary trait scale, the essays written by young students there. In the first instance, the rubric that we devised from actual papers, and, in the latter instance, the rubric that we obtained from the National Assessment of Educational Progress (NAEP), enabled us to approach both tasks with the same care we give our local or state exams. In the same vein, we found that English teachers from many school levels in our county who attended the portfolio training workshop were able to score successfully the portfolios created by one class of seventh graders. My view seems supported by Michael Allen's research (1995), which showed that portfolio readers were largely able to agree on their evaluations of portfolios from other college programs throughout the country even when they disliked some of the programs themselves. Thus, while contextualized assessment that is tied to the curriculum may be preferred, it is not the only form in which a meaningful writing assessment can be undertaken.

Placement Context

Likewise, I do not think that one has to be immersed in teaching first-year composition in order to place students effectively in the appropriate course. For several years, many first-year students at my institution were placed into the appropriate composition class by means of the SAT-II written essay, combined with multiple-choice results. But when students did not take the national exam beforehand, we—as local scorers and local English teachers at varying educational levels—were able to use the same rubric as the national scorers and place students at the appropriate level of first-year composition. To be sure, the students were part of a local context (and our English Department determined the necessary scores for placement), but they were part of a larger context as well—namely, new students at a competitive university, and not unlike many entering first-year students at other institutions across the country. Likewise, the scorers were part of both a local and a larger discourse community, one in which, despite varying grade levels and varying emphases, concerns about writing prevailed. Such scoring was, furthermore, not irrevocable in that a student who was placed inappropriately could often be placed satisfactorily once classes began.

Scoring Rubrics

In my view, the strength of scoring rubrics or guides—especially those derived descriptively rather than prescriptively—lies in the openness with which scoring criteria are revealed, not only for scorers but also for students. It is precisely this demystifying of criteria that has contributed to the increased use of scoring rubrics and to efforts by parents and teachers to devise these rubrics themselves for some subject areas (Kirby-Linton, Lyle, & White, December 1996–January 1997). The rubrics suggest that external criteria do exist, criteria that readers, when trained and monitored in their use, can apply effectively to particular essays or portfolios. These criteria are, as Louise Rosenblatt (1988) suggests, important for transactional (or what she calls "efferent") writing, which is what is being assessed in most instances of student writing.

Furthermore, just as the new *Standards for the English Language Arts* (1996) stresses the importance of motivating students to link their knowledge with their own lives (p. 44), the existence of criteria serves to guide students toward the self-assessment that is the ultimate goal. The emphasis on descriptive criteria in particular is important because it addresses not only the demand for criteria that reflect reality rather than an abstract ideal, but also the need for teachers to be involved at all stages of writing assessment. External writing assessment need not be implemented by top-down decree; rather, it should be based on the bottom-up expertise of teachers who are knowledgeable, trained, and involved.

Training and Reliability

My doctoral dissertation (Wolcott, 1989) corroborates the importance of training and monitoring as a way of providing scorers with guidance and enabling them to respond as real readers of a text, not just as evaluators. However, the real value of the training—in addition to the rubrics—is that a reader's individual response is tempered by a sense of group expectations established *usually by consensus* through the interpretive discourse community formed by readers. This effort to establish some reliability among readers—some sense of agreement in a writing assessment—is, I believe, crucial. I personally find appalling the current efforts as noted in Chapter 12 to obtain higher interrater reliability by means of computer scoring. But the idea of reliability, at least when it applies to human scorers, is linked to the notion of fairness, so that each student's essay or portfolio is being evaluated by readers who are looking at it through somewhat comparable prisms, and not through idiosyncratic lenses that may make one reader decide an essay is worth a *4* on a six-point scale and another reader rate the same work on the same scale as a *1*. Of course, some differences among readers can be genuine and legitimate, but wide variations would surely be confusing or difficult for writers to interpret. (How is a student-writer likely to interpret a high score given by one reader and a bottom score given by another, other than as "proof" that there are no commonalities at all for acceptable writing?) While interrater reliability, as discussed in Chapter 9, should not be the sole objective of writing assessment—and should never be obtained at the expense of human readers—the notion of reliability suggests that readers are attempting to evaluate writing on a comparable basis, which is certainly fairer to the students whose writing is being assessed. Even with rubrics, assessing writing is not an exact science (as is surely illustrated when an essay receives one score on one occasion and a different score on a different occasion). But the explicit criteria of the rubrics, combined with the training and monitoring of scorers, enable scorers to assess writing at least somewhat comparably in a context beyond that of personally situated knowledge. The current development of rubrics for the written portion of many content-area performance assessments is a natural extension of their use in writing assessment.

Holistic Scoring and Analytic Scoring

I believe holistic scoring to be the best method for large-scale assessments, not only because it enables large numbers of papers to be scored at a reasonable expenditure of time and personnel, but also, and more significantly, because it requires scorers to weigh each essay *as a whole.* While holistic scoring can be used productively in a classroom as well, and while I certainly agree that writing is more than a sum of its separate components, I still find analytic scoring to be most useful for instructional purposes. Analytic scoring provides specific feedback for students so that they have a sense of what they can do to improve on their revisions. Even when they are given holistic scoring rubrics, for instance, students often cannot tell exactly what particular element of each score point on the rubric—for example, language, organization, or development—may need to be improved in their own essays. In my view, then, holistic scoring and analytic scoring both have their uses, depending on the purpose of the assessment.

Portfolio Assessment and Direct Writing Assessment

Furthermore, I heartily endorse portfolios, both for classroom instruction and for external assessment. They take time—time to prepare for, to reflect upon, and to revise—but the finished record they provide is far more complete and rewarding than single assessments can ever be. They blend the writing process with the writing product and tie assessment closely to instruction within a student-centered classroom. Despite my preference for portfolios as an assessment tool, I still find impromptu essays to be very useful in some circumstances. Such pre-post essays, for example, served effectively to provide, along with portfolios, one means of evaluating my developmental writing program. Other than being factored into students' final course grades, the essays were not high-stakes for the students. I applaud the efforts undertaken by some school systems to provide for prewriting, revising, and use of resources in the assessment period so that the impromptu essay at least approximates the conditions of the writing process.

Portfolios are more time-consuming to score than single essays, whether the scoring approach used is holistic or analytic, and indeed it can be hard for readers to retain mentally all the entries of a portfolio before assigning it a single score. However, a random sampling of portfolios appears to suffice for most program purposes. With sufficient training, teachers are likely to be able to score portfolios as effectively as they can single samples. In fact, I favor having portfolios offered as a possible alternative to impromptu essays for high-stakes assessments. For example, when students who speak English as a second language or a second dialect, or who have learning disabilities, are unable after several tries to pass the single impromptu essay component of the state college exam, I would like to see them given the chance to demonstrate their writing proficiency through portfolios. When I wear my "teaching hat," as opposed to my "assessment hat," I know full well the struggle that many of these students undergo. Thus, I would like the same alternatives to exist for them in high-stakes assessments that Holt and Baker (1991) described at Southeast Missouri State—alternatives that take into account students' particular situations. Although authorship might arise as an issue in such high-stakes portfolios, the possibility of plagiarism or other forms of cheating could be reduced if drafts and some impromptu entries were made a part of the portfolio requirements.

The apparent conflict between the statistical requirements of classical test theory and writing assessment is as troublesome to me as it is to many of my English colleagues. I chafe at some statistical concepts—at the idea that two adjacent holistic scores on a four-point holistic scale may not always demonstrate sufficient rater reliability, for example, since many papers do indeed exemplify a straddle between two scores, such as a 3 and a 2. And when I have been thrilled at pre-post program improvement as shown in our students' impromptu essays, I do not like to hear of the statistical limitations that prevent me from drawing that conclusion with absolute confidence. At the same time, I recognize the importance of such technical requirements, and I acknowledge, with my test and measurement colleagues, the limitations of having only single writing samples on which to base decisions. I am pleased to see serious attention being paid to "consequential validity," to what Linn, Baker, and Dunbar (1991) call the "intended and unintended effects of assessments on the ways teachers and students spend their time and think about the goals of education" (p. 17). In the course of helping students to prepare for portfolio assessments, for example, will teachers end up having to restrict their curriculum? Or, alternately, will formulaic writing be the result of helping students to prepare for direct writing assessments? As Linn, Baker, and Dunbar stress, thinking through the unintentional, as well as the direct, results of assessment becomes imperative. Moreover, the cautionary words of Blaine Worthen (1993) have remained fixed in my mind—namely, that not only must authentic assessment be genuine and meaningful in order to be effective, but also it must meet enough technical criteria to represent faithfully what students can do in certain areas (p. 448).

Significance of Writing Assessment

I believe that writing assessment, as a forerunner of the entire alternative assessment movement, has indeed improved teaching and learning. Despite its limitations (of which there are many), writing assessment has resulted in a new emphasis on actual writing in all levels of many schools—that is, emphasis on the thinking and composing processes and stages that result in the better *understanding* and *production* of writing, and not merely the *recognition* of writing elements as multiple-choice tests often required. To the teachers who come together to form scoring discourse communities (and I remain a strong advocate of having teachers, rather than external agencies, score the writing assessments), each essay or portfolio remains a unique piece of communication between a student-composer and a teacher-scorer who do not know each other. As such, a writing assessment presents one occasion on which students write for a broader literacy community than their classroom teacher or peers. Indeed, in the requirement it makes of students to write to a *different* audience, a writing assessment serves to fulfill one part of the *Standards for the English Language Arts* (1996, p. 35). Similarly, writing assessment represents one of the occasions on which teachers see and evaluate the work of a broader literacy community than that of their own students whose work they regularly grade. This broadening of perspective and purpose—in contrast to focusing inward on only the local classroom context—surely befits the growing tendency toward global communication and remains one value of external writing assessment.

Willa Wolcott
February 1998

References

Abbott, A., Bonnick, L., Bultman, G., & Henry, D. J. (1994, November). *Portfolios: Tilling, sowing, and reaping in the field of student writing.* Paper presented at the Conference of the National Council of Teachers of English, Orlando, FL.

Allen, M. S. (1995). Valuing differences: Portnet's first year. *Assessing Writing, 2,* 67–90.

American Educational Research Association, American Psychological Association, & National Council on Measurement in Education. (1985). *Standards for educational and psychological testing.* Washington, DC: Author.

Applebee, A., Langer, J., & Mullis, I. V. S. (1989). *Understanding direct writing assessments: Reflections on a South Carolina writing study.* Princeton, NJ: Educational Testing Service.

Applebee, A., Langer, J., Mullis, I. V. S., & Jenkins, L. (1990). *The writing report card, 1984–88: Findings from the nation's report card.* Princeton, NJ: Educational Testing Service, National Assessment of Educational Progress.

Atwell, N. (1987). *In the middle: Writing, reading, and learning with adolescents.* Portsmouth, NH: Boynton/Cook, Heinemann.

Ball, A. (1992). Cultural preference and the expository writing of African-American adolescents. *Written Communication, 9,* 501–532.

Barritt, L., Stock, P., & Clark, F. (1986). Researching practice: Evaluating assessment essays. *College Composition and Communication, 37,* 315–327.

Bartholomae, D. (1985). Inventing the university. In M. Rose (Ed.), *When a writer can't write: Studies in writer's block and other composing-process problems* (pp. 134–165). New York: Guilford Press.

Belanoff, P. (1991). The myth of assessment. *Journal of Basic Writing, 10*(1), 54–66.

Belanoff, P., & Elbow, P. (1991). Using portfolios to increase collaboration and community in a writing program. In P. Belanoff & M. Dickson (Eds.), *Portfolios: Process and product* (pp. 17–36). Portsmouth, NH: Boynton-Cook/Heinemann.

Bereiter, C. (1980). Development in writing. In L. Gregg & E. Steinberg (Eds.), *Cognitive processes in writing* (pp. 73–97). Hillsdale, NJ: Erlbaum.

Boomer, G. (1985). The assessment of writing. In P. J. A. Evans (Ed.), *Directions and misdirections in English evaluation* (pp. 63–64). Ottawa, Canada: Canadian Council of Teachers of English.

Braddock, R., Lloyd-Jones, R., & Schoer, L. (1963). *Research in written composition.* Urbana, IL: National Council of Teachers of English.

Breland, H., Camp, R., Jones, R., Morris, M., & Rock, D. (1987). *Assessing writing skill* (Research Monograph No. 11). New York: College Board Publications.

Breland, H. M., & Jones, R. J. (1984). Perceptions of writing skills. *Written Communication, 1,* 101–119.

Breland, H. M., & Jones, R. J. (1988). *Remote scoring of essays.* (College Board Report No. 88-3, ETS RR No. 88-4). New York: College Entrance Examination Board.

Bridgeman, B., Hale, G. A., Lewis, C., Pollack, J., & Wang, M. (1992). *Placement validity of a prototype SAT with an essay.* (RR-92–28). Princeton, NJ: Educational Testing Service.

Britton, J., Burgess, T., Martin, N., McLeod, A., & Rosen, H. (1975). *The development of writing abilities (11–18).* Schools Council: Project on Written Language of 11–18 Year-Olds. London: MacMillan Education.

Brossell, G., & Ash, B. H. (1984). An experiment with the wording of essay topics. *College Composition and Communication, 35,* 423–425.

Brown, A., & Palincsar, A. (1989). Guided, cooperative learning and individual knowledge acquisition. In L. Resnick (Ed.), *Knowing, learning, and instruction: Essays in honor of Robert Glaser* (pp. 393–453). Hillsdale, NJ: Erlbaum.

Bruffee, K. A. (1986). Social construction, language, and the authority of knowledge: A bibliographical essay. *College English, 48,* 773–790.

Buschman, L. (1993). *Sharing portfolios: Students and teachers doing assessment together.* Portland, OR: NWEA Institute of Alternative Assessment.

Calfee, R. C., & Perfumo, P. (1993). Student portfolios: Opportunities for a revolution in assessment. *Journal of Reading, 36,* 532–537.

Calfee, R., & Perfumo, P. (1994, December). Portfolio assessment: For better or worse? *National Center for the Study of Writing and Literacy [NCSWL] Briefs on Writing,* 1–4.

Camp, R. (1990). Thinking together about portfolios. *Quarterly of the National Writing Project and the Center for the Study of Writing and Literacy, 12*(2), 8–14, 27.

Camp, R. (1993). Changing the model for the direct assessment of writing. In M Williamson & B. Huot (Eds.), *Validating holistic scoring for writing assessment* (pp. 45–78).Cresskill, NJ: Hampton Press.

Camp, R., & Levine, D. S. (1991). Portfolios evolving: Background and variations in sixth- through twelfth-grade classrooms. In P. Belanoff & M. Dickson (Eds.), *Portfolios: Process and product* (pp. 194–205). Portsmouth, NH: Boynton-Cook/Heinemann.

Campbell, D. T., & Fiske, D. W. (1959). Convergent and discriminant validation by the multitrait-multimethod matrix. *Psychological Bulletin, 56,* 81–105.

Cantor, N. K., & Hoover, H. D. (1986). *The reliability and validity of writing assessment: An investigation of rater prompt within mode, and prompt between mode sources of error.* University of Iowa.

Carlson, S., & Bridgeman, B. (1986). Testing ESL student writers. In K. Greenberg, H. Wiener, & R. Donovan (Eds.), *Writing assessment: Issues and strategies* (pp. 126–163). New York: Longman.

Carson, C. (1991, Winter). Why math portfolios? *Portfolio News, 2*(2), 6.

CCCC Committee on Assessment. (1995). Writing assessment: A position statement. *College Composition and Communication, 46,* 430–437.

Charney, D. (1984). The validity of using holistic scoring to evaluate writing: A critical overview. *Research in the Teaching of English, 18,* 65–81.

Charney, D., & Carlson, R. (1995). Learning to write in a genre: What student writers take from model texts. *Research in the Teaching of English, 29*(1), 88–125.

Cherry, R., & Meyer, P. (1993). Reliability issues in holistic assessment. In M. Williamson & B. Huot (Eds.), *Validating holistic scoring for writing assessment* (pp. 109–141). Cresskill, NJ: Hampton Press.

Clark, I. (1993a). Portfolio evaluation, collaboration, and writing centers. *College Composition and Communication, 44,* 515–524.

Clark, I. (1993b). Portfolio grading and the writing center. *Writing Center Journal, 13*(2), 48–62.

College Entrance Examination Board. (1993). *College Board Writing Service Leader's Guide and Reader's Scoring Guide.* Author.

Cooper, C. (1977). Holistic evaluation of writing. In C. R. Cooper & L. Odell (Eds.), *Evaluating writing: Describing, measuring, judging* (pp. 3–31). Urbana, IL: National Council of Teachers of English.

Cooper, W. (1990, Fall). Look what they've done to my song (Editorial). *Portfolio News, 2*(1), 8–10.

Costa, A. (1993). How world-class standards will change us. *Educational Leadership, 50*(5), 50–51.

Cronbach, L. J. (1971). Test validation. In R. L. Thorndike (Ed.). *Educational measurement* (2nd ed., pp. 443–507). Washington, DC: American Council on Education.

Crowhurst, M., & Piché, G. L. (1979). Audience and mode of discourse effects on syntactic complexity in writing at two grade levels. *Research in the Teaching of English, 13,* 101–109.

Darling-Hammond, L. (1994). Performance-based assessment and educational equity. *Harvard Educational Review, 64,* 5–30.

Davies, J. (1991, Summer). Portfolios for good or evil (Editorial). *Portfolio News, 2*(4), 8.

Davis, A., & Felknor, C. (1994). The demise of performance-based graduation in Littleton. *Educational Leadership, 51*(6), 64–65.

Davis, B. G., Scriven, M., & Thomas, S. (1987). *The evaluation of composition instruction.* New York: Teachers College Press.

Despain, L., & Hilgers, T. (1992). Readers' responses to the rating of non-uniform portfolios: Are there limits on portfolios' utility? *WPA: Writing Program Administration, 16,* 24–37.

Diederich, P. B. (1974). *Measuring growth in English.* Urbana, IL: National Council of Teachers of English.

Diederich, P., French, J., & Carlton, S. (1961). *Factors in judgments of writing ability.* Princeton, NJ: Educational Testing Service. (ERIC Document Reproduction Service No. ED 002 172)

Dorans, N. J., & Schmitt, A. P. (1990, November). *Constructed response and differential item functioning: A pragmatic approach.* Paper presented at the ETS Conference, Constructed vs. Choice in Cognitive Measurement, Educational Testing Service, Princeton, NJ.

Duke, D. R., & Strong, W. J. (1988). *Utah pilot writing assessment for grades 3 and 8: Final report.* Salt Lake City, UT: Utah State Office of Education. (ERIC Document Reproduction Service No. ED 301 886)

Dunbar, S. B., Koretz, D., & Hoover, H. D. (1991). Quality control in the development and use of performance assessments. *Applied Measurement in Education, 4,* 289–303.

Eisner, E. (1993). Why standards may not improve schools. *Educational Leadership, 50*(5), 22–23.

Elbow, P. (1986). *Embracing contraries: Explorations in learning and teaching.* New York: Oxford University Press.

Elbow, P. (1991). Foreword. In P. Belanoff & M. Dickson (Eds.), *Portfolios: Process and product* (pp. ix–xvi). Portsmouth, NH: Boynton-Cook/Heinemann.

Elbow, P. (1993). Ranking, evaluating, and liking: Sorting out three forms of judgment. *College English, 55,* 187–206.

Emig, J. (1971). *The composing processes of twelfth graders.* Urbana, IL: National Council of Teachers of English. (ERIC Document Reproduction No. ED 058 205)

Engelhard, G., Gordon, B., & Gabrielson, S. (1992). The influences of mode of discourse, experiential demand, and gender on the quality of student writing. *Research in the Teaching of English, 26,* 315–336.

Faigley, L., Cherry, R., Jolliffe, D., & Skinner, A. (1985). The development of performance assessment. In L. Faigley (Ed.), *Assessing writers' knowledge and processes of composing* (pp. 103–117). Norwood, NJ: Ablex.

Farr, M. (1993). Essayist literacy and other verbal performances. *Written Communication, 10,* 4–38.

Fitzgerald, K. (1994). Computerized scoring? A question of theory and practice. *Journal of Basic Writing, 13*(2), 3–17.

Fitzpatrick, A. R., Erickan, K., & Yen, W. M. (1994, April). *The consistency between ratings collected in different test years.* Paper presented at the annual meeting of the National Council on Measurement in Education.

Flower, L., & Hayes, J. (1981). A cognitive process theory of writing. *College Composition and Communication, 32,* 365–387.

Fox, T. (1993). Standards and access. *Journal of Basic Writing, 12*(1), 37–45.

Freedman, R. L. H. (1993, Winter). Writing, student portfolios, and authentic assessment in science. *Portfolio News, 4*(2), 6, 17.

Freedman, S. W. (1979). How characteristics of student essays influence teachers' evaluations. *Journal of Educational Psychology, 71,* 328–338.

Freedman, S. W. (1981). Influences on evaluators of expository essays: Beyond the text. *Research in the Teaching of English, 15,* 245–255.

Freedman, S. W. (1984). The registers of student and professional expository writing: Influences on teachers' responses. In R. Beach & L. S. Bridwell (Eds.), *New directions in composition research* (pp. 334–347). New York: Guilford Press.

Freedman, S. W., & Calfee, R. C. (1983). Holistic assessment of writing: Experimental design and cognitive theory. In P. Mosenthal, L. Tamor, & S. A. Walmsley (Eds.), *Research on writing: Principles and methods* (pp. 75–98). New York: Longman.

French, R. (1991). *Issues and uses of student portfolios in program assessment.* Paper presented as part of a "Symposium examining assessment strategies of the Next Century Schools Project" at the American Educational Research Association, Chicago, IL.

Fuller, D. A. (1985). Evaluation and curriculum: A case study of primary trait scoring. *Dissertation Abstracts International, 46*(09), 2601A. (University Microfilms No. DA8525327)

Gearhart, M., Herman, J., Novak, J., & Wolf, S. (1995). Toward the instructional utility of large-scale writing assessment: Validation of a new narrative rubric. *Assessing Writing, 2,* 207–242.

Gentile, C. (1992). *Exploring new methods for collecting students' school-based writing: NAEP's 1990 Portfolio Study.* Washington, DC: National Center for Education Statistics, Office of Educational Research and Improvement, U.S. Department of Education.

Gilbert, P. (1980). The effects of a primary trait scoring guide on the reliability, validity, and time used in teacher evaluation of student writing. *Dissertation Abstracts International, 41*(10), 4370A. (University Microfilms No. DA8107326)

Godshalk, F., Swineford, F., & Coffman, W. E. (1966). *The measurement of writing ability.* New York: College Entrance Examination Board.

Gorrell, D. (1988). *Writing assessment and the new approaches.* St. Cloud, MN: St. Cloud State University. (ERIC Document Reproduction Service No. ED 296 334)

Graham, S., Harris, K., MacArthur, C., & Schwartz, S. (1991). Writing instruction. In B. Y. L. Wong (Ed.), *Learning about learning disabilities* (pp. 309–343). Orlando, FL: Academic Press, Inc.

Graves, D. H. (1983). *Writing: Teachers and children at work.* Exeter, NH: Heinemann Educational Books.

Greenberg, K. (1981). The effects of variations in essay questions on the writing performance of college freshmen. *Dissertation Abstracts International, 42*(02), 685A. (University Microfilms No. DA8115492)

Greenberg, K. (1992). Validity and reliability issues in the direct assessment of writing. *WPA: Writing Program Administration, 16,* 7–22.

Guskey, T. (1994). *High stakes performance assessment: Perspectives on Kentucky's educational reform.* Thousand Oaks, CA: Corwin Press.

Hake, R. (1986). How do we judge what they write? In K. Greenberg, M. Wiener, & R. Donovan (Eds.), *Writing assessment: Issues and strategies* (pp. 153–168). New York: Longman.

Hamp-Lyons, L. (1995). Uncovering possibilities for a constructivist paradigm for writing assessment (Review). *College Composition and Communication, 46,* 446–455.

Hamp-Lyons, L., & Condon, W. (1993). Questioning assumptions about portfolio-based assessment. *College Composition and Communication, 44,* 176–190.

Hancock, C. L. (1995). Implementing the assessment standards for school mathematics: Enhancing mathematics learning with open-ended questions. *Mathematics Teacher, 88*(6), 496–499.

Harris, W. H. (1977). Teacher response to student writing: A study of the response patterns of high school English teachers to determine the basis for teacher judgment of student writing. *Research in the Teaching of English, 11,* 175–185.

Haswell, R. (1988). Dark shadows: The fate of writers at the bottom. *College Composition and Communication, 39,* 303–315.

Haviland, C. P., & Clark, J. M. (1992). What can our students tell us about essay examination designs and practices? *Journal of Basic Writing, 11*(2), 47–60.

Hewitt, G. (1995). *A portfolio primer: Teaching, collecting, and assessing student writing.* Portsmouth, NH: Heinemann.

Hills, J. R. (1993, Fall). Regression effects in educational measurement. *Educational Measurement: Issues and Practice, 12,* 31–34.

Hinojosa, T. (1993, Spring). A proposal for a science student portfolio system. *Portfolio News, 4*(3), 6, 17.

Hoetker, J. (1982). Essay examination topics and students' writing. *College Composition and Communication, 33,* 377–392.

Hoetker, J., & Brossell, G. (1986). A procedure for writing content-fair essay examination topics for large-scale writing assessments. *College Composition and Communication, 37,* 328–335.

Holt, D., & Baker, N. (1991). Portfolios as a follow-up option in a proficiency-testing program. In P. Belanoff & M. Dickson (Eds.), *Portfolios: Process and product* (pp. 37–45). Portsmouth, NH: Boynton-Cook/Heinemann.

Horton, P., Fronk, R., & Walton, R. (1985). The effect of writing assignments on achievement in college general chemistry. *Journal of Research in Science Teaching, 22*(6), 535–541.

Howard, K. (1990). Making the writing portfolio real. *The Quarterly of the National Writing Project and the Center for the Study of Writing and Literacy, 12,* 4–7.

Hrach, E. (1983). The influence of rater characteristics on composition evaluation practices. *Dissertation Abstracts International, 45*(02), 440. (University Microfilms No. DA8410956)

Hult, C. (1987). Assessment topics: The importance of the rhetorical frame. *Writing Program Administration Journal, 10,* 19–28.

Huot, B. (1988). The validity of holistic scoring: A comparison of the talk-aloud protocols of expert and novice holistic raters. *Dissertation Abstracts International, 49*(08A), 2188A. (University Microfilms No. DA8817872)

Huot, B. (1990). The literature of direct writing assessments: Major concerns and prevailing trends. *Review of Educational Research, 60,* 237–263.

Huot, B. (1993). The influence of holistic scoring procedures on reading and rating student essays. In M. Williamson & B. Huot (Eds.), *Validating holistic scoring for writing assessment* (pp. 206–236). Cresskill, NJ: Hampton Press.

Huot, B. (1996). Toward a new theory of writing assessment. *College Composition and Communication, 47*(4), 549–566.

Janopoulos, M. (1993). Comprehension, communicative competence, and construct validity: Holistic scoring from an ESL perspective. In M. Williamson & B. Huot (Eds.), *Validating holistic scoring for writing assessment* (pp. 303–327). Cresskill, NJ: Hampton Press.

Johnston, P. (1987). Assessing the process, and the process of assessment, in the language arts. In J. R. Squire (Ed.), *The dynamics of language learning: Research in reading and English* (pp. 335–357). Urbana, IL: ERIC Clearinghouse on Reading and Communication Skills and the National Conference on Research in English.

Keech, C. (1982). Practices in designing writing test prompts: Analysis and recommendations. In J. Gray & L. Ruth (Eds.), *Properties of writing tasks: A study of alternative procedures for holistic writing assessment.* Berkeley: University of California, Graduate School of Education, Bay Area Writing Project. (ERIC Document Reproduction Service No. 230 576)

Kegley, P. H. (1986). The effect of mode discourse on student writing performance: Implications for policy. *Educational Evaluation and Policy Analysis, 8,* 147–154.

Kinzer, C., Carroll, K., & Murphy, S. (1982). The writing prompt: Differences in expectations among participants in a writing test episode. In J. Gray & L. Ruth (Eds.), *Properties of writing tasks: A study of alternative procedures for holistic writing assessment* (pp. 397–410). Berkeley: University of California, Graduate School of Education, Bay Area Writing Project. (ERIC Document Reproduction Service No. 230 576)

Kinzer, C., & Murphy, S. (1982). The effects of assessment prompt and response variables on holistic score: A pilot study and validation of an analysis technique. In J. Gray & L. Ruth (Eds.), *Properties of writing tasks: A study of alternative procedures for holistic writing assessment* (pp. 317–332). Berkeley: University of California, Graduate School of Educaiton, Bay Area Writing Project. (ERIC Document Reproduction Service No. 230 576)

Kirby-Linton, K., Lyle, N., & White, S. (Dec. 1996/Jan. 1997). When parents and teachers create writing standards. *Educational Leadership, 54*(4), 30–32.

Kirszner, L., Jussawalla, F., & Mandell, S. (1990). *Writing in the disciplines.* Fort Worth, TX: Holt, Rinehart and Winston.

Koretz, D., Stecher, B., Klein, S., & McCaffrey, D. (1994). The Vermont Portfolio Assessment Program: Findings and implications. *Educational Measurement: Issues and Practice, 13*(3), 5–16.

Langer, J. (1984). Where problems start: The effects of available information on responses to school writing tasks. In A. N. Applebee (Ed.), *Contexts for learning to write: Studies of secondary school instruction* (pp. 135–148). Norwood, NJ: Ablex.

Leahy, R. (1992). Competency testing and the writing center. *WPA: Writing Program Administration, 15,* 41–56.

Leder, J. R. (1991). An echo of genesis: An assessment of the business-writing portfolio. In P. Belanoff & M. Dickson (Eds.), *Portfolios: Process and product* (pp. 123–136). Portsmouth, NH: Boynton-Cook/Heinemann.

Lederman, M. J. (1986). Why test? In K. Greenberg, H. Wiener, & R. Donovan (Eds.), *Writing assessment: Issues and strategies* (pp. 34–46). New York: Longman.

Legg, S., Wolcott, W., Henry, D. J., Bonnick, L., Christensen, V., Howland, R., Ketts, S., Martin, S., & Shaughnessy, A. (1994). *A framework for training teachers in portfolio assessment.* Tallahassee, FL: Florida Department of Education.

Leki, I. (1992). *Understanding ESL writers: A guide for teachers.* Portsmouth, NH: Boynton-Cook/Heinemann.

Linn, R. L. (1993). Linking the results of distinct assessments. *Applied Measurement in Education, 6,* 83–102.

Linn, R., Baker, E., & Dunbar, S. (1991). Complex, performance-based assessment: Expectations and validation criteria. *Educational Researcher, 20*(8), 15–21.

Lloyd-Jones, R. (1977). Primary trait scoring. In C. Cooper & L. Odell (Eds.), *Evaluating writing: Describing, measuring, judging* (pp. 33–69). Urbana, IL: National Council of Teachers of English.

Lucas, C. (1993, Spring). Writing portfolios: Changes and challenges. *Portfolio News, 4*(3), 1, 7–11.

MacIsaac, D., & Jackson, L. (1992, Fall). Portfolio assessment processes and outcomes. *Portfolio News, 4*(1), 1, 12–13.

Martin, M., Miller, G., & Delgado, J. (1993, Fall). Preliminary research results of portfolio assessment: California's Golden State Examinations in Science. *Portfolio News, 5*(1), 1, 12–16.

Mathematics Portfolio Project. (1990, Summer). Portfolios in the mathematics curriculum. *Portfolio News, 1*(2), 2–3.

McCandless, A. T. (1994). Reconstructing the history major at the College of Charleston: A focus on skills. *The History Teacher, 28*(1), 64–71.

Mcclymer, J. F., & Moynihan, K. J. (1977). The essay assignment: A teaching device. *The History Teacher, 10*(3), 359–371.

McGlohn, R. (1991, Fall). Portfolios for science. *Portfolio News, 3*(1), 6–7.

McLeod, S. (1996, January). Learning to write: Strategies for teaching writing in various disciplines. CCCC Winter Workshop on Teaching Composition to Undergraduates. Clearwater Beach, FL.

Messick, S. (1989). Validity. In R. L. Linn (Ed.), *Educational measurement* (3rd ed., pp. 13–103). New York: American Council on Education, Macmillan.

Meyer, C., Schuman, S., & Angello, N. (1990, September). *NWEA white paper on aggregating portfolio data* (2nd ed.). Lake Oswego, OR: Northwest Evaluation Association.

Mills-Courts, K., & Amiran, M. R. (1991). Metacognition and the use of portfolios. In P. Belanoff & M. Dickson (Eds.), *Portfolios: Process and product* (pp. 101–112). Portsmouth, NH: Boynton-Cook/Heinemann.

Mountford, R. (in press). Beyond academic prose: Accommodating cultural difference in large-scale writing assessment. In C. Cooper & L. Odell (Eds.), *Evaluating writing* (2nd ed.). Urbana, IL: National Council of Teachers of English.

Mullis, I. V. S. (1980). *Using the primary trait system for evaluating writing.* No. 10-W-51, Princeton, NJ: Educational Testing Service, National Assessment of Educational Progress.

Murphy, K. R., & Davidshofer, C. O. (1991). *Psychological testing: Principles and applications.* Englewood Cliffs, NJ: Prentice Hall.

Murphy, S., & Smith, M. A. (1990). Talking about portfolios. *Quarterly of the National Writing Project and the Center for the Study of Writing and Literacy, 12*(2), 1–3, 24–27.

Myers, M. (1980). *A procedure for writing assessment and holistic scoring.* Urbana, IL: ERIC Clearinghouse on Reading and Communication Skills and the National Council of Teachers of English.

Myers, M. (1994). NCTE's role in standards projects. *English Education, 26,* 67–76.

NCTE Council-Grams. (1991). Portfolio assessment: Will misuse kill a good idea? Reprinted in *Portfolio Assessment Newsletter, 3*(1).

Noguchi, R. (1991). *Grammar and the teaching of writing: Limits and possibilities.* Urbana, IL: National Council of Teachers of English.

Northwest Evaluation Association. (1991). Portfolios. *Portfolio News, 2*(3), 4.

Odell, L. (1981). Defining and assessing competence in writing. In C. Cooper (Ed.), *The nature and measurement of competency in English* (pp. 95–138). Urbana, IL: National Council of Teachers of English.

Oliver, E. (1995). The writing quality of seventh, ninth, and eleventh graders, and college freshmen: Does rhetorical specification in writing prompts make a difference? *Research in the Teaching of English, 29*(4), 422–450.

O'Neil, J. (1993). On the new standards project: A conversation with Lauren Resnick and Warren Simmons. *Educational Leadership, 50*(5), 17–21.

O'Neil, J. (1994). Aiming for new outcomes: The promise and the reality. *Educational Leadership, 51*(6), 6–10.

Page, E., & Petersen, N. (1995, March). The computer moves into essay grading: Updating the ancient test. *Phi Delta Kappan, 76*(7), 561–565.

Paulis, C. (1985). Holistic scoring: A revision strategy. *Clearing House, 59,* 57–60.

Paulson, F. L., & Paulson, P. (1991). *The ins and outs of using portfolios to assess performance.* Chicago, IL: National Council on Measurement in Education. (ERIC Document Reproduction Service No. ED 334 250)

Pelavin Associates. (1992). *Evaluating education reform: Assessment of student performance. A review of the current state of the field.* Washington, DC: Author.

Perkins, K., & Brutten, S. (1990). Writing: A holistic or atomistic entity? *Journal of Basic Writing, 9*(1), 75–84.

Perl, S. (1978). Five writers writing: Case studies of the composing processes of unskilled college writers. *Dissertation Abstracts International, 39*(08), 4788A. (University Microfilms No. 7824104)

Popham, W. J. (1988). *Educational evaluation.* Englewood Cliffs, NJ: Prentice-Hall.

Pula, J., & Huot, B. A. (1993). A model of background influences on holistic raters. In M. Williamson & B. Huot (Eds.),*Validating holistic scoring for writing assessment* (pp. 237–265). Creskill, NJ: Hampton Press.

Purves, A. (1992). Reflections on research and assessment in written composition. *Research in the Teaching of English, 26*(1), 108–122.

Radmacher, S., & Latosi-Sawin, E. (1995). Summary writing: A tool to improve student comprehension and writing in psychology. *Teaching of Psychology, 22*(2), 113–115.

Rafoth, B. A., & Rubin, D. L. (1984). The impact of content and mechanics on judgments of writing quality. *Written Communication, 1,* 446–458.

Raley, C. R. (1986). An assessment of freshman high school students' persuasive writing performance. *Dissertation Abstracts International, 47*(08), 2875A. (University Microfilms No. DA8625717)

Reckase, M. D. (1993, April). *Portfolio assessment: A theoretical prediction of measurement properties.* Paper presented at the meeting of the American Educational Research Association, Atlanta, GA.

Rief, L. (1990). Finding the value in evaluation: Self-assessment in a middle school classroom. *Educational Leadership, 47,* 24–29.

Rodgers, M. L. (1995). How holistic scoring kept writing alive in chemistry. *College Teaching, 43*(1), 19–22.

Rosenblatt, L. M. (1988). *Writing and reading: The transactional theory* (Tech. Rep. No. 13). Berkeley: University of California and Carnegie Mellon University, Center for the Study of Writing.

Roy, E. (1993). Computerized scoring of placement exams: A validation. *Journal of Basic Writing, 12*(2), 41–54.

Ruth, L., & Murphy, S. (1988). *Designing writing tasks for the assessment of writing.* Norwood, NJ: Ablex.

Severino, C. (1992). Where the cultures of basic writers and academia intersect: Cultivating the common ground. *Journal of Basic Writing, 11*(1), 4–15.

Shanker, A. (1996, April 7). Where we stand: What standards? *The New York Times,* E7.

Shavelson, R. J., Baxter, G. P., & Pine, J. (1992). Performance assessments: Political rhetoric and measurement reality. *Educational Researcher, 21,* 22–27.

Simmons, W., & Resnick, L. (1993). Assessment as the catalyst of school reform. *Educational Leadership, 50*(5), 11–15.

Sizer, T., & Rogers, B. (1993). Designing standards: Achieving the delicate balance. *Educational Leadership, 50*(5), 24–26.

Skaggs, G., & Lissitz, R. (1995). *A comparison of strategies for equating single prompt writing assessments.* Paper presented at the annual meeting of the American Educational Research Association, San Francisco, CA.

Smith, W. L. (1993). Assessing the reliability and adequacy of using holistic scoring of essays as a college composition placement technique. In M. Williamson and B. Huot (Eds.) *Validating holistic scoring for writing assessment* (pp. 142–205). Cresskill, NJ: Hampton Press.

Sommers, J., Black, L., Daiker, D., & Stygall, G. (1993). The challenges of rating portfolios: What WPAs can expect. *WPA: Writing Program Administration, 17,* 7–29.

Soven, M. (1996). *Write to learn: A guide to Writing Across the Curriculum,* Cincinnati, OH: South-Western.

Spady, W. G. (1994). Choosing outcomes of significance. *Educational Leadership, 51*(6), 18–22.

Stach, C. L. (1987). The component parts of general impressions: Predicting holistic scores in college-level essays. *Dissertation Abstracts International, 48*(07), 1683A. (University Microfilms No. DA8722706)

Standards for the English language arts. (1996). Urbana, IL: National Council of Teachers of English and Newark, DE: International Reading Association.

Standards project for English language arts. (1994). The Center for the Study of Reading at the University of Illinois, The International Reading Association, and the National Council of Teachers of English. Excerpts from Professional Collection #2.

Stiggins, R. (1987). NCME instructional module on design and development of performance assessments. *Educational Measurement: Issues and Practice, 6,* 33–42.

Stiggins, R. (1995, November). Assessment literacy for the 21st century. *Phi Delta Kappan, 77*(3), 238–245.

Storms, B. (1990, Winter). Interdisciplinary portfolios. *Portfolio News, 1*(1), 3.

Stotsky, S. (1995). The uses and limitations of personal or personalized writing in writing theory, research, and instruction. *Reading Research Quarterly, 30,* 758–776.

Taylor, H. C., & Russell, J. T. (1939). The relationship of validity coefficients to the practical effectiveness of tests in selection: Discussion and tables. *Journal of Applied Psychology, 23,* 565–578.

Tchudi, S., & Yates, J. (1983). *Teaching writing in the content areas: Senior high school.* Washington, DC: National Education Association Professional Library.

Tierney, R., Carter, M., & Desai, L. (1991). *Portfolio assessment in the reading-writing classroom.* Norwood, MA: Christopher-Gordon.

Turk, P. (1992, Fall). Here comes the bandwagon. *Portfolio News, 4*(1), 5.

Vermont Department of Education. (1991). *This is my best.* Montpelier, VT: Author.

Vermont Department of Educaiton. (1991). *Vermont Mathematics Portfolio Project: Grade eight benchmarks.* Montpelier, VT: Author.

Westcott, W., & Gardner, P. (1984). Holistic scoring as a teaching device. *Teaching English in the Two-Year College, 11,* 35–39.

White, E. (1985). *Teaching and assessing writing.* San Francisco: Jossey-Bass.

White, E. (1993). Holistic scoring: Past triumphs, future challenges. In M. Williamson & B. Huot (Eds.), *Validating holistic scoring for writing assessment* (pp. 79–108). Cresskill, NJ: Hampton Press.

White, E. (1994). *Teaching and assessing writing: Recent advances in understanding, evaluating, and improving student performance* (2nd edition). San Francisco: Jossey-Bass.

White, E. (1995). Apologia for the timed impromptu essay test. *College Composition and Communication, 46,* 30–45.

Wiggins, G. (1993a, November). Assessment: Authenticity, context, and validity. *Phi Delta Kappan, 75,* 200–214.

Wiggins, G. (1993b). *Assessing student performance: Exploring the purpose and limits of testing.* San Francisco: Jossey-Bass.

Winograd, P., & Jones, D. (1993, Summer). The use of portfolios in performance assessment. *Portfolio News, 4*(4), 1, 9–13.

Witte, S., & Faigley, L. (1983). *Evaluating college writing programs.* Carbondale, IL: Southern Illinois University Press.

Wolcott, W., with Legg, S. (1988). *The effectiveness of essay topic formats.* Tallahassee, FL: Florida Department of Education.

Wolcott, W. (1989). Perspectives on holistic scoring: The impact of monitoring on writing evaluation. *Dissertation Abstracts International, 51*(05–06), 1499A (University Microfilms No. DA9028582)

Wolcott, W. (1990). *Issues in designing a direct eighth-grade writing assessment.* Tallahassee, FL: Florida Department of Education.

Wolcott, W. (1992). *A feasibility study of large-scale writing portfolio assessment: Phase I, literature review and definition of issues.* Tallahassee, FL: Florida Department of Education.

Wolcott, W., with Hoffman, A. (1994). *Moving forward: A survey of alternative assessment in literature and current practice.* Tallahassee, FL: Florida Department of Education.

Wolf, D. P., & Reardon, S. F. (1996). Access to excellence through new forms of student assessment. In J. Baron and D. Wolf (Eds.), *Performance-based student assessment: Challenges and possibilities* (pp. 1–31), Ninety-fifth yearbook of the

National Society for the Study of Education. Chicago: University of Chicago Press.

Woodworth, P., & Keech, C. (1980). *The write occasion: Collaborative research study No. 1.* Berkeley, CA: University of California, School of Education, Bay Area Writing Project. (ERIC Document Reproduction Service No. ED 198 534)

Worthen, B. R. (1993). Critical issues that will determine the future of alternative assessment. *Phi Delta Kappan, 74,* 444–454.

Writing Assessment Specialists, Inc. (1990). *Feasibility study of an analytic scale for rating CLAST essays.* Tallahassee, FL: Florida Department of Education.

Yager, R., & McCormack, A. (1989). Assessing teaching/learning successes in multiple domains of science and science education. *Science Education, 73*(1), 45–58.

Young, A. (1994). *Writing across the curriculum.* Englewood Cliffs, NJ: Prentice-Hall, Blair Press.

Index

Authors

Willa Wolcott is the director of the Reading and Writing Center and an assistant director of the Office of Instructional Resources at the University of Florida. A former secondary English teacher, she taught composition for many years to first-year college developmental writers, developed and administered writing programs, and supervised other instructors. She serves as one of the chief readers of holistic scorings for state-mandated essay tests. She has completed for the State of Florida several research grants on portfolio assessment and other aspects of reading and writing assessment, often collaborating on assessment projects with area elementary, secondary, and college teachers to fulfill these grants. She has published articles in *College Composition and Communication,* the *Journal of Basic Writing,* the *Journal of Teaching Writing, Focuses,* the *Writing Center Journal,* and the *Writing Lab Newsletter.* Her research interests include basic writing and writing assessment. Wolcott received her B.A. in English from Wellesley College, Wellesley, Massachusetts; her M.A. in English from the University of Denver, Colorado; and her Ph.D. in instruction and curriculum (English education) from the University of Florida, Gainesville, Florida.

Photo: J. R. Hermsdorfer, Univ. of Florida

Sue M. Legg is a specialist in measurement and evaluation with extensive experience in the development of assessment programs for teachers and students. These measures include both multiple-choice and performance assessments. She is responsible for the administration of contracts from the Florida Department of Education for the Florida Teacher Certification Examination, the Florida Educational Leadership Examination, and the College Level Academic Skills Test. In addition, she has assisted in the development of a five-year plan for targeted assessment for the State of Florida and developed (with Willa Wolcott) a teacher training program for portfolio assessment in mathematics, science, and English for grades 3, 5, and 10. Legg also serves as the measurement consultant to the Florida Bar Board of Legal Certification and Education. In this capacity, she provides guidance for the development and scoring of ten certification area committee examinations. In addition, she is co-editor (with James Algina) of *Cognitive Assessment of Language and Math Outcomes* (1990), and they have a chapter addressing technical issues in *What's Happening in Teacher Testing* (1988), published by the Office of Educational Research and Development in Washington, D.C. Currently, Legg directs the Office of Instructional Resources (OIR) at the University of Florida. Among the responsibilities of OIR is the oversight of the Reading and Writing Center and the Teaching Center at the university. These centers offer instruction and instructional support in reading, writing, and mathematics. Legg received her baccalaureate degree from the University of California, Berkeley, and has taught in the California public school system. She received her doctorate in research, measurement, and evaluation from the University of Florida.

*This book was typeset in Palatino by Omegatype Typography, Inc.
Typefaces used on the cover and spine were Journal Ultra and Helvetica.
The book was printed on 50-lb. smooth offset by Versa Press, Inc.*

ALTERNATIVES TO GRADING STUDENT WRITING

Stephen Tchudi, editor

Evaluating a student's progress as a writer requires striking a delicate balance between the student's needs and the school's needs. This up-to-date collection of essays, assembled by NCTE's Committee on Alternatives to Grading Student Writing, offers several innovative and interesting options. An introductory essay by Tchudi, chair of the Committee, delineates the field of possibilities—or "degrees of freedom"—determined by these often competing needs. The book begins by reviewing research on grading (which resoundingly argues against grading papers) and the paradigm shifts in composition that make paper grading a questionable practice. Further sections address ways of making response to writing an increasingly productive part of the writing process and offer specific classroom strategies. The volume concludes with ideas for formulating plans of action for introducing grading alternatives in classrooms, schools, and districts. *308 pp. 1997. Grades K–Coll. ISBN 0-8141-0130-5.*

No. 01305-4044 $22.95 ($16.95)

NCTE National Council of Teachers of English
1111 W. Kenyon Road, Urbana, IL 61801-1096
Telephone: 800-369-6283 or 217-328-3870
Web: http://www.ncte.org   Fax: 217-328-9645

NEW RELEASES

DEEP REVISION
A Guide for Teachers, Students, and Other Writers

Meredith Sue Willis

Geared toward writers of all ages, *Deep Revision* is filled with practical and interesting ways to revise both fiction and nonfiction. It explores how the ability to revise develops and how people can use one another's responses to improve their writing. It offers techniques for adding more material and deepening the material you have; it also discusses form, structure, and finishing. *176 pp. 1993. Teachers & Writers Collaborative. Grades 3–Coll. ISBN 0-915924-41-2.*
No. 10754-4044 $22.95 ($16.95)

NCTE National Council of Teachers of English
1111 W. Kenyon Road, Urbana, IL 61801-1096
Telephone: 800-369-6283 or 217-328-3870
Web: http://www.ncte.org   Fax: 217-328-9645

NEW RELEASES

WRITING PROCESS REVISITED
Sharing Our Stories

Donna Barnes, Katherine Morgan,
and Karen Weinhold, editors

In this collection, elementary, secondary, and college teachers candidly discuss their experiences with implementing the writing-process approach in their classrooms—the struggles and successes, and the differences between their imagined ideal and the everyday reality. Though the results don't always match their expectations, the teachers learn that they can often adapt to meet the challenges of their unique situations. Whether using picture books to model elements of successful writing to fourth graders, arguing for the teaching of grammar, punctuation, and mechanics along *with* writing process, or grappling with portfolios as tools for assessment, these educators share their teaching stories with honesty and humor. *188 pp. 1997. Grades K–Coll. ISBN 0-8141-2815-7.*
No. 28157-4044 $21.95 ($15.95)

NCTE National Council of Teachers of English
1111 W. Kenyon Road, Urbana, IL 61801-1096
Telephone: 800-369-6283 or 217-328-3870
Web: http://www.ncte.org   Fax: 217-328-9645

NEW RELEASES

SITUATING PORTFOLIOS
Four Perspectives

Kathleen Blake Yancey and Irwin Weiser, editors

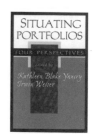

Both reflective and forward-looking, *Situating Portfolios* brings together 31 writing teachers from diverse levels of instruction, institutional settings, and regions to create an inviting volume on current practice in portfolio writing assessment. Contributors to the volume reflect on the explosion in portfolio practice over the past decade, why it happened, and what comes next; discuss portfolios in hypertext, the Web, and other electronic spaces; report on current and new contexts, from emergent literacy to faculty development, in which portfolios now appear; and consider emerging trends and issues that are involving portfolios in teacher assessment, faculty development, and graduate student experience. Contributors include Peter Elbow and Pat Belanoff, Gail Hawisher and Cynthia Selfe, Brian Huot, Sandra Murphy, William Condon, and many others. *416 pp. 1997. Utah State University Press. Grades K–Coll. ISBN 0-87421-220-0.*
No. 44756-4044 $26.95 ($19.95)

NCTE National Council of Teachers of English
1111 W. Kenyon Road, Urbana, IL 61801-1096
Telephone: 800-369-6283 or 217-328-3870
Web: http://www.ncte.org   Fax: 217-328-9645